1975

may be kept

THE CHEKHOV PLAY

THE CHEKHOV PLAY

A New Interpretation

BY

HARVEY PITCHER

Lecturer in Russian
University of St. Andrews

BARNES & NOBLE

BOOKS

10 East 53d St., New York 10022
(a division of Harper & Row Publishers, Inc.)

Published in the U.S.A. 1973 by
HARPER & ROW PUBLISHERS, INC.
BARNES & NOBLE IMPORT DIVISION

ISBN 06 495585 0

Printed in Great Britain

CONTENTS

ACKNOWLEDGEMENTS

Acknowledgements are made to the following publishers and authors: Geoffrey Bles Ltd., for quotations from *My life in the Russian Theatre* by V. I. Nemirovich-Danchenko; Bradda Books Ltd., Letchworth, Hertfordshire, for quotations from their editions of *The Seagull* and *The Cherry Orchard*; E. J. Brill, Leiden, for quotations from *Anton Čechov: 1860–1960. Some Essays*, edited by T. Eekman; the Cambridge University Press for the quotation from *Tolstoy: A Critical Introduction* by R. F. Christian; the Columbia University Press for the quotation from *Anton Chekhov: The Voice of Twilight Russia* by Princess Toumanova; Faber and Faber Ltd., for the quotations from *Somerville and Ross* by Maurice Collis; Alfred A. Knopf, Inc., New York, for quotations from *A History of Russian Literature* by D. S. Mirsky, edited and abridged by Francis J. Whitfield; David Magarshack for quotations from *Chekhov the Dramatist*, published as a Dramabook edition by Hill and Wang, New York; the Oxford University Press, New York, for quotations from *The Breaking String. The Plays of Anton Chekhov* by Maurice Valency; Prentice-Hall, Inc., Englewood Cliffs, New Jersey, for quotations from *Chekhov. A Collection of Critical Essays*, edited by Robert Louis Jackson; and Ernest J. Simmons for the quotation from *Chekhov: A Biography*, published in Britain by Jonathan Cape Ltd.

Foreword

'THE time has come to speak up about Chekhov!'

It is the kind of remark that Trofimov, the earnest young student in *The Cherry Orchard*, might make: 'Let there be no shilly-shallying, my friends, let us speak up now or forever remain silent!'

Yet more and more it expresses the feeling that I have about Chekhov. In our insensitive, action-centred world we seem to be continually losing touch with the spirit that informs these beautiful and remarkable plays. The time has come to rescue Chekhov from his admirers: from the drama critics who refer with such knowing confidence and lack of insight to what is 'typically Chekhovian'; from the experts who have never learned a word of Chekhov's language, let alone visited his country or spoken to any of his fellow-countrymen; from those vocal partisans for whom Chekhov is not the voice of twilight Russia, but the stormy petrel of the Russian Revolution (or the other way round, depending on political persuasion), and from the sophisticated critics who see in Chekhov a precursor of the theatre of the absurd or an ironist who smiled wryly at the tragicomedy of life. As Russians would say, scorning the niceties of academic debate: *Chort s nimi!* Away with them all!

What I have set out to do in this book is to give an interpretation of Chekhov's plays that differs sharply from those which are current in the West and the Soviet Union, and in this I hope that I have succeeded; but few books are more tedious than those which spell out in solemn detail where the author disagrees with his predecessors, and this is not a work of extended refutation. It is the new approach that matters. My starting point was a feeling of dissatisfaction with critics who failed to make clear their general attitude towards Chekhov's plays, and whose comments, however interesting in themselves, were ultimately no more persuasive than the next man's, since they did not lead to any verifiable conclusions. This feeling made me try to work out before anything else a simple but reasoned *explanation* of what makes the Chekhov plays fascinating, and which would give my comments an overall sense of direction. The results of this enquiry are summarized early in the opening chapter, so that the reader may see very clearly at the outset what he is being asked to agree and disagree with. This chapter attempts to define the essential nature and characteristics of the

Chekhov play and is intended to act as a key to subsequent chapters; it may be regarded as both introduction and conclusion. In thinking about how to define the Chekhov play, a picture began to emerge of the way in which the plays had evolved, and it is with this evolutionary aspect that the chapters on *The Seagull* and *Uncle Vanya* are largely concerned. The chapters on *Three Sisters* and *The Cherry Orchard*, while they continue and round off this evolutionary theme, are more in the nature of appreciations, intended to present these plays in a new light and to communicate my feelings about them.

I am grateful to Professor R. F. Christian, of the University of St. Andrews, for his encouragement, and to James Forsyth, of the University of Aberdeen, for reading the manuscript and making a number of valuable suggestions.

The Chekhov Play

i. what's the point of it all?

ONE of the earliest and most outspoken critics of Chekhov as a dramatist was Tolstoy. He could see no point at all in Chekhov's plays, and said so. Chekhov visited him once during the winter of 1901–02 when Tolstoy, then well over seventy, was convalescing in the Crimea at Gaspra, not far from Chekhov's home in Yalta:

> He was still confined to bed but talked a great deal about every-thing and about me, among other things. When eventually I get to my feet and make my farewells, he pulls me back by the arm, saying: 'Kiss me!', and after giving me a kiss, he suddenly bends over swiftly to my ear and says in that energetic quick-fire old man's voice of his: 'But I still can't stand your plays. Shakespeare's are terrible, but yours are even worse!'[1]

Chekhov told this story with much amusement, flattered perhaps that his name had been bracketed, however negatively, with Shakespeare's; and he was tickled too when Tolstoy, complaining of the purposeless-ness of Chekhov's characters, once remarked: 'And where does one get to with your heroes? From the sofa to the privy and from the privy back to the sofa?'[2] Chekhov had his own explanation for Tolstoy's antipathy towards Shakespeare:

> What I especially admire in Tolstoy is his contempt for all us other writers, or rather, not so much contempt, as that he considers us all to be complete nonentities. There are times when he praises Maupassant, Kuprin, Semyonov, myself . . . Why does he praise us? Because he regards us all as children. Our tales, our stories, our novels—for him these are just children's games . . . But Shakespeare is a different matter. Shakespeare is an adult and annoys him because he doesn't write à la Tolstoy . . .[3]

Tolstoy's exceptional irritation with Chekhov's plays might be seen in a similar light. That these plays were considered worthy of criticism, rather than praise, seems like a grudging acknowledgement by Tolstoy that Chekhov had achieved some kind of 'adult status' as a dramatist. But whatever his private feelings may have been (and there is some evidence, as we shall see later, to suggest that he was more deeply affected by Chekhov's plays than he cared to admit), in his public pronouncements Tolstoy remained consistently damning. 'I could not even force myself to read his *Three Sisters* through to the end,' he is reported as saying. 'Where does it all lead us to?'[4]

Where *does* it all lead us to? What is the point of Chekhov's plays? What are they all about?

Chekhov himself would no doubt have turned such questions aside. 'I was just trying to write a few good parts for the Moscow Art Theatre company', he would have said of *Three Sisters* and *The Cherry Orchard*, and refused to participate further in the discussion.

Tolstoy was certainly right when he pointed out that actions do not form an important part of Chekhov's plays—a criticism that he could not level at Shakespeare, whatever his other shortcomings. The events of *The Cherry Orchard* can be described in a single sentence. Chekhov was reacting strongly against the kind of popular action-filled drama that was entirely divorced from everyday experience. Half a century earlier, another famous writer, Gogol', had bewailed the state of the Russian theatre, where lurid, sensational melodrama was the order of the day, and had called for a dramatist of genius (Nikolai Vasil'evich Gogol' himself?), who would be capable of presenting on stage what was ordinary and recognizable in Russian life. During the nineteenth century Russian fiction had explored human behaviour with increasing subtlety, but in drama there had been no comparable developments: Gogol's censures would still have been widely applicable to the theatre of the 1880's. A study of the evolution of Chekhov's plays shows that he too needed some time to break away entirely from the existing conventions. His first attempt at drama, *Platonov* (1880), which was only discovered in manuscript form after his death, is crowded out with theatrical effects and melodramatic incident. But as the plays progress, so this element of strong action decreases, until in his last play, *The Cherry Orchard*, he found himself able to dispense for the first time with that prerequisite of conventional action drama: the pistol-shot.

If Chekhov's plays are not plays of action, can they be described as plays of ideas? One imagines the scornful eyebrow which Tolstoy might have raised at that suggestion! From time to time, it is true, some of Chekhov's characters indulge in an occupation which is referred to as 'philosophizing', but a student of Chekhov does not take long to realize that whatever else it may be, this philosophizing cannot be equated with rational argument or the vigorous exchange of ideas.

A more serious case may be made out for saying that Chekhov's plays are valuable because of the picture and interpretation which they give of Russian society at a particularly interesting stage in its development. Soviet critics are bound ultimately to take their stand on this proposition. There is nothing new about such an approach, for throughout the nineteenth century literature and literary criticism had provided much of the most perceptive comment on the Tsarist regime (of the kind that in other societies might have been provided by a free press or a political opposition). Chekhov's later plays evoke a memorable picture of the social landscape of his time, none more so than *The Cherry Orchard*, in which the playwright manages to freeze that critical moment in social evolution when the traditional ruling class is forfeiting its position of superiority, and other classes are rising to take its place.

But this case is very much weakened for two reasons. The first is that the social themes which stand out in Chekhov's plays—the bankruptcy, both economic and spiritual, of the Russian upper class, and the futility of so many of its members' lives—were themes which had already been very fully covered in Russian literature before Chekhov. The type of the 'superfluous man', for example—the talented man for whom there is no place in contemporary society—had long since become a literary cliché. It did not need Chekhov to make the point that the Russian nobility was moribund.

The second and perhaps stronger reason is that although these plays evoke a vivid impression of Russian society, how Chekhov himself interprets or wishes to comment on that society is by no means so clear-cut. If one considers only the most obvious instance, *The Cherry Orchard*, there are those who feel that in this play Chekhov is taking a fond and nostalgic last look at the old regime, while others claim that he was instead cheerfully laughing the old regime on its way to oblivion. Distortions of emphasis can soon be detected in both viewpoints. But the two extremes seem to cancel one another out. Chekhov's own attitude remains equivocal, and one begins to suspect that he was not concerned to make his own position clear for the very simple reason that this consideration was never in the forefront of his mind anyway. My view is that because of subsequent events in Russia, far too much attention has continued to be paid to the social content of *The*

Cherry Orchard, and that the social landscape, however vividly evoked, was only an incidental part of Chekhov's plays. Their point remains elusive.

Once, after he had been watching a performance by the Moscow Art Theatre of *Uncle Vanya*, Chekhov expressed dissatisfaction with the way in which the actress playing the part of Sonya had at one point in Act III thrown herself at her father's feet and started to kiss his hand. 'That's quite wrong,' he commented, 'after all, it isn't a drama. The whole meaning, the whole drama of a person's life are contained within, not in outward manifestations . . . A shot, after all, is not a drama, but an incident.'[5] This is a helpful indication of Chekhov's general approach to playwriting, and suggests that his presentation of the characters' inner lives might be regarded as the central feature of Chekhov's plays. Is he then to be thought of primarily as a psychological dramatist?

In one sense, beyond any doubt. 'When psychological mistakes are made,' remarked Tolstoy, 'when the characters in novels and stories do what, from their spiritual nature, they are unable to do, it is a terrible thing.'[6] This test of psychological plausibility is one that the characters of Chekhov's later plays all pass with flying colours.

On the other hand, critics sometimes write about Chekhov's plays as if they were vast coded documents which can only be deciphered with the utmost patience, and in which every remark, however innocent on the surface, is full of hidden psychological meaning and conceals a most complex web of motivation. I have become increasingly sceptical of this approach, for it seems to me that the best of Chekhov's dramatic characters are quite ordinary people, leading unremarkable lives, and that from a psychological point of view, they are neither particularly complex nor unusual. Moreover, in tracing the evolution of Chekhov's approach to dramatic characterization, a significant progression emerges. His first four-act play to be performed, *Ivanov* (1887), is a very full study of a psychologically complex figure. In a letter of untypical length to his friend, the publisher Suvorin, Chekhov analyses his hero's past and present life in the most thorough psychological detail, even making use of his medical knowledge and drawing little graphs in order to explain Ivanov's neurasthenic condition.[7] Kostya in *The Seagull* (1895) is another psychologically complex portrait: Chekhov seems to anticipate the psychoanalytical approach when he makes Kostya unconsciously reveal the contradictions of his personality through what he says about himself, his past life and especially about his mother.

But this deep probing of the individual personality comes to an abrupt halt with *The Seagull*. In *Uncle Vanya* (1896), *Three Sisters* (1900) and *The Cherry Orchard* (1903), Chekhov reveals enough about his characters to enable us to understand their situation, and to feel with them in the crises which they pass through; but the characters do not analyse themselves, nor do we learn very much about the influences that have shaped their lives. There is even a certain bluntness about the way in which Chekhov gives background information on the characters early in the play, as if anxious to dispose of such unimportant matters as quickly as possible. Chekhov's correspondence no longer contains any letters comparable to the one about Ivanov; and when Chekhov became closely associated with the Moscow Art Theatre, both Nemirovich-Danchenko and Stanislavsky, the co-directors, noted in him a peculiar feature. 'Chekhov', wrote Nemirovich, 'was incapable of advising actors ... Everything appeared so comprehensible to him: "Why, I have written it all down," he would answer.'[8] And Stanislavsky observed:

> When the actors began to read his play aloud and turned to Anton Pavlovich for explanations, he would become terribly embarrassed and be unable to reply, saying: 'Look, I've written down all there is to know.'
> And indeed he was never able to criticize his own plays and listened to the opinions of other people with great interest and even astonishment.[9]

The impression that such remarks may give of a primitive, inarticulate dramatist of genius who did not even understand his own characters, is quickly dispelled by a glance at Chekhov's letters. He knew his own characters well enough. But the details that he now gives about them are not analytical but descriptive, sometimes bordering on the impressionistic. Here is his thumbnail sketch to Nemirovich of the merchant Lopakhin in *The Cherry Orchard*: 'white waistcoat, light brown boots, waves his arms about as he walks, taking long strides, thinks as he walks about, walks in a straight line. Hair not short, and so he often throws his head back; when he is thinking, combs his beard from back to front, i.e. from the neck towards the mouth.'[10] Chekhov's approach seems to have become much more intuitive, making reasoned explanations, of the kind that the actors would have appreciated, a far from easy task. 'He wears checked trousers and there are holes in his socks,' Chekhov told Stanislavsky, who was playing the part of Trigorin in

The Seagull, as if to imply that from these two features everything about the character became immediately comprehensible.[11] The label of 'psychological dramatist' is thus to be applied with some caution, for in the later plays the *analyst* seems to have retired into the background.

Yet it still seems clear that Chekhov's plays do stand or fall by their ability to involve our interest in the inner lives of the characters. The question is: involve in what way?

What Chekhov certainly avoids is entering into any kind of moral dialogue with his audience. Tolstoy would have liked to see him take up a much clearer moral position towards his characters. But this he never does. The elderly playgoer who said that she did not like Chekhov's plays 'because the men spend all their time chasing after other men's wives', had a point. Problems of conscience seem not to exist. One might have expected Chekhov to explore the moral dilemma that faces Trigorin in *The Seagull* (the successful middle-aged writer confronted by a naive young girl who is prepared to make any sacrifice that he requires of her), or Masha and Vershinin, who are both already married, when they find themselves attracted to one another in *Three Sisters*; but such themes are conspicuous by their absence. Chekhov seems to have had no interest in putting his characters through any kind of moral test.

But although explicit moral judgements may be absent, are we being invited to judge the characters in more subtle ways? By suggesting his approval of one quality in human behaviour and his disapproval of some other quality, by inducing us to feel deeply for some of his characters and to despise others, is Chekhov tacitly passing on his own complex system of human values?

Unless an audience is made to sympathize with such characters as Uncle Vanya, Sonya or the three sisters, Chekhov's plays will obviously have failed. Behind much that is written there seems however to be the further assumption that Chekhov intended us to *take sides* among his characters: to take the part, for example, of the 'virtuous victim', Uncle Vanya, against that 'evil exploiter', the Professor, or to fly to the defence of the sisters, so charming, so talented and so unworldly, against their ruthlessly wicked sister-in-law, Natasha; and that in this taking of sides, this giving or withholding of sympathy and approval, the whole point of Chekhov's plays is to be found.

Studying how the plays evolved yields an interesting observation here too: that with each new play the incidence of unsympathetic characters decreases. By the time of *The Cherry Orchard* there are no un-sympathetic characters at all, unless one counts the very minor figure of the manservant, Yasha; and the mild contempt that the audience may feel for him takes second place to the affection that is felt for all the characters, for the characters as a group. Certainly, though, the Professor in *Uncle Vanya* and Natasha in *Three Sisters* are to be re-garded as unsympathetic figures. But the taking of sides can lead to obvious errors. To regard the Professor, for example, as an 'evil exploiter' and Vanya as a 'virtuous victim' misses the whole point of Vanya's portrayal, which is to show the plight of a man who really has no one but himself to blame for the mess that he has made of his life. Nor is the depiction of the sympathetic characters by any means clear-cut. The sisters seem to be very likeable people, but did Chekhov seriously intend us to approve of, or even indeed to sympathize at all deeply with characters who show such an extraordinary inability to accomplish the simple task of moving to Moscow? Vershinin is perhaps even more ambiguous: he has fine and stirring things to say, yet his personal life strikes us as an absolute disaster.

Trying to work out whether Chekhov meant us to approve or disapprove of Vershinin seems to me to be on the same unrewarding level as trying to decide whether Chekhov was glad or sorry that the cherry orchard had to be chopped down. The most that one can hope to do is to produce some rather complicated equivocation that will satisfy nobody. As with the social approach to the plays, one begins to wonder whether the reason for this might be that Chekhov's attention was not focussed on his characters in this kind of way in the first place. But how else are the characters being presented, if not as individuals, with individual qualities to which we react favourably or unfavourably?

ii. NATURE OF THE CHEKHOV PLAY

It was after studying a particularly revealing episode in the evolution of Chekhov's plays—his transformation of *The Wood Demon* into *Uncle Vanya*—that an answer to this question became rather more than just a faint glimmer on the horizon. *The Wood Demon* was Chekhov's second full-length play, which failed disastrously when it was per-formed in December 1889. At some time between the beginning of 1890 and December 1896, probably in 1896 itself, Chekhov converted *The Wood Demon* into *Uncle Vanya*, using all the main characters from the earlier play and taking over the entire second act with only minor alterations.

In *The Wood Demon* Voinitsky is a talented man of psychological complexity, whose life has been ruined by the curse of 'irony', which poisons all his relations with other people. His niece, Sonya, an attractive but rather formidable young bluestocking with much of her uncle's critical disposition, is in love with the 'Wood Demon' (Doctor Khrushchov); but she cannot make up her mind whether he is 'genuine' or not, for the Doctor, a man of sternly upright principle and strong views, seems almost obsessional in the way that he concerns himself more with preserving Russia's forests than with his medical practice. In the course of the play Voinitsky commits suicide after a row with his brother-in-law, the Professor, but Sonya and the Wood Demon finally resolve their misunderstandings and are presumed to live happily ever after.

It may well have been as a result of witnessing Russian rural life at first hand after the purchase of his small country estate at Melikhovo in 1891 that Chekhov transformed the generally light-hearted *Wood Demon* (Voinitsky's suicide notwithstanding) into the much more sombre *Uncle Vanya*: a play in which frustration is the dominant theme. How the three main characters were transformed is very striking and significant. Voinitsky ceased to be an intellectual figure with a low opinion of his fellow men, and became instead the much more ordinary, hardworking Uncle Vanya, who is overwhelmed in middle age by the feeling that his life has been a complete waste of time. Sonya is no longer an attractive bluestocking, but a plain, sensitive girl who has been in love with the Doctor for the past six years without ever receiving a word of encouragement; while Doctor Astrov (Chekhov's new name for Khrushchov) no longer gives the impression of a rich dilettante who practises medicine in the occasional intervals between preserving Russia's forests, but has become instead the grossly overworked and frustrated provincial doctor, in whose life, as he puts it, 'there is no light shining in the distance'.

The essential difference in characterization, I believe, is this: that in the later play Chekhov is not so concerned with what kind of people his characters are, but is focussing his attention directly on their *emotional preoccupations*. The individual qualities are still there, but they have become more blurred and peripheral; they are no longer at the centre of Chekhov's vision. What the characters are feeling has become the focus of attention. And whereas it is natural for an audience to adopt a detached and critical attitude towards individual qualities, such a response seems far less appropriate in the case of feelings or emotions.

In contrast therefore to the general tradition of Western drama, an audience is under no obligation to pass judgement on the characters as individuals, but is rather being invited to respond on an emotional level to the feelings that the characters experience. This constitutes for me the single most important element in an understanding of 'the Chekhov play' (using that term to refer to *Uncle Vanya*, *Three Sisters* and *The Cherry Orchard*, but scarcely at all to *Ivanov*, and only partly to *The Seagull*, which, like *The Wood Demon*, represents a transitional stage in the play's evolution).

What each character brings to the Chekhov play may be described as a particular set of emotional preoccupations. Chekhov presents his characters in terms of what they feel about themselves and other people, about their situation in life and about life in general. It is true, of course, that the characters can also be distinguished from one another by virtue of certain individual qualities. Of the three sisters it may be said that Olga is considerate, Masha outspoken and Irina dreamy. But if asked what was important about this trio, it is unlikely that we should start by isolating these qualities. We are more likely to say that what stands out about them, what seems to *define* them, is their longing for a better life, their longing for 'Moscow'. What Chekhov's characters *do* is important only in so far as their actions (or in the sisters' case, inaction) illustrate these emotional preoccupations, and in particular, as the expression of some inner emotional crisis: 'A shot, after all, is not a drama, but an incident.' What the characters *say* is likewise primarily important as an indication of what they are feeling.

In practice, Chekhov's important characters are to be defined in terms of such emotions as their hopes, longings, yearnings, aspirations, optimism about the future, nostalgia for the past, regrets, frustrations, disappointments and disillusionments. There is a peculiar quality about all these emotions. On the face of it, they are not in the least dramatic. They do not include the strong emotions—the desires and passions, hatreds and jealousies—that one might expect to find in drama centred upon the emotions. These strong emotions had been the stock-in-trade of melodrama, because of their obvious dramatic potentialities: flaring up suddenly, they could be shown as intensely active for a while to the exclusion of all other emotions, and might then be excitingly resolved through some violent sequence of events. But in the experience of the vast majority of people, such emotions are exceedingly rare occurrences. In portraying them, dramatists often had recourse to unfamiliar settings, recognizing that no audience would

B

find such emotions credible if they were presented against a background of normal everyday life. By contrast, the emotions that Chekhov portrays are the undramatic, long-term ones. They do not appear and vanish suddenly but remain largely unresolved, persisting perhaps for a lifetime and being momentarily highlighted during the course of the play. And they are pervasive emotions, in the sense that they do not take sudden and exclusive possession of a person, but tend to colour the whole of his behaviour in a much more subtle and pervasive manner. To depict these pervasive long-term emotions, Chekhov did not have recourse to unfamiliar settings but took his material from life round him, so that there is nothing esoteric about the emotions he presents. Just as the outstanding quality of his best short stories is their ability to generalize, to take a simple story about a handful of people and to make it seem relevant and important to everyone, so too in the Chekhov play the kind of emotions portrayed are never just of importance to those involved, but can always be widely recognized and appreciated.

What happens in the course of the Chekhov play is that the characters are shown responding and reacting to one another on the emotional level: Chekhov creates among them what may be called an emotional network, in which it is not the interplay of character but the interplay of emotion that holds the attention of the audience. George Calderon, who was responsible for translating and producing *The Seagull* at the Glasgow Repertory Theatre in November 1909, the first occasion on which a Chekhov play had been performed in this country, wrote an introduction in 1912 to his translation of *The Seagull* and *The Cherry Orchard* that still remains one of the liveliest pieces of writing on Chekhov the dramatist. Calderon found Chekhov a pioneer in recognizing and portraying on the stage that 'there is nothing of which we are more urgently, though less expressly conscious than the presence of other life humming about us, than the fact that our experiences and our impulses are very little private to ourselves, almost always shared with a group of other people'.[12] A kind of electric field exists among all the persons in a Chekhovian group. No one has ever matched his ability to put on stage the infectiousness of a mood. It may be a mood of youthful gaiety, as in the first act of *Three Sisters*, when even the usually staid schoolmaster, Kulygin, and the middle-aged Colonel Vershinin are affected by what is going on around them, and start to behave like schoolboys; or it may be a mood of contemplation, as in Act II of *The Cherry Orchard*, when even the ebullient

Ranyevskaya is affected by the general atmosphere and falls silent, and all the characters hear in the distance the mysterious sound of 'a breaking string'.

But it is not only when a large group is assembled that these 'vibrations' of the emotional network begin to operate. Emotional preoccupations in the Chekhov play do not remain private and submerged, but are brought to the surface as the characters intermingle and become emotionally involved with one another. This as it were activates the emotional network, and emotions may come to vibrate between particular individuals. At one extreme, these emotional vibrations may be full of tension and disharmony: as when one person is seeking from another an emotional response that is not forthcoming, or when a character feels that someone else is standing in the way of the fulfilment of his desires. At the other extreme, there are occasions when emotions vibrate with unusual sympathy and harmony: as when individuals come to share a common outlook, a common yearning or a common grief. It is on occasions such as these, when the emotional network is vibrating with an unusually high degree of harmony or disharmony, that the characters' emotional preoccupations are likely to be most clearly revealed.

There is one more feature of the Chekhov play that is very distinctive and deserves to be pointed out at this early stage. I mentioned above that Chekhov presents his characters not only in terms of what they feel about themselves (their emotional preoccupations) and about other people (the emotional network), but also in terms of what they feel about their situation in life and about life in general. Characters like Astrov in *Uncle Vanya* and especially Vershinin in *Three Sisters* react to their situation by evolving for themselves a 'philosophy of life'; and this philosophy of life can best be described as a way of coming to terms with life emotionally. When a Chekhov character is philosophizing, it is likely that he will be expressing what he *feels* about life. When characters are philosophizing together, it is likely that they will be comparing what they feel—comparing notes, as it were, about life, trying to discover whether their feelings have anything in common. This philosophizing involves the individual in the need to look beyond his private life and fortunes, to forget about his *own* problems, and to speculate on the significance of his life within the scheme of human life as a whole. These philosophies of life do not however stand outside the emotional network of the plays. On the contrary, they may acquire within the network a special importance: for other characters respond

emotionally to the philosophy that is being put forward and may come
to share it (as happens in the case of the three sisters and Vershinin), so
attaining an unusual degree of emotional harmony.

George Calderon used a helpful term when he said that Chekhov's
plays were 'centrifugal' rather than self-centred.[13] An audience's
attention does not remain fixed on the fates of the characters as individuals but moves beyond those individual fates to considerations
of a much wider nature. Partly this centrifugal effect comes about
because Chekhov is able to make his characters' emotions seem of
universal relevance, so that what those characters are feeling strikes us
as part of our common lot. But it derives also from the way in which
the audience finds itself drawn into this distinctively Chekhovian philosophizing: responding to Vershinin, for example, not so much as a
person—what do we think of him as an individual?—but more as the
embodiment of an outlook: how do we feel about his philosophy of
life? An audience is prompted by the Chekhov play to explore what it
feels in general about life and the world we live in; and to explore in
many and varying directions, for the emotional implications of the
Chekhov play are very open-ended. This centrifugal quality is present
in *Uncle Vanya*, *Three Sisters* and *The Cherry Orchard*, but especially
in *Three Sisters*, where Chekhov, as I shall hope to illustrate, explores
most fully different ways of coming to terms with life emotionally.

In conclusion, the Chekhov play may be described as subtly and
deeply concerned with emotion, whether in respect of the playwright's
approach to his characters, or of what happens in the course of the
plays, or of the likely responses of the audience. More than any other
dramatist before or since, Chekhov is the dramatist of the emotional
side of man's nature.

iii. CHEKHOV'S FORMULA

In looking carefully at Chekhov's four major plays, one becomes
aware that they have all been put together according to a certain
formula, which Chekhov adheres to quite closely; and it is this formula
which I now wish to consider, especially in relation to the thesis above
about the nature of the Chekhov play. *The Seagull* is included here,
alongside *Uncle Vanya*, *Three Sisters* and *The Cherry Orchard*, since
it does largely correspond to this dramatic formula, even though it
represents a transitional stage so far as the nature of the Chekhov play is
concerned.

In these four plays Chekhov presents his characters within a single location. Sometimes we may see them in the house, sometimes in the garden or the grounds of their estate, but this is almost the only variation that Chekhov allows himself. When he does on one occasion venture away from the estate into 'open country' nearby, the result is the very striking second act of *The Cherry Orchard*. As in his short stories, Chekhov seems to have felt that it was impossible to portray his characters' lives adequately unless one gave a clear indication of the kind of house that they lived in, and of the landscape or townscape against which they moved. Precisely where they are living is not stated, but their general environment is always subtly conveyed: the lakeside setting of *The Seagull*, backward rural Russia in *Uncle Vanya*, the uninspiring provincial capital of *Three Sisters*, or the twentieth-century world of advancing towns and railway lines that threatens to engulf the nineteenth-century estate in *The Cherry Orchard*. During the play these Chekhov estates begin to seem like little worlds of their own, so isolated do the characters feel within an alien environment. When Trigorin says in Act IV of *The Seagull* that he'll be 'travelling on to Moscow next day', Moscow sounds terribly remote. In reality it is no great distance, but the world that the characters live in has come to seem so self-absorbed and self-contained that Moscow is psychologically remote, even if not physically so.

The characters whom Chekhov assembles in this little island world may be described as a very democratic group, for one of Chekhov's most important innovations was to decentralize his cast. The traditional idea of a hero and heroine has been discarded. No single character is allowed to stand out as more central than any other; instead, there are always at least four roles of comparable importance, and in *Three Sisters* it is difficult to distinguish between the relative importance of no less than ten characters. Even the obviously minor characters stand out as independent figures, and are never just an incidental part of someone else's world, as in conventional drama. Often Chekhov achieves this effect by giving his minor characters a strong colouring of the comic, the absurd or the eccentric. This is a way of ensuring that these characters are memorable and not just lost within the group, while at the same time it helps to strike a lifelike balance within the play as a whole between serious and comic elements.

Moreover, every member of the group knows everyone else; or if they do not when the play begins, they very quickly become acquainted. All of them are presented in Act I; none disappears in the course of the play, nor are there any unexpected new arrivals; and in the final

act everyone is accounted for. This circumscribed group is clearly
essential to the Chekhov play, but for what reason? It means that from
the outset an atmosphere of psychological intimacy is present. Chekhov
comes to rely less and less on the kind of emotions that arise among
strangers who meet one another for the first time during the play.
He prefers to concentrate on the emotional network among a group
of people whose lives are already connected, and who are thus in
varying degrees emotionally attuned and sensitive to one another.
Where the paths of communication have already been laid down, it is
possible for characters to communicate with one another by the most
subtle and indirect emotional means.

If we exclude the various servants and a few important but exceptional figures such as Astrov in *Uncle Vanya*, Natasha in *Three Sisters*
and Lopakhin in *The Cherry Orchard*, the members of Chekhov's group
are drawn by and large from the same social class: the Russian gentry
(*dvoryanstvo*). This feature is the more striking when one remembers
that Chekhov himself was the grandson of a serf and the son of a
shopkeeper. He did not know the gentry very well; he had only observed
this class as an outsider. But if the Chekhov play is concerned primarily with the emotional side of man's nature, two reasons come to
mind that might explain his choice. The first is that because of their
education and their frequently introspective lives, members of this
class were most likely to be able to put their emotions into words,
to be sufficiently articulate, that is, to convey at least a part of what they
were feeling to an audience. The second concerns the *kind* of emotions
that these people experienced. Chekhov may well have felt that the
greatest depth and subtlety of feeling were to be found among representatives of the gentry; and it was the fine shades of emotion,
not the crude colours of melodrama that he wanted to experiment with
in his plays. Writing in January 1900 to the actress Olga Knipper,
a member of the Moscow Art Theatre company and soon to become his
wife, Chekhov told her that he had advised Meierhold, another young
actor, not to be too obvious in depicting a nervous person on stage.
'Where,' asks Chekhov, 'either indoors or outdoors, will you see
people rushing about, jumping up and down or seizing hold of their
head in their hands? ... The subtle emotions which are characteristic
of cultured people must also be given subtle outward expression.'[14]

A further basic element in Chekhov's formula is that an immediate
distinction is to be made in all four plays between residents and
outsiders. The residents are those characters who belong permanently

to the play's setting, and who form part of a well-established way of life. The outsiders are attached to the setting of the play only temporarily: though temporarily in this context may mean a period of several years, as in the case of the officers in *Three Sisters*. What may be called the plot in the Chekhov play is best described as the working-out within the group of a process of disruption. The irruption of the outsiders into the lives of the residents leads to friction, emotional tension, and in time, emotional crises. Disruption results in *The Seagull* from the impact of Arkadina and Trigorin on the lives of Kostya and Nina, and in *Uncle Vanya* from the impact of the Professor and his wife on the lives of Vanya, Sonya, and Astrov. In *Three Sisters* it results partly from the impact of Natasha on the lives of Andrei and his sisters, but also from the way in which the sisters' lives become linked with those of the officers; while in *The Cherry Orchard* disruption or more accurately, disintegration, is provoked not so much by individuals (Lopakhin after all does his best to help) as by the pressure of outside circumstances, which makes the sale of the beloved family estate inevitable and leads to the break-up of a well-established way of life. It would be misleading though to suggest that this disruption is *caused* by the outsiders or outside events. All the makings of an emotional crisis are present before the outsiders arrive. Kostya and Nina were not really suited to one another; Vanya had already reached a crisis of middle age; whether the sisters could ever achieve the kind of happiness they dreamed of was in doubt before Natasha and the officers entered on the scene; and the upper-class way of life depicted in *The Cherry Orchard* was under sentence long before the accumulation of debts made it necessary to sell the estate. What the arrival of the outsiders does is to act as a catalyst, which works upon these latent forces and brings the crisis to a head.

It is disruption then which generates movement in the Chekhov play, and which provides the framework around which the play is constructed. If we exclude the untypical last act of *The Seagull*, all four plays show a marked similarity of construction. The third act is pivotal. It is here that the process of disruption comes to a head. This is always the most dramatic act in the Chekhov play, the act of emotional crisis: 'scenes' occur, harsh words are spoken, confessions are made, hopes are dashed, in *Uncle Vanya* shots are fired, and so on; and this applies to *The Cherry Orchard* too, even though the crisis itself, the sale of the estate by auction, is occurring off-stage. In the first act, Chekhov is building up his emotional network. This act takes place either during or shortly after arrivals: the residents' background and way of life are carefully suggested, and the interaction of outsiders and residents already set in motion. If Act III is dramatic, then the second act of the Chekhov play is decidedly undramatic and leisurely. It is here that the talk is likely to be most discursive, and the longest discussions are to be found, though the atmosphere is often brooding and uneasy, relations become strained, and the ground is well prepared for the crises to come. After the climaxes in the third act, anti-climax follows in Act IV. This is the act of departures, complementing the arrivals of Act I (in *The Seagull* this departure scene provides the finale of Act III). At the end of *Uncle Vanya* and *Three Sisters*, the outsiders depart, leaving the residents behind to resume their lives as best they can, and at the end of *The Cherry Orchard*, all the characters leave apart from the old servant, Firs.

In building his plays around this framework of disruption, Chekhov was not interested in the disruption for its own sake, as a dramatic spectacle. It was the means whereby he might activate the play's emotional network. In moments of stress or crisis, people's underlying preoccupations become highlighted and emotions flow between them most uninhibitedly. Disruption may also very often be followed by its opposite, by some kind of reconciliation or emotional recovery, and this enabled Chekhov to range widely between the extremes of harmony and disharmony. A similar emotional range is implicit in the scheme of arrivals and departures. Such occasions are always liable to be highly charged with emotion, whether with the joy of establishing and re-establishing emotional ties, or with the sadness of having to break them off. At the same time, Chekhov's downbeat departure endings enabled him to break away from the artificial convention, which he himself still follows in *The Seagull*, of saving up the dramatic climax for the end of the final act. Chekhov's anti-climaxes suggest rather that life goes on willy-nilly, and has merely been interrupted for a brief period by the action of the play. A third reason for the scheme of arrivals and departures is of a more formal, aesthetic nature. The departure act does not merely complement the arrival act, but constantly echoes it. By such means Chekhov gives the play an overall shape and symmetry, and imposes a pattern on the life that he has created.

Chekhov's career as a dramatist developed much less smoothly than his career as a writer of short stories. There was more than one painful setback, and after the disastrous first night of *The Seagull* in 1896, of which he wrote two months later that 'I can't forget what happened any more than I could forget, for example, if I'd been struck by some-one',[15] Chekhov vowed that he would never write another play again. But he did eventually return to the drama, and he did persist in writing plays according to a formula which he knew well enough was far from being widely appreciated. Why risk his reputation in this way? One means of approaching the problem would be to compare in detail the nature of Chekhov's plays and stories, a subject that I can touch on only briefly here. Short stories like *Ward Six*, *A Boring Story* or *The Black Monk* give the reader far more food for thought than any of the plays; and the stories are often psychologically subtle in ways that the drama cannot be. Chekhov the short story writer plays delicately on his reader's sympathies, so that one hesitates how to feel about a certain character: our attitude to Gurov, for example, the hero of Chekhov's famous *Lady with a Little Dog*, is switched right round by Chekhov—from dislike at the beginning of the story, when he appears as no more than a cynical womanizer, to sympathy at the end, where he discovers a deeper side to his nature when it is too late to do anything about it. Such subtleties are not to be found in the Chekhov play. Here the characters enter the play much more 'ready-made', and where predictions occur about how they will behave, these are always fulfilled. Chekhov realized that if you are watching a play in the theatre, you cannot turn back the pages or mull it over as you go along; and it may well have been for this reason that he dropped the 'deep probing of the individual personality' approach to characterization which is still to be found in *The Seagull*.

On the other hand, whereas in his short stories Chekhov seldom concentrates on more than two or three main figures, it is much easier in a play to present a group of characters with a reasonably even degree of emphasis; and the Soviet critic, Roskin, suggests that Chekhov's plays might be regarded 'as a kind of substitute for the work that he never accomplished as a novelist'.[16] The play's other obvious advantage is its directness. However brilliant the writing, the word can never quite jump off the page with the emotional intensity that may be achieved by a line spoken in the theatre. Fiction reaches its audience through the cerebral process of reading; and while this is no drawback in conveying the thoughts that pass through a person's mind, it is far less suitable for transmitting what a person feels. A writer has to work hard to convey in words that which in the theatre can be conveyed directly, as in life itself, by a gesture, an inflection or a tone of voice. Words are very ponderous when it comes to following the rapid shifts in a person's emotional processes. And because fiction can only describe each character's feelings in turn, it is at a grave disadvantage in trying to keep up with the still more rapid ebb and flow of emotion between two individuals, let alone with the infectiousness of mood among a group. All this needs to be perceived by an audience directly, and in these respects, as Chekhov realized, the drama always wins out.

iv. HOW THE CHEKHOV PLAY IS WRITTEN: THE CHARACTERS ON STAGE

In 1881 Sarah Bernhardt and her company made a tour of Russia. Her performances in Moscow were a big social event, as Tolstoy recorded in *The Death of Ivan Ilyich* (1886). Chekhov was twenty-one at the time, and a contributor of theatrical reviews to the Moscow journals. During her visit he found himself 'thinking, talking, reading and writing of nothing but Sarah Bernhardt'.[17] His reporter's nerves were stretched to the limit: no sooner had he returned from the matinée at the Bolshoi Theatre, scribbled a few lines and snatched a meal, than he was setting out for the Bolshoi again to see the evening performance. Then he would sit up until 4 a.m. completing his review. The whole business was playing havoc with his digestion, and he looked forward to the time when the revered *diva* had left Russia for good, and he could enjoy a fortnight's uninterrupted sleep.

Chekhov was not one of Bernhardt's converts. However intently he gazed, he could see in her nothing more exceptional than 'a good artist', whose reputation had been much inflated. The Moscow audience, Chekhov claimed, was only mildly enthusiastic, but this did not affect the way in which Bernhardt took her curtain-calls, 'advancing slowly and grandly towards the footlights, looking straight ahead, like a high priestess about to offer up a sacrifice'. What Chekhov objected to in her acting was its artificiality. 'Every sigh,' he wrote, 'all her tears, her convulsions in the death scenes, the whole of her acting is nothing more than a cleverly, faultlessly learned lesson. A lesson, readers, simply a lesson! ... When she acts, she is not trying to be natural, but to be unusual. Her aim is to strike the audience, to astonish and to dazzle them ...' Chekhov's insistence at the age of twenty-one on the artificiality of Bernhardt's performance is of particular interest, since the avoidance of anything artificial was to be one of his major concerns in the writing of drama. 'That's not how it is in real life' was the most severe judgement that Chekhov could pass on a work of drama or fiction.

There was one respect, however, in which Chekhov felt able to pay Bernhardt a genuine compliment, however back-handed: this was her *ability to listen.* 'She is not the only one to possess this ability,' he wrote, 'the whole of the company has it too. The French actors are excellent listeners, and because of this they never feel out of place on the stage, they know what to do with their hands and do not get in one another's way. Not like our people . . . We have our own methods. With us Mr. Maksheyev is delivering his speech, while Mr. Vil'de, who is supposed to be listening to him, is gazing at some distant point and clearing his throat impatiently; and the expression on his face seems to be saying: "Well, after all, none of that's got anything to do with *me!*"'

This lesson too Chekhov would later put into practice in his own plays. He rejected that artificial stage convention, amusingly depicted by Calderon when he writes: 'as each actor opens his mouth to speak, the rest fall petrified into an uncanny stillness, like the courtiers about the Sleeping Beauty, or those pathetic clusters that one sees about a golf-tee, while one of the players is flourishing at his ball in preparation for a blow'.[18] It was important to Chekhov that everything on stage should be done as naturally and informally as possible. With him it is not particular individuals but the group that should command attention. There could be no question of directing the spotlight on to one character to the exclusion of the others, and it is rare for a character to hold the stage for any length of time. Trigorin's long speeches at the end of Act II in *The Seagull* are decidedly exceptional. As the plays progress, the old-fashioned soliloquy disappears completely, and even duologues become less frequent. In Chekhov, it has been said, it is the listeners whom you watch; and certainly, one always feels that Chekhov knows what every member of his group is doing at any given moment, whether or not the person happens to be contributing to the conversation.

Not that the group itself is ever very static. There is a great deal of informal coming and going by the characters, and wandering about on stage. Spectators at the first performance of *The Seagull* who were used to more formal dramatic conventions must have been taken aback by the curious sight of Masha hopping off the stage in Act II because her leg had gone to sleep; or by the way in which all the characters near the end of Act III troop off to say goodbye to Arkadina and Trigorin, and the stage remains for some moments completely empty. The Moscow Art Theatre likewise caused a stir when they made the characters watching Kostya's play sit with their backs to the audience. While some members of the group are talking together, others may be engrossed in their own thoughts, or doing something quite different—such as reading a book or a newspaper, knitting stockings, playing patience or solitaire, humming a little tune or dropping off to sleep. And here it is also appropriate to mention the informal effect that Chekhov creates by making his characters participate in some everyday pastime or domestic occasion: amateur theatricals and the game of lotto in *The Seagull*, drinking tea in the garden and the family conclave in *Uncle Vanya*, Irina's party in *Three Sisters*, and Charlotte's conjuring displays and the ball in *The Cherry Orchard*.

In all these respects Chekhov's approach to drama coincided with the methods adopted by the Moscow Art Theatre, founded in 1898. The new theatre had abolished the 'star' system. Members of the company were told that 'there are no small parts, there are only small actors', and they might find themselves playing an important role one day, and a walk-on part the next. But the walk-on part was to be treated with the same seriousness as the big role, and here Chekhov's small parts, which are not really small at all, offered ample scope for creative interpretation. All playing to the audience and theatrical histrionics were to be avoided, anything that smacked even slightly of 'theatricality' was taboo. Instead acting must be 'stage-centred', the audience must be ignored, the actor must live his part on stage and let his inner feelings dictate his outward behaviour. The absence of leading roles in the Chekhov play, his interest in the group rather than the individual, his reliance on what is implied or hinted at rather than what is actually said—all this was perfectly suited to the 'ensemble' approach and introspective style of acting that became characteristic of the Moscow Art Theatre.

v. THE CHARACTERS CONVERSING

How the characters converse in the Chekhov play is likewise dominated by the feeling of informality.

The simplest dialogue Chekhov ever wrote is the one recalled by Nemirovich-Danchenko in his autobiography.[19] When he was a young writer contributing to the comic journals, Chekhov was paid for his stories 'by the line', which made it very much to his advantage to write in short, terse paragraphs. On one occasion he claimed that he could receive as much for ten words as for ten solid lines. Challenged by the editor to prove his claim, Chekhov thought for a moment and then produced the following dialogue:

'Listen!'
'What?'
'Native?'
'Who?'
'You.'
'I?'
'Yes.'
'No.'
'Pity!'
'H'm!'

Though he may not have achieved such startling brevity as this, Chekhov in his major plays evolved a kind of dialogue which is remarkable for its great outward simplicity and naturalness. He tried to create on the stage the impression of the casual, haphazard flow of ordinary conversation. He wanted his audience to feel that they were in the position of eavesdroppers, and that the author had stepped down and was allowing his characters to talk among themselves. After the unsuccessful run of *The Seagull* in 1896, it was of some consolation to Chekhov when a friend wrote to him that in the play, 'life is so close to you, so easily apprehended that sometimes you forget you are sitting in the theatre and feel that you could join in the discussions taking place in front of you.'[20] To achieve such an effect, Chekhov had to undermine the persistent dramatic convention, whereby dialogue is arranged in the kind of neat and rational sequence that is seldom to be heard in life itself. He gave his dialogue a much more unpredictable, 'broken-up' quality. A significant part of a Chekhov play consists of small talk, where the conversation is likely to switch rapidly from person to person, or from subject to subject. The thoughts of the person speaking may veer off in an unexpected direction; and the reply that is given often bears an unexpected relation, sometimes no relation at all, to what has gone before. Chekhov's last two plays are especially rich in techniques of this kind by which he 'deformalizes' the dramatic dialogue.

It would be wrong, however, to imagine that the Chekhov dialogue is inconsequential merely for its own sake. Stanislavsky rightly observed that 'behind each word of Chekhov's there stretched a whole range of many-sided moods and thoughts, of which he said nothing, but which arose of their own accord in one's mind'.[21] In watching or reading the four major plays, one is constantly aware that the words spoken by the characters are not hollow, but are backed up by that emotional density which Stanislavsky had in mind. It is the ability to suggest through a few simple lines of speech the complex inner lives of his characters that represents the fine art of Chekhov's dialogue. This dialogue might be described as a kind of emotional shorthand—but a shorthand, one must add, that is related only *indirectly* to what the characters are feeling or thinking inwardly. In the earlier plays, *Ivanov* and *The Wood Demon*, his characters do describe their inner feelings in some detail; but Chekhov came to realize that this is very much an artificial dramatic convention. People are seldom at all articulate about their own feelings; often, they do not even *know* what these feelings are. They are more likely to reveal themselves obliquely, through the inconsequential remark or half-expressed thought, and hence the emotional undercurrents that form such a vital part of the Chekhov play. To become aware of these undercurrents demands from the audience a special kind of alertness and sensitivity, a willingness to become involved in the inner lives of the characters, and to feel for the implications of barely perceptible hints in the dialogue itself. The idea of the characters in the Chekhov play responding to one another on the emotional level needs to be extended, for the audience too must respond on the emotional level to all the characters in the play.

A glance at a short scene from Act I of *The Seagull* may help to make these points clearer. When she realizes that Kostya's play is not to be resumed, Nina decides to come out from behind the stage and has just been introduced to Trigorin by Arkadina:

NINA (*to Trigorin*). It's a strange play, isn't it?
TRIGORIN. I didn't understand it at all. But I enjoyed watching. You acted so genuinely. And the scenery was beautiful.
(*Pause.*)
There must be a lot of fish in that lake.
NINA. Yes.
TRIGORIN. I love fishing. There's nothing I enjoy more than to sit by the water early in the evening and to watch my float.
NINA. But I imagine that for anyone who's tasted the pleasure of creative work, all other pleasures cease to exist.
ARKADINA (*laughing*). You mustn't talk like that. When people make him pretty speeches, he never knows what to say.
SHAMRAYEV. I remember one night at the Moscow Opera hearing the great Silva take a lower C. Now it so happened that a bass from our parish choir was sitting in the gallery, and all of a

sudden—you can imagine how astonished we were—from up in the gallery there comes this voice: 'Bravo, Silva!'—a whole octave lower ... Like this, it was. (*In a deep bass.*) 'Bravo, Silva!' ... You could have heard a pin drop.

(*Pause.*)

DORN. The angels are passing!

This passage shows the Chekhov dialogue at its most relaxed and casual, and succeeds completely in satisfying our sense of the unpredictability of human conversation. There is the unexpected change of direction in Trigorin's speech, which takes him from discussing the merits of Kostya's play to the question of how many fish there are in the lake; the discursive small talk, switching rapidly from character to character, and from subject to subject; and the complete breakdown of continuity in the dialogue, when Shamrayev comes in with his anecdote which is apparently unconnected with anything that has been said before. Yet clearly there is rather more to it than this. Trigorin is polite about Nina's performance, but the pause, and the sudden jump in his thoughts, give the impression that he is not—as yet—very interested in this naive young girl, still less in the World Spirit of Kostya's play; and that what really interested him, as he sat there staring at the lake, was the thought of carp, and perch, and fishing rods. Nina's 'Yes' expresses bewilderment: she does not know what to make of this unexpected remark from the famous author; and even when Trigorin has explained himself more fully, she still cannot quite grasp it and feels sure that he is not being serious. Her earnest comment about 'the pleasure of creative work' amuses Arkadina, who is glad of the opportunity to suggest how familiar she is with all Trigorin's little idiosyncrasies. Shamrayev's clumsy entrance into the conversation shows him to be on a different wavelength from the other characters. He would like to be able to talk about art in this artistic company, but the only thing that comes into his head that seems at all relevant is this anecdote about the bass from the church choir. It may be an anecdote that he is fond of telling in other company, because he likes the sound of his own deep bass voice. Its inappropriateness here seems to be felt by the rest of the characters, who greet the story with a silence of embarrassment or indifference. It is left to Dorn to break the prolonged silence by his remark that 'the angels are passing' (literally, 'the quiet angel has flown over').

The pauses used by Chekhov in this passage show that he is able, by means of stage directions, to give his audience at least some help in becoming aware of the dialogue's emotional undercurrents. These two pauses indicate that some kind of 'deviation' is in the air: Trigorin is about to deviate from his original line of thought, while the pause following Shamrayev's anecdote suggests that a certain tension has temporarily interrupted the spontaneous flow of conversation. Chekhov made extensive and subtle use of these pauses, which elsewhere may consist of some stage direction, such as 'looking at his watch', or simply of dots in the text. The dots especially are ubiquitous in the Chekhov play and a translator omits them at his peril, for Chekhov seems to have deployed them with the same kind of unconscious artistry that a painter reveals when he uses shading to soften the harsh outlines of a sketch.

These pauses are less significant, however, than the stage directions whereby Chekhov indicates a character's tone of voice, and hence his emotional state. In *The Seagull* these directions are mostly straight-forward: 'thoughtfully', 'excitedly', 'coldly', 'tearfully' or 'through tears', etc. (This last direction, *skvoz' slyozy*, is common in all the plays, and liable to misinterpretation. 'You'll often find "through tears" in my stage directions,' Chekhov wrote in connection with *The Cherry Orchard*, 'but that shows only the mood of the characters and not actual tears.')[22] A more complex example occurs in the course of Kostya's play, when Arkadina comments that 'this is something decadent' and Kostya reproves her, 'imploringly and reproachfully', which in itself reveals the whole ambivalence of Kostya's feelings towards his mother. Professor Nilsson has pointed out that as the plays progress, these directions are used with increasing frequency and subtlety, and may sometimes consist of apparently opposing parts, for instance: 'cheerfully, through tears' (*radostno, skvoz' slyozy*).[23] A good example of Chekhov's technique is to be found in the following ex-tract from Act I of *The Cherry Orchard*. Varya has been talking about herself and Lopakhin:

> VARYA. Everyone keeps mentioning the wedding and con-gratulating me, when really nothing's happened at all and it's just a kind of dream . . . (*Changing her tone.*) That brooch of yours looks like a bee.
> ANYA (*sadly*). Mamma bought it me. (*Goes into her room and talks gaily, like a child.*) Do you know, I went up in a balloon in Paris!

But all these pauses and stage directions, however subtle, can only take us so far. There remain vast areas in the Chekhov play where the audience is bound to rely on its own intuition. And this raises one of the trickiest problems in Chekhov interpretation. Chekhov's method of emotional suggestion and implication is necessarily elusive. Whereas qualities like courage and cowardice, being directly linked to human actions, can be demonstrated without difficulty on the stage and are likely to be universally recognized and agreed upon, emotional yearnings or regrets are by their nature obscure and intangible, often they can only be hinted at, and these hints may be interpreted differently by different members of the audience. It is this situation which helps to explain why there has been so much diversity in the interpretation of Chekhov's plays. What chance is there that non-Russian audiences will be able to appreciate Chekhov's emotional vocabulary? And for that matter, is a Soviet audience, separated from Chekhov by such profound social changes, in any better a position to understand him than we are?

My own reading of Chekhov's emotional vocabulary will, I hope, be made clear in the course of subsequent chapters. For the moment I would like to concentrate on one particular view of Chekhov's dialogue which is very widespread in the West and which, I believe, badly needs to be challenged.

In his celebrated *History of Russian Literature*, Prince Mirsky wrote that 'the dialogue form is also admirably suited to the expression of one of Chekhov's favourite ideas: the mutual unintelligibility and strangeness of human beings, who cannot and do not want to understand each other'.[24] Since the 1920's, when Mirsky was writing, these sentiments have been echoed time and again, so that today it is scarcely possible to read a Western review of one of Chekhov's plays that does not refer sooner or later to the 'tragic lack of communication' among the characters. The whole purpose of the plays, it would often seem, was to illustrate this tragic failure.

As a general comment on the nature of the Chekhov play, such a view is undoubtedly misleading. It is true that there are certain obviously unsympathetic characters, like the Professor in *Uncle Vanya* or Natasha in *Three Sisters*, who seem to be operating on an entirely different wavelength from everyone else; but these characters are deliberate exceptions, who show up by contrast the degree of emotional responsiveness among those around them—especially the depth of understanding and feeling for one another that distinguish the more central characters: Sonya and Uncle Vanya, or the three sisters. Then it is also true that some of the eccentric characters, like Solyony or Chebutykin in *Three Sisters*, or Charlotte Ivanovna in *The Cherry*

c

Orchard, feel themselves to be emotionally alienated from other people; but at the same time Chekhov makes it clear that they all crave a greater degree of intimacy. Where the 'tragic lack of communication' view seems more apt is in describing those relationships where one character seeks from another an emotional response that is not forthcoming: Sonya and Astrov in *Uncle Vanya*, Tuzenbach and Irina in *Three Sisters*, Varya and Lopakhin in *The Cherry Orchard*. Sonya feels very deeply about Astrov and tries to intimate her feelings to him, whereas Astrov does not feel deeply about her and fails to understand. But this is really an exceptional case. In the two later plays the situation is not the same. Tuzenbach and Irina are both very much *aware* of the gap that divides them, of how they would like to bridge it but are unable to; and the depth of emotional contact between them is considerable. Likewise, the acute tension that characterizes the scene where Lopakhin is expected to propose to Varya arises not because they are too little, but because they are too much, aware of what the other person is feeling.

So that the world of Chekhov's plays is not one in which the characters 'cannot and do not want to understand each other'. Some characters do already understand one another very well. Others strive to achieve such understanding, with varying degrees of success.

But there is a second criticism of the 'tragic lack of communication' view, namely, that it involves a misunderstanding of the emotional conventions that govern the behaviour of Chekhov's characters. It may be argued in favour of 'tragic isolation' that Chekhov's characters are often talking past one another; that they seem to be absorbed in their own thoughts and enclosed in their own worlds; that they can be rude and outspoken to one another, sometimes quarrelling bitterly; and that even the most sensitive of them may be so preoccupied with their own feelings that they are indifferent to the sufferings of people round them. Against this I shall argue that these outward features of the Chekhov play have none of the tragic significance so often ascribed to them, and can only be properly understood against the background of a different set of emotional conventions.

As an example of Chekhov's characters talking past one another here is a passage of dialogue from Act I of *The Cherry Orchard*:

LYUBOV' ANDREYEVNA. Varya hasn't changed a bit, she still looks like a nun. And I knew Dunyasha straight away. (*Kisses Dunyasha.*)

GAYEV. The train was two hours late. How's that, eh? How about that for efficiency?

CHARLOTTE (*to Pishchik*). My dog eats nuts as well.

PISHCHIK (*astonished*). Just fancy that!

It might be supposed that the disconnectedness of the dialogue here should be taken to imply a similar disconnectedness among the characters. But it seems to me unlikely that we are dealing with anything more significant than an example of Chekhov's deformalization technique. Such dialogue captures the haphazardness of everyday speech. There is indeed nothing peculiarly Russian about this. One need only listen with sufficient care to the sequence of a conversation—especially if there is no set topic, and different people are involved in different parts of a room—to realize just how disjointed human talk can be; and where an intimate group is involved, such disconnectedness can be expected to increase, since there is no need to be so formal and explicit.

An example of a character pursuing his own thoughts and, supposedly, being enclosed in his own world occurs in Act I of *Uncle Vanya*. After Yelyena has gone into the house, Voinitsky (Uncle Vanya) gazes longingly after her, while Telyegin goes on talking to Marina:

VOINITSKY. But isn't she lovely? Isn't she? Never in my life have I seen a more beautiful woman.

TELYEGIN. Do you know, Marina Timofeyevna, whether I'm driving through the fields, or strolling in a shady garden, or just looking at this table—I can't explain how blissfully happy I feel! The weather's enchanting, the birds are singing, and we're all living together in peace and harmony—what more can we ask for? (*Accepting a glass of tea.*) I'm exceedingly obliged to you.

VOINITSKY (*dreamily*). Her eyes . . . A wonderful woman!

There can be no doubt that Vanya is so preoccupied with his own thoughts that he probably does not hear a single word of Telyegin's little speech. But can this be cited as evidence that Chekhov's characters all live in their own enclosed worlds? If this exchange were transposed to our own social context, it would look as if Vanya had flouted a convention—that convention which says that you should pay attention (or at least appear to do so!) when other people are talking; and therefore the only conclusion to be drawn must be that Vanya is alienated from other people. The experience of living among Russians suggests, however, that this convention does not apply. On the contrary, it seems more likely that in their culture it is generally accepted that there may be occasions when you just have to follow out and express the emotion uppermost in you; and far from implying the alienation of individuals, this is to be regarded as a perfectly normal part of social behaviour.

Later in the same act there is another striking example of the greater latitude which Chekhov's characters are allowed in expressing their emotions publicly:

> YELYENA ANDREYEVNA. The weather's nice today . . . Not too hot . . .
>
> (*Pause.*)
>
> VOINITSKY. Yes, nice weather for hanging oneself . . .
>
> (*Telyegin tunes the guitar. Marina walks about near the house, calling the hens.*)

What is remarkable here is not just that Voinitsky gives vent to his feelings with such obvious bitterness. It is more that none of the other characters seems to find his remark in the least surprising. They do not, as English listeners might, rush to cover up this breach of social convention with cries of 'Vanya, how *could* you say such a thing!', or 'Cheer up, old chap, things can't be that bad!' It is quite natural for Vanya to express himself in that way, and not worthy of comment.

Elsewhere in the plays there are instances where the characters seem unexpectedly rude or outspoken to one another, but again we must be careful not to interpret their remarks in terms of familiar social conventions. Chekhov's characters, for example, frequently break one of our most strictly observed conventions when they go around telling other people how old they look or how much they've aged. A case of rudeness? No one in Chekhov is ever at all offended when spoken to in this way. On the contrary, it often seems as if a certain emotional satisfaction is to be derived from sharing with someone else an awareness of this common human predicament; only a very hard and individualistic character like Arkadina, the middle-aged actress in *The Seagull*, tries to assert human self-sufficiency by defying the passage of the years.

As an example of the abrupt rudeness to be found in the Chekhov play, here is an exchange from Act I of *The Cherry Orchard*:

YEPIKHODOV. I bought these boots the day before yesterday and they keep on squeaking, if you'll pardon the temerity, like nobody's business. What can I put on them?

LOPAKHIN. Go away. I'm tired of you.

YEPIKHODOV. Every day some misfortune happens to me. Not that I'm complaining, I'm used to it. I can even raise a smile.

The brusqueness of Lopakhin's two words (*Otstan'. Nadoyel.*) cannot be reproduced in translation. Lopakhin is not inhibited by social convention from expressing what he feels, and makes no attempt to conceal his irritation with Yepikhodov; while Yepikhodov is not at all put out by Lopakhin's remarks and does not regard them as any kind of personal affront. Care must likewise be taken not to jump to wrong conclusions about the occasional quarrels in the Chekhov play. One critic interprets the row in Act III of *The Seagull* between Kostya and his mother in Western terms as a kind of stand-up fight in which Arkadina delivers 'a shrewd blow', Kostya is 'utterly beaten', etc.[25] Is it not more of a childish squabble, in which they are infected by one another to say what they know will hurt most, and which finishes up in tears?

Finally, let us look at a scene from *Uncle Vanya* which might be regarded as a test case. It comes shortly before the end of Act II:

YELYENA ANDREYEVNA. And as for me, I'm just a tiresome person, an 'incidental figure'. In my music, in my husband's house, in all my romantic affairs—in absolutely everything—I've always played a minor role. When you come to think of it, Sonya, I'm really very, very unhappy! (*Walks agitatedly up and down the stage.*) There's no happiness for me in this world. None at all! Why are you laughing?

SONYA (*laughs, hiding her face*). I'm so happy . . . so happy!

YELYENA ANDREYEVNA. I feel like playing the piano . . . I'd like to play something now.

At first sight this scene might appear to provide striking confirmation of the 'tragic lack of communication' view. How bitterly ironical that it should be the sensitive Sonya of all people who is so absorbed in her own thoughts of what she has just said to Astrov that she pays no attention to Yelyena's *cri de cœur*! But can this really be the comment that Chekhov would have expected? First, it contradicts the earlier characterization of Sonya as someone who is very sensitive to other people, and who is alarmed, for example, when she sees tears in her uncle's eyes; though this, it might be argued, makes her reaction here all the more ironical. But secondly, it contradicts that feeling of harmony and emotional responsiveness which pervades the whole of this scene, both before and after the passage quoted, and which derives from the reconciliation and newly-found friendship between the two characters. And finally, Yelyena's response seems inappropriate if she really does feel that Sonya is indifferent to her plight. The alternative comment is to say that Sonya here simply cannot help herself, that she must follow out and express the emotion that is uppermost in her, and that she is the more encouraged to reveal her emotion because she is aware that Yelyena too is in a 'soul-revealing' emotional state. Yelyena is not in the least offended; she understands that Sonya feels emotionally moved, as she does herself, and this prompts her to suggest playing the piano.

So it is important to bear in mind that the social conventions governing the expression of emotion do not always coincide from one culture to another. There are dangers in referring to Chekhov as a universal dramatist, in so far as it may be necessary to learn a slightly different set of emotional conventions in order to appreciate him fully. It is, however, only the *expression* of emotion that may vary; the emotions themselves can be widely appreciated.

A general conclusion to be drawn from this discussion of Chekhov's dialogue is that one should always be sensitive to the emotional colouring of what is said, as well as to the meaning of the words themselves. On some occasions, as Professor Nilsson points out, the words used have no meaning, and are there only for the sake of the way in which they are to be spoken; Gayev's meaningless billiard phrases in *The Cherry Orchard*, which are often accompanied by an indication of his tone of voice, are an obvious example. Nilsson also suggests that an important principle in Chekhov's mind as he composed his dialogue was to vary the emotional key, so that he frequently juxtaposes 'a lyrical or elated with a banal, everyday atmosphere, a melancholy and serious with a comic atmosphere, a lively and active with a calm and pensive atmosphere'. Such variations, one might add, can even be found within the course of a single short speech, as in this example from *The Cherry Orchard*:

VARYA (*to Trofimov*). Of course, our student has to show how clever he is! (*In a gentle tone of voice, tearfully.*) How ugly you've become, Petya, how much older you look! (*Addressing Lyubov'*

Andreyevna, without any sign of tears.) The one thing I can't stand, Mamma, is having nothing to do. I need to be doing something every minute of the day.

Nilsson explains these variations by saying that it is as if Chekhov 'were keen that no one key become too dominating or last too long. There must be change and rhythm if his plays are really to give a picture of everyday life.' But as Nilsson adds, these contrasting emotional keys 'not only succeed each other, but are also to be found in balance in the same scene'.[26] Here Chekhov seems to have been pursuing the effect of harmonious balance for its own sake, as with his balancing of arrivals and departures within the play as a whole.

Nilsson's idea of varying the emotional key is particularly helpful in interpreting two brief passages of dialogue that have aroused some controversy. In Act II of *The Cherry Orchard*, there is a long discussion between Lopakhin and Trofimov about the sad state of Russia. The conversation pauses, and in the distance the estate clerk, Yepikhodov, walks past, 'softly and sadly playing his guitar'. 'There goes Yepikhodov . . .', says Ranyevskaya, *thoughtfully*; and her daughter, also *thoughtfully*, echoes her words exactly. One recent critic comments that for Ranyevskaya, Yepikhodov 'represents the half-emancipated peasantry', whereas for her daughter 'he is an argument for redoubling one's efforts in behalf of the lower classes'.[27] But nowhere else does Ranyevskaya show any social awareness, nor has her daughter as yet revealed a social conscience, and in any case is it likely that either of them would entertain serious thoughts in connection with such a completely unserious character as Yepikhodov? Confusion may arise because the Russian word for 'thoughtfully' (*zadumchivo*) implies in this instance not so much a thinking state as an emotional one—a state of reflection, contemplation, almost absentmindedness. Nilsson is surely right when he comments:

> After the serious conversation between Trofimov and Lopakhin the appearance of Yepikhodov comes in marked contrast, as a change in the emotional key. It communicates something comic and trivial, concepts connected with the figure of Yepikhodov. And further, after the lively, active conversation, a contrast of rest: Lyubov' Andreyevna's and Anya's pensive, abstracted lines.[28]

The second brief moment is very similar. It comes in Act II of *Three Sisters*, after Vershinin and Tuzenbach have been discussing whether life is ever likely to improve. During a lull in the conversation,

Chebutykin for no apparent reasons reads out from his newspaper that 'Balzac was married in Berdichev'; and Irina, who is playing patience, echoes his words, once again *thoughtfully*. Nilsson is sceptical of ingenious attempts to discover psychological import in Irina's remark— e.g. if *Balzac* was willing to be married in the provinces, why am I so obsessed with Moscow? Instead he points the emotional contrast: the serious discussion is followed by something trivial and everyday, the lively conversation by 'Irina's abstracted, dreamy repetition'.[29]

Finally, let us turn from conversation between the characters to consider briefly their individual styles of speech. Mirsky is again provocative when he refers to the 'complete lack of individuality'[30] in the way that Chekhov's characters speak, whereas Calderon comments that 'each line is so unmistakably coloured with the character of its speaker that there is no need for the rest to hold their breath and "point" that we may know who utters it'.[31] Mirsky's remark seems at first to have no application to the plays. One thinks straight away of the singsong speech that distinguishes peasant characters like Anfisa and Ferapont in *Three Sisters*, or Marina in *Uncle Vanya* ('My legs is throbbing too, throbbing away like anything'); and of the comic linguistic pretensions and distortions of Medvyedyenko in *The Seagull* or Yepikhodov in *The Cherry Orchard* ('forgive my frankness, but you've reduced me to an absolute state of mind'). Among the central characters a more educated norm prevails, but there is still plenty of room for variation. Astrov in *Uncle Vanya* conceals his slight awkwardness in company by being rather loud and facetious ('There's a chap in one of Ostrovsky's plays with a very big moustache and a very small brain. Just like me in fact . . .'), though he can speak very eloquently on his favourite themes; while Masha in *Three Sisters* has an attractively forthright style all her own. Chekhov also makes an indirect comment on some of his characters through their ugly use of Russian. The Professor in *Uncle Vanya* speaks in a stilted fashion, and his sense of humour is ponderously Teutonic: 'Now, ladies and gentlemen. Allow me to coin a phrase by asking you to hang your ears up on the nail of attention' (a remark that he enjoys, if no one else does). Of all the characters in *Three Sisters*, Natasha alone is denied any elegance of speech. Her diminutives are especially repellent. The sugary diminutives which she uses to address her husband—*Andryúsha* and *Andryúshanchik*—contrast sharply with the obvious contempt in which she holds him. The diminutives become sentimental when she is referring to her beloved offspring:

He's such a little sweetie (*takoi milashka*), I said to him today:
'You're mine, Bobik! All mine!' And he just gazed up at me with
his darling little eyes (*svoyimi glazyonochkami*).

But it is arguable nonetheless that Chekhov's primary concern was
not that his characters' speech should be vividly colloquial and life-
like. Certainly, he makes them speak simply and naturally, without
false pathos or false rhetoric; so that the general impression of his
dialogue is of good timeless Russian, in which the colloquialisms too
are good colloquialisms. But one will not find in the Chekhov play
the kind of racy dialogue that was a speciality of the Russian drama,
as in Gogol's famous comedy, *The Inspector General* (1836), or even
in Chekhov's own one-act plays. What seems to have concerned
Chekhov more was the musical content of his dialogue, and any translation ought to attempt the difficult task of suggesting this musicality
in English. One feels that it may have been with considerable reluctance
that Chekhov allowed characters like Natasha and the Professor to
abuse the Russian language, and how they speak certainly grates on
the ear. This musicality is in evidence not only in the play's climaxes,
such as the highly musical finale of *Three Sisters*, but may also be discovered in quite minor scenes and speeches, like the reminiscences by
Olga with which *Three Sisters* begins.

What Mirsky might have had in mind is that if one considers only
the most eloquent and musical speeches in Chekhov's plays (Astrov
talking about the forests and Sonya's closing speech in *Uncle Vanya*,
Vershinin's philosophizing speeches and the finale of *Three Sisters*,
Trofimov's 'All Russia is our orchard' speech from *The Cherry Orchard*),
one may distinguish them by content, but little by style or tone of
voice. The reason is perhaps quite simply that if anyone's distinctive
voice makes itself heard on these occasions, it is the playwright's:
speaking on his characters' behalf as well as he is able, and endeavour-
ing to find not so much the words appropriate to a particular character,
as the kind of simple but eloquent words that would be universally
moving.

*   *   *

In this opening chapter I have tried to do two things: to say what I
think the Chekhov play is all about, and to outline what I take to be
its most important features. My aim has been to persuade; or if not to

persuade, then at least to challenge. For unless one raises these questions at the outset, further discussion becomes pointless: it can never be more than a dialogue between those who are talking past one another, failing to see that their disagreement is not at all on the level of 'how to play that scene in Act II' but concerns their fundamental attitudes towards Chekhov and his plays. In reading Soviet critics, I soon find myself disagreeing with them, but I am seldom left in any doubt as to *why* we disagree. Either explicitly stated, or close to the surface, there is an over-all attitude to Chekhov, the result of a need to assign this revered and widely-read author to his allotted place within the framework of a political ideology. When one perceives that, it becomes obvious that though many of the incidental observations may be valuable (and the best Russian critics, simply by virtue of being Russian, are able to appreciate details in Chekhov's plays that non-Russians are bound to miss), total agreement is out of the question; it would be necessary to go back to the ideological scheme and to discuss that. In reading Western critics, the sense of disagreement is just as strong, if not stronger, but the reasons are less immediately evident. The underlying attitudes, I suspect, are there just the same and are every bit as rigid, but they are never so clearly exposed. While Soviet critics would be very willing to answer the question—what are Chekhov's plays all about?—among Western critics such a question is felt to be not worthy of attention, even in some way shameful. That is why I have spent a long time discussing the 'tragic lack of communication' approach to Chekhov's plays, because it is here that one seems closest to the underlying attitude to Chekhov that is now prevalent among Western critics. I have argued that a careful re-examination of the plays shows that this approach cannot be justified, that it is mistaken. And not only is it mistaken but also harmful, for it interferes no less than any overtly ideological attitude with the freedom of emotional response that is necessary for a full en-joyment of Chekhov's plays. Yet all the signs are that Western criti-cism is moving more and more in this direction, and that Chekhov will be increasingly regarded as the detached and ironical, if not cynical, observer of man's triviality and futility. The time has come, to echo an earlier rallying cry, to speak up against this attitude and to proclaim that at the heart of the Chekhov play there lies not emotional isolation but emotional contact between human beings.

But the time has also come to leave the Chekhov play, and to con-sider how the individual plays conform, or fail to conform, to the pattern that has been outlined above.

'The Seagull'
A Testing Ground?

i. THREE ASPECTS

CHEKHOV'S first full-length play to be performed was *Ivanov*, which he wrote in 1887, at the age of twenty-seven. The play caused a considerable stir in Chekhov's time, and given a virtuoso performer in the title role, it can still make a strong impression today; but it is very much the outsider in the family of Chekhov plays, more so indeed than his next play, the notoriously unsuccessful *Wood Demon* (1889), and we shall say little about it here. Only in the occasional blending of the serious and the comic can the later Chekhov be glimpsed. From the technical point of view the play was quite orthodox, whereas the critics of the less conventional *Wood Demon* had no hesitation in telling Chekhov that he did not understand the first thing about stagecraft.[1] Chekhov felt obliged to follow the tradition of strong action by giving the audience 'a good punch on the jaw'[2] at the end of each act, culminating in the traditional dramatic climax at the end of Act IV, when the hero is made to commit suicide on his wedding morning (or, in an earlier version, to collapse and die shortly after receiving a mortal insult). In accordance with current theatrical practice, Chekhov intended the title role for a star performer: the part of Ivanov is unusually long, with some striking dramatic scenes. What stands out in relation to the Chekhov play is the extent to which the central character overshadows everyone else in *Ivanov*. There is no 'decentralization' here, no atmosphere of the intimate group. The play does include quite a collection of minor characters, but none of them is more than slightly interesting: they simply inhabit Ivanov's world.

Where *Ivanov* did depart from tradition was in the psychological depth which the author gave to the portrait of his hero. The play has affinities with Chekhov's *A Boring Story* (1889): both portray the disintegration of a man of ideals and ability, who finds that his life is collapsing around him. That Ivanov, 'a type of literary significance',[3] might have made a better fictional hero than the hero of a play is suggested by Chekhov's letter to his publisher friend Suvorin, from which Ivanov's character can be understood much better than from the play itself.[4]

Chronologically, it would be appropriate to turn now to Chekhov's second full-length play, *The Wood Demon* (1889). At some stage, however, between 1890 and 1896—probably in 1896 itself—Chekhov converted *The Wood Demon* into *Uncle Vanya*. To compare these two is of particular interest for the evolution of the Chekhov play; so we shall defer discussion of *The Wood Demon*, and turn instead to Chekhov's third full-length play, and the first of his major quartet: *The Seagull*. Chekhov's third play is his most heterogeneous. It contains elements which seem to belong to orthodox, traditional drama; in some respects it may be thought of as an example of the Chekhov play; while it also includes certain unorthodox, experimental features which are not characteristic of the Chekhov play and were not repeated later on. This section aims to bring out these three aspects of *The Seagull*, starting with the play's traditional elements.

Chekhov had known Nemirovich-Danchenko for some years before the founding of the Moscow Art Theatre, and Nemirovich, already a successful dramatist himself, was one of those to whom Chekhov sent a copy of the original draft of *The Seagull*. In his autobiography Nemirovich describes how Chekhov visited him to hear his verdict, and 'stood at the window, his back towards me, his hands as always in his pockets, never turning towards me once during at least half an hour, and not missing a single word'. Nemirovich does not attempt to re-create their conversation, but one detail did stick firmly in his memory:

> In the version which I criticized the first act ended in a great surprise: in the scene between Masha and Dr. Dorn it was suddenly revealed that she was his daughter. Not a word was again said in the play concerning this circumstance. I said that one of two things must be done: either this idea must be developed, or it must be wholly rejected, all the more so if the first act was to end with this scene. According to the very nature of the theatre, the end of the first act should turn sharply in the direction in which the drama is to develop.
>
> Chekhov said: 'But the public likes seeing a loaded gun placed before it at the end of the act!'
>
> 'Quite true', I said, 'but it is necessary for it to go off afterwards, and not be merely removed in the intermission!' It seems to me that

later Chekhov more than once repeated this rejoinder. He agreed with me. The end was changed.[5]

The story is a useful reminder that Chekhov at this time was still thinking to some extent in terms of 'what the public likes'. Had he retained the revelation about Masha, this would have added another complication to what is already a very involved emotional intrigue. In *The Seagull* Chekhov appears to have decided that the public likes the kind of intrigue in which a large number of characters, and several different plots, are involved. Apart from the interlocking love relations among the four central characters, there is the sub-plot revolving round Masha, and yet another sub-plot around Masha's mother, Polina. These sub-plots involving minor characters had been a feature of *Ivanov* as well. Moreover, the revelation about Masha would have contributed another strong effect to *The Seagull*. Reduced to their simplest terms, the main events of the play sound very much like the conventional fare of melodrama: an unsuccessful attempt at suicide, the seduction of a young girl by an older man who then abandons her, though the girl remains 'desperately in love' with him, the death of the girl's baby, and finally a second, and on this occasion successful, attempt at suicide. Although the punch on the jaw may be less vigorous than in *Ivanov*, Chekhov ends each act on a strongly dramatic note; and as in *Ivanov*, the play concludes with a knock-out blow—the revelation that Kostya has shot himself. 'Anyone who can discover new endings for a play', Chekhov wrote to Suvorin in 1892, 'will open up a new era . . . The hero either has to be married off or made to shoot himself, there's no other way out.'[6] Nor was there in the case of *The Seagull*, where the dramatic shock is further increased by lulling the audience into believing, along with Arkadina and the others, that it was only a phial of ether in the doctor's medical kit that had caused the explosion.

These links with traditional drama are nonetheless no more than vestigial. They do not prevent us from describing *The Seagull* as a psychological drama. Chekhov rescued the central emotional intrigue from conventionality by making it psychologically complex, and by involving all four participants in the world of art. He rescued the sub-plot around Masha by making her and Medvyedyenko into such unusual figures. Even the sub-plot around Polina is saved by its touches of humour. As for action, it is never presented for its own sake, but only as part of the psychological drama. All the dramatic events described above take place off-stage. The details of the affair between Nina and Trigorin are included only so that we shall now understand her state of mind, and the play's finale is to be regarded as the culmination of a psychological process. Traditional elements in *The Seagull* are an incidental accompaniment to the psychological drama.

If that is the case, to what extent can *The Seagull* be described as an example of the Chekhov play?

So far as our description of 'the characters on stage' and 'the characters conversing' is concerned, it does meet all the requirements.

The opening of *The Seagull* might even be said to go too far in the direction of deformalization! When the curtain rises, the audience is visually taken aback by the unexpected sight of the improvised garden theatre to which workmen behind the scenes are putting the final touches; and then further startled by the extraordinary opening exchange between Masha and Medvyedyenko:

MEDVYEDYENKO. Why do you always wear black?
MASHA. I'm in mourning for my life. I'm unhappy.

Perhaps it was not so surprising that some of the audience at the ill-fated first night decided that this was the beginning of one of Chekhov's farces (like his enormously popular one-act plays, *The Bear* and *The Proposal*, both frequently repeated since their original performance in 1888), especially when soon after, Masha hands Medvyedyenko her snuff-box with the curt invitation: 'Help yourself' —just as the fat Ivan was wont to do in Gogol's comic *Tale of How Ivan Ivanovich Quarrelled with Ivan Nikiforovich* (1834). Certainly the other three major plays all start on a much more ordinary note. But we may guess that Chekhov's aim with this opening was, as it were, to throw down the gauntlet and challenge the traditional theatre, where everything had become so dull and predictable. He wanted to capture the freshness of the first impression, to evoke the kind of sensation that we might feel if plunged without warning into someone else's well-established but unfamiliar way of life; to create something that was unusual, yet intensely alive and memorable in a way that the existing theatre singularly failed to be.

Elsewhere in the play there are numerous instances of deformalization, some of which have already been mentioned in the previous chapter. Informal movement about the stage occurs in preparation for

Kostya's play, and as the spectators occupy their seats; while the departure of Arkadina and Trigorin at the end of Act III is accompanied by much bustling to and fro, and then, unexpectedly, by the complete vacating of the stage. Masha's leg goes to sleep and she has to hop her way across the stage into the house, while Sorin is pushed about the stage in a wheel-chair. Several conversations take place against the background of some ordinary domestic activity: as when Trigorin is having his breakfast, while Arkadina is changing Kostya's bandage or when Polina and Masha are making up a bed on the settee for Sorin. Domestic pastimes are also much in evidence in *The Seagull*: amateur theatricals, reading aloud in the garden, playing lotto. The game of lotto in the final act, and the sound of the characters enjoying their supper in the next room, are used by Chekhov to offset the decisive last meeting between Kostya and Nina, and to prevent it from seeming too obviously dramatic in the old sense. And the dialogue too in *The Seagull* is frequently deformalized: not only by pauses and inconsequential remarks, but by making Sorin, for example, fall asleep every so often and begin to snore, or Dorn walk off humming to himself in the middle of a conversation. Sorin contributes an informal effect by his semi-coherent way of talking—he puts in superfluous phrases, and cannot always manage to finish a sentence—and he has the habit, said to have been Chekhov's own, of referring back to something much earlier in a conversation. His reaction to Kostya's anguished speech in Act I about the problems of having a famous mother is to ask him what kind of a person Trigorin is!

The dialogue of *The Seagull* also possesses that emotional suggestivity which is so characteristic of the Chekhov play. Towards the end of their long talk in Act II, Nina rhapsodizes to Trigorin about the artist's life, and her dream of glory is so intense that it makes her feel quite giddy. Then Arkadina is heard calling from the house, and the dialogue continues:

TRIGORIN. That's for me. . . . Time to pack, I suppose. I don't feel like leaving though. (*Looks round at the lake.*) What a superb view that is! . . . Wonderful!

NINA. Do you see the house and garden on the other side?

TRIGORIN. Yes.

NINA. That was my mother's estate until she died. I was born there. I've spent all my life near this lake, I know every little island on it.

TRIGORIN. Yes, this is a wonderful spot! (*Catching sight of the seagull.*) But what's that?

NINA. It's a seagull. Killed by Konstantin Gavrilovich.

TRIGORIN. A beautiful bird. You know, I really don't feel like leaving. Couldn't you persuade Irina Nikolayevna to stay? (*Writes in his notebook.*)

NINA. What are you writing?

TRIGORIN. Just making a note. . . . Idea for a plot. (*Putting his notebook away.*) A plot for a short story: a young girl like you has lived beside a lake since childhood; she loves the lake like a seagull, and like a seagull she is free and happy. But a man happened to pass that way, saw her, and for want of anything better to do destroyed her, just like this seagull.

(*Pause. Arkadina appears at the window.*)

ARKADINA. Boris Alekseyevich, where are you?

TRIGORIN. Coming! (*Walks off and looks back at Nina; by the window, to Arkadina.*) What is it?

ARKADINA. We're staying.

(*Trigorin goes indoors.*)

NINA. (*Comes to the front of the stage; after reflecting for a while.*) I must be dreaming!

CURTAIN

What is most fascinating about this passage is its suggestivity: its emotional undercurrents and trains of thought. It is very natural for Nina to point out her home on the far side of the lake; but there is also the suggestion that her thoughts turn in this direction because she knows that to realize her dream of glory, she will have to part irre-vocably from the home and the lake that mean so much to her. Such emotional implications are however lost on Trigorin, who is pursuing his own line of thought. When he asks Nina about the seagull, her reply is curtly dismissive: she doesn't have much time any more for Kostya and his dramatic, symbolic gestures. Trigorin's 'I don't feel like leaving' is emotionally open-ended. Is it the beautiful scenery that he is reluctant to part from? Or is he thinking of the unexpected pleasure that he has just derived from revealing his innermost thoughts to Nina? His reaction to the seagull seems offhand, and his conscious thoughts return to the unpleasant prospect of departure. But at a less conscious level his ever-active writer's mind (too active, he would argue) has been working on the idea of the seagull, and the result is the plot for a short story. This plot has been well prepared. Its components—the lake, the young girl who has spent all her life beside it, and the shot seagull—have all just figured in the conversation. Trigorin supplies one extra link: the identification of the seagull with the young girl. What he could not know was that Nina already thought of herself as a seagull ('I feel drawn towards the lake like a seagull', she says to Kostya early in Act I); so that Trigorin's story must almost seem like an act of clairvoyance. The impression made upon her is immediately unpleasant, and—although this is not apparent at the time—very deep. In early versions of the play Nina was made to give a start after hearing the story, and to reply: 'You mustn't say that';[7] but in Chekhov's revision of 1901 this was simply replaced by a pause. The alteration is significant. It means that Chekhov was placing greater reliance both on the sensitivity of the actress, who must convey the depth of Nina's reaction without the benefit of words, and also on the sensitivity of the audience. Nina's final 'I must be dreaming!' is again emotionally open-ended. Is it the dream of glory that still intoxicates her? Is she simply bowled over by the realization that she has been talking on equal terms to this famous author, and has suggested the plot for a story to him? Or was it the look that Trigorin gave her when he turned round before going into the house which has so overwhelmed her?

So much then for the characters on stage and the characters conversing; the next question is whether *The Seagull* is written in accordance with the Chekhov formula.

In contrast to *Ivanov*, where the setting alternates between Ivanov's home and that of the Lyebedevs, *The Seagull* makes use of one setting only, the characters being seen either inside the house or in the grounds of their isolated lakeside estate. The impression of a self-contained world is strongly conveyed, and all the characters who appear early in Act I continue to be present throughout the play. There is not however the same sense of continuity as in the later plays, because of the important interval of two years dividing Acts III and IV; and some contrivance is required to reassemble everyone again on the estate for the final act. Where *The Seagull* contrasts sharply with *Ivanov* is in its elimination of a central character, who is replaced by an inner quartet of characters treated on equal terms; but the atmosphere is more like that of a country house party than of an intimate family group. Nor does *The Seagull* strike us as a play about

D

upper class people, since the inner quartet are all members—or aspiring members—of the artistic profession before they are members of any particular class. This contravention of the formula is unimportant however: it does not mean that the characters are unable to put their emotions into words, or to experience subtle emotions. Chekhov's distinctive contrasts between arrivals and departures, and between outsiders (Arkadina, Trigorin) and residents (Kostya, Nina and the others)—leading to disruption—are obvious in *The Seagull*; though qualifications need to be made here also. It is Act III in *The Seagull* which is the departure act, Act IV leading up to a more conventional dramatic climax; and this affects the formula of outsiders and residents as well, since Nina has become very much an outsider when she returns to the house in Act IV, while Kostya has remained a resident.

One respect in which *The Seagull* does establish an important feature of the Chekhov play is in the treatment of minor characters; and since the minor characters are not going to figure prominently in our main discussion of *The Seagull*, we may pause here to consider this feature of the Chekhov play in some detail. What is distinctive about Chekhov's treatment of his minor characters is that he gives them independent status, so that they do not strike the audience as being subordinate to those characters who are more in the limelight. This applies less to Shamrayev and Polina; they are closer to the minor characters in *Ivanov*, who merely inhabit someone else's world. It does apply to Masha, Medvyedyenko and Sorin. In spite of the attempt by the current Moscow Art Theatre production to turn Masha into a major figure by giving exceptional prominence to everything that she says and does, there is little doubt that Chekhov conceived of these three roles as minor ones; but though minor, they are independent. To see how Chekhov achieves this, let us go back to the opening of *The Seagull*:

MEDVYEDYENKO. why do you always wear black?
MASHA. I'm in mourning for my life. I'm unhappy.
MEDVYEDYENKO. But why? (*Thoughtfully.*) I don't understand it. You're healthy, your father may not be rich, but he's comfortably off. Life's a lot harder for me than for you. I only get twenty-three roubles a month, and there's my superannuation to be deducted from that. But I don't go about in mourning. (*They sit down.*)
MASHA. It's not a question of money. Even a poor man can be happy.

MEDVYEDYENKO. In theory, yes, but what happens in practice? There's me, my mother, my two sisters and my young brother. My salary's only twenty-three roubles, but we must have food and drink, mustn't we? And what about tea and sugar? And tobacco? It's a job making ends meet.

MASHA. (*Glances back at the stage.*) The play'll be starting soon.

MEDVYEDYENKO. Yes. Acted by Zaryechnaya, and written by Konstantin Gavrilovich. They're in love with one another, and today their souls will be merged in an attempt to create one and the same artistic image. But between my soul and yours there are no mutual points of contact. I love you, I can't stay at home because of my longing for you, every day I come over on foot, four miles here and four miles back, and I meet nothing but indifferentism on your part. It's understandable. I've no money, we're a large family. . . . Why should you want to marry a man who has to go hungry himself?

MASHA. Rubbish. (*Takes snuff.*) I'm touched by your love, but I can't reciprocate it—that's all there is to say. (*Holds out the snuff-box.*) Help yourself.

MEDVYEDYENKO. I don't feel like it.

(*Pause.*)

MASHA. It's so close, there's bound to be a thunderstorm tonight. You're always philosophizing or else talking about money. You think there's no greater misfortune than being poor, but in my opinion it's a thousand times easier to go about in rags and beg than to. . . . But that's something you wouldn't understand. . . .

These exchanges impart basic information about the two characters (and also about Kostya and Nina); but it is characteristic of Chekhov that at the same time, both Masha and Medvyedyenko impress themselves on the audience by describing how they *feel* about their situation in life.

How they speak on this, their first appearance, is also used by Chekhov as a means of making these characters memorable. Masha speaks brusquely, like a man. She is fond of saying 'Rubbish'. She tries to sound determinedly matter-of-fact about her emotions: 'I'm touched by your love, but I can't reciprocate it—that's all there is to say.' Medvyedyenko's case is more complex. At the risk of seeming incompetent, a translator should try to retain something of the mixture of styles and occasional clumsiness that characterize his way of talking.

He aspires towards a poetic turn of phrase—'today their souls will be merged in an attempt to create one and the same artistic image'—but the effect is merely pompous and stilted. He would like to sound cultured and introduces a foreign borrowing, *indifferentism*, into his speech, but he misuses the term when a perfectly good Russian word, *ravnodushiye*, was available. These linguistic aspirations contrast with his catch-phrase—'It's a job making ends meet'—which is undoubtedly more typical of his natural way of talking. Like Yepikhodov in *The Cherry Orchard*, Medvyedyenko has swallowed a certain amount of culture without being able to digest it properly.

The other Chekhovian means of making the minor characters memorable is to give them some fixed preoccupation which they constantly reveal throughout the play. With Medvyedyenko it is money, 'making ends meet'. He at least finds something of interest in Shamrayev's anecdote about the bass from the local church: 'And tell me, what sort of pay do they get in a church choir?' Masha's preoccupation is only hinted at in this opening passage—by the dots, suggestive of unspoken thoughts and deep yearnings, which accompany her remark that 'it's a thousand times easier to go about in rags and beg than to. . . . But that's something you wouldn't understand. . . .' The preoccupation turns out to be her unrequited love for Kostya. That determinedly matter-of-fact attitude towards her own emotions is no more than wishful thinking. In the course of the play poor Masha is constantly resolving to tear her love for Kostya out 'by the roots'—and just as constantly failing to do so!

Where Chekhov's treatment of these two minor characters diverges is that Medvyedyenko is made memorable by giving him a strong colouring of the comic and the absurd, whereas Masha is given a strong colouring of the comic and the eccentric. Absurdity and eccentricity in Chekhov's work can both be traced back to the comic anecdotes and vaudevilles which Chekhov produced in such quantities as a young man. Masha's eccentricities—the black dress, her fondness for snuff and the vodka-bottle, speaking like a man (one almost expects her to start smoking a pipe!)—create a comic effect at first, but the lasting impression is more serious; and this is true generally of eccentricity in the Chekhov play. It is used as a means of showing the extent to which characters are dissatisfied with, or dissociated from, the situation in which they find themselves. Masha's behaviour is eccentric because she is not willing to accept without registering some kind of protest a life that falls so far short of the life that she would wish for herself. This protest is essentially personal, not intended to impress other people at all: wearing a black dress is not meant to be a way of drawing attention to herself. There is in general no element of self-satisfied individualistic posturing in the behaviour of Chekhov's eccentrics; they are not 'characters' in the English sense. On the contrary, fundamentally they do not feel that they are any different from anyone else. If you were in my position, Masha seems to imply, you would behave in just the same way that I do. When she says that she is in mourning for her life, she is merely stating what to her seems obvious. To behave abnormally appears to her the only normal response to what she sees as her abnormal situation.

Chekhov's eccentrics (and here we have in mind, apart from Masha in *The Seagull*, her namesake in *Three Sisters*—who likewise wears black all the time and is given to whistling and using strong language at a period when well-bred young Russian ladies just did not do that kind of thing; also from *Three Sisters*—Solyony and Chebutykin; and from *The Cherry Orchard*—the governess, Charlotte Ivanovna) do not stand outside the emotional network of the Chekhov play. Their relation to the other characters is oblique. They feel themselves to be emotionally isolated from them, yet crave a greater degree of intimacy; and their inability to find it leads them into eccentric behaviour.

But to return once more to the question of the Chekhov formula. Though there are some qualifications to be made, *The Seagull* does correspond in general terms to the pattern outlined in the opening chapter. It is when we move further back, to the hard core of the Chekhov play—namely, its emotional content—that doubts arise about referring to *The Seagull* as an example of the Chekhov play. What of the characters' emotional preoccupations in *The Seagull*, their emotional network, and the centrifugal quality arising out of different ways of coming to terms with life emotionally? Does *The Seagull* match the earlier description? I think the answer is that it does not, that Chekhov was not yet concentrating on these features; and later we shall discuss in more detail why it does not match the description. I would regard *The Seagull* more as a testing ground; and when Chekhov wrote to Suvorin, while composing the first draft, that he was 'sinning dreadfully against the conventions of the stage',[8] he was perhaps himself aware of feeling his way, of casting around for new approaches. Let us turn finally to those experimental features of *The Seagull* which, though interesting in themselves and not necessarily unsuccessful, do not occur again in the later plays. From the point of

view of the Chekhov play, it looks as if Chekhov felt that they were
not quite what he was after, that these were blind alleys.

Prominent among these blind alleys are a number of features which
can be generally described as autobiographical. Alone of his major
plays, *The Seagull* is about the kind of people Chekhov mixed with
and knew best. The central characters in the play—the talented actress
who always wants to be the centre of attention, the distinguished
author who feels unable to direct his own talents, the obscure young
writer experimenting with 'new forms', and the stage-struck young
girl prepared to leave home in her search for fame and glory—would
all have fitted in well with the visitors and 'permanent guests' at
Melikhovo, the small estate not far from Moscow, where Chekhov
and his family lived from 1891 to 1898; to say nothing of the local
doctor and the local schoolmaster. When Nina makes the discovery
that 'well-known people . . . cry, go fishing, play cards, laugh and get
angry, just like anyone else', she might well be speaking of life at
Melikhovo. Chekhov did in fact borrow all the external details of the
Trigorin–Nina story from the affair between his friend, the Ukrainian
writer Potapenko, and the attractive young Lika Mizinova, a close
friend of the Chekhov family, and of Chekhov in particular. Lika and
Potapenko had first met at Melikhovo in 1893. As well as the kind
of people to be found at Melikhovo, *The Seagull* also reflects the kind
of subjects that were discussed there: the question of 'new forms' in
art, for example, must have been hotly debated by Chekhov and his
friends. Crowding into the play too are Chekhov's own literary preoccupations, such as his admiration for Maupassant, and his lifelong
interest in *Hamlet*. Even those opening lines of *The Seagull*, about
Masha's black dress, sound like an amusing echo of Hamlet's 'inky
cloak' and 'customary suits of solemn black'. Finally, it has been
suggested that Chekhov incorporated elements from his own experience into at least three of the characters: Trigorin, Kostya and Doctor
Dorn.

This autobiographical element is not however the only important
feature of *The Seagull* that was not repeated in the later plays. There
is the elaborate poetic use which Chekhov makes of an exotic natural
setting: the beautiful lake. There is also the use of a recurrent symbol,
the seagull, which can be identified with particular individuals—a
feature which drew down upon Chekhov's head the official disapproval
of the Theatrical Literary Commission, who criticized the play for
bearing too close a resemblance to Ibsen's *The Wild Duck*. Most

important, there is Chekhov's choice of four very distinctive main characters, and the varying means which he used to depict them. The account of *The Seagull* that follows will be particularly concerned with these methods of characterization, since this can be regarded as the most sensitive area for the evolution of the Chekhov play.

ii. THE LAKE AND THE THEME OF ART

In trying to visualize *The Seagull* as a whole, we may well think first of all of the play's unusual setting: the country house with its large terrace and a garden that runs down to the shores of a beautiful lake. This lakeside setting was not inspired by Melikhovo, which boasted nothing grander than a large pond, but by an estate in the Novgorod province which Chekhov visited briefly in July 1895 to see his friend, the painter Levitan, who, like Kostya, had tried to shoot himself. When the curtain rises, the lake cannot be seen, however, as it is obscured by Kostya's improvised garden theatre; and his play cannot begin without Nina. At last she appears, excited and out of breath. 'The sky was red,' she tells Kostya, 'the moon was beginning to rise, and I kept making my horse go faster and faster.' Now the spectators arrive from the house and take up their places. All of a sudden, the stage is completely transformed:

> The curtain rises; it reveals a view of the lake; the moon above the horizon and its reflection in the water; Nina Zaryechnaya, dressed entirely in white, is sitting on a rock.

It is clear now why the lake was not allowed to be visible at the beginning of *The Seagull*. Chekhov has reserved the play's most dramatic 'entrance' for the lake—appropriately, since it is not only the outstanding feature of the natural setting, but will also be constantly referred to as the play progresses.

The lake is associated with the residents, in particular with Kostya and Nina. Both have lived near the lake for a long time, and Nina knows 'every little island on it'. At the end of Act I, Doctor Dorn comments on his companions:

> How overwrought they all are! How overwrought! And there's so much love about . . . Oh, you spellbinding lake!

Dorn may well be suggesting how Chekhov intends us to feel about the lake, since on several occasions he seems to act as Chekhov's spokesman (another feature of *The Seagull* that was not to be re-peated). The adjective which he uses to describe the lake is *koldovskoye*, which has suggestions of magic and witchcraft. Calm and beautiful in normal conditions, but covered by huge waves when the weather is stormy, the lake is like a lake of folk legend, with magic powers for good and evil. It casts a spell over those who live round it. For both Kostya and Nina the lake seems to symbolize the source of all happi-ness, and inspires in them vivid dreams of a happy and successful future. When Kostya feels that Nina has grown cold towards him, it is as if he had 'woken one morning and seen that this lake had sud-denly dried up or run away into the ground'. In times of distress, they both turn back to the lake in search of solace. After his play has failed, Kostya 'spends whole days beside the lake'; and in Act IV, Nina says: 'Ever since I arrived I've been walking about here . . . by the lake.' Yet the lake's spell is full of danger. Those vivid dreams are mis-leading; life has nothing so wonderful to offer them; and the more they turn back to the lake, with its poetry and its beauty, the harder it becomes to reconcile themselves to the prosaic realities of life and to shattered dreams.

To the estate by the lake come the outsiders, Arkadina and Trigorin. Middle-aged and successful in the world of art, they are immediately contrasted with Kostya and Nina, who are young and striving after artistic success. The lives and emotions of these four characters become increasingly interwoven, but what is common to all four of them is the depth and constancy of their dedication to art. This artistic involve-ment of the four main characters, who between them are engaged in and hold views about the arts of acting, fiction-writing and writing for the stage, is the most distinctive feature of the subject matter of *The Seagull*; and there are no important scenes in the play in which the question of art does not figure prominently. Chekhov also handles the theme of art in a distinctive way—for in working out the personal destinies of his characters, he seems at the same time to have been writing a commentary on the nature of artistic talent.

To appreciate the full force of this theme of art in *The Seagull* requires some awareness of the intellectual climate of nineteenth-century Russia. When Sorin says that 'we can't manage without the theatre', he would have had the backing of all the Russian intelli-gentsia (if not of the establishment, as witness the horror which the thought of Nina becoming an actress inspires in her father and step-mother). The intellectuals of Chekhov's day felt that whatever its shortcomings, the theatre was a vital institution which should be wholeheartedly supported. One must remember that there was no political opposition in Tsarist Russia, no freedom of speech or of the press, and that literature, drama, and even literary and dramatic criticism acquired unusual importance as a forum for the veiled discussion of social issues. But there seems also to have been a belief among enlightened Russians that literature and the theatre represented a powerful spiritual force which might exercise a profound influence for the better upon human life generally. Art and its practitioners were regarded with a kind of religious veneration. Kostya recognizes this when he refers, however contemptuously, to his mother's belief that she was 'serving humanity and the sacred cause of art'; and it is significant that when Nina at the climax of *The Seagull* reaffirms her determination to become a genuine actress, she also uses religious language, saying that what is important is to learn how to 'bear one's cross' and to 'have faith'. The function of the serious artist was not so much to entertain as to raise people on to a higher spiritual level, by the inspiration of his acting, or by the beauty and profundity of his writing.

iii. METHODS OF CHARACTERIZATION:
KOSTYA, TRIGORIN, ARKADINA

Each act of *The Seagull* has a distinctive quality, which comes about largely because each act is dominated by one of the play's four principal characters. Act I belongs to Treplyov or, as we have been calling him, Kostya (an affectionate diminutive of Konstantin). His play provides the focal point of the act: we are shown the preparations for it, its performance and aftermath. But we also come to know closely the play's author—with his complicated yet immature personality, especially as seen in his confused feelings towards Arkadina, and with his outspoken views on the contemporary theatre. In the second act Kostya appears only briefly, presenting Nina with the seagull that he has shot and threatening to shoot himself in the same way. It is Trigorin who overshadows Act II. Until this point Chekhov has held him in reserve: Trigorin in Act I scarcely opens his mouth. But the speeches in which he now reveals himself to Nina are the longest by any character in Chekhov's four major plays. The third act is dominated by Arkadina. She is on stage almost throughout, and is at the centre of three dramatic scenes which follow in rapid succession: with Sorin, when her stinginess helps to bring on his fainting spell (in

Stanislavsky's production, an extra element of drama was added here by making it seem to Arkadina that Sorin had actually died); with Kostya—the famous 'bandage' scene which generates more emotional electricity than any other passage in the play; and with Trigorin, when she persuades him not to abandon her for Nina.

Although the final act of *The Seagull* is not a departure act (in some ways it resembles a new first act, with its element of fresh exposition when Kostya recounts what has happened to Nina and Trigorin in the previous two years), it does illustrate a characteristic feature of the Chekhov play, in that it frequently echoes and refers back to earlier passages, particularly from Act I, and so gives the play a sense of overall shape. When the act begins, Masha and Medvyedyenko are talking together, as they were when the play started, and there are immediate references to the lake and to Kostya's theatre, which now stands 'bare and shapeless, like a skeleton'. Masha is still pulling herself together, Medvyedyenko still trying to make ends meet, and Sorin complaining that the doctor refuses to give him any medicine. The comments on Kostya's writing echo the comments on his play in Act I, and in their last conversation Kostya and Nina are repeatedly calling up the past. Nina talks of the lake and of her youthful love for Kostya, she refers to herself as a seagull and recalls Trigorin's 'subject for a short story', and in her final speech she quotes the opening sentences from Kostya's play.

Chekhov uses the stormy weather in Act IV for symbolic purposes —an effect that is not characteristic of the Chekhov play but is more associated with the novels of Turgenev. Indoors it is warm and cheerful, and the game of lotto proceeds at a leisurely pace until it is time for supper. But outside the wind is howling, the trees are rustling, and there are huge waves on the lake. The outdoors–indoors contrast underlines the contrast between the turmoil of Nina's life as an unrecognized actress, and the lives of Arkadina and Trigorin, so cosily successful and unchanged since we last saw them; and between Nina, who went out into the world as a 'homeless wanderer' and faced up to its difficulties, and Kostya, who was so absorbed in himself that he remained safely at home near the lake. In the course of the act, the 'lines' of Kostya and Nina may be said to cross over. At first it seems that Kostya's life has taken a turn for the better: he seems more composed and independent, even his appearance has improved, and the suicidal frame of mind which provoked his unsuccessful attempt to shoot himself earlier is apparently a thing of the past. Nina, however, seems to be living out Trigorin's story; and when she comes in out of the stormy night, she looks thinner, she is exhausted, and her state of mind is obviously distraught. But these appearances are deceptive. It is not Kostya but Nina who is on the way to becoming independent. Act IV belongs to Nina, and the play reaches its climax when she declares her faith in her vocation as an actress; Kostya's subsequent suicide is a logical anti-climax to this.

Although none of the four characters is ever out of sight for long, it does look as if Chekhov found himself concentrating on each of the characters in turn, and in discussing them individually we shall follow the same order as Chekhov. What I hope will emerge from these individual accounts is not only that the characters are very different from one another, but that they differ in ways which demanded very contrasting *methods* of presentation.

Any discussion of Kostya must begin, as Chekhov begins, with Arkadina. 'I love my mother, I love her deeply,' Kostya tells Sorin early in the play; but this does not prevent him from listing her faults with brutal frankness. His judgements prove correct, but their very harshness, combined with the excessive length at which he talks about her, suggests that she is still abnormally important in his life. The trouble with Kostya is that he has only *partly* detached himself from Arkadina: he sees all her weaknesses, yet he still craves her affection; he despises the theatre that she represents, yet still aspires to be a successful dramatist himself. Where he is least free of her influence is in the excessive importance that he attaches to success and failure; and this makes him very touchy and aware of his own lack of reputation:

> ... And when all those artists and writers in my mother's drawing-room were so kind as to notice my presence, I could feel that they were thinking to themselves just how insignificant I was— and as I read their thoughts, I suffered agonies of humiliation ...

Kostya, like his mother, is immediately jealous of the success of other people. He resents the fact that Trigorin is 'a long way off forty, but already he's famous and thoroughly spoilt'. He accurately describes Trigorin's work, using the same adjectives—'charming and talented' —that Trigorin will later use of himself, but when Nina comments shortly after on Trigorin's 'wonderful stories', Kostya denies that he has ever read them. He is afraid that Trigorin may turn Nina's head, even before Nina has set eyes on him. In Kostya's love for Nina we might see an attempt to detach himself completely from Arkadina's influence, but Chekhov suggests that he seeks a very dependent relationship with Nina, one in which she would act as little more than a substitute for his mother. When Kostya exclaims to Sorin: 'I can't live without her'; or when, after Nina has returned home, he says despairingly to Dorn at the end of Act I: 'Whatever am I going to do? I want to see her . . . I simply must see her'—his words are rather more than sentimental effusions: Kostya's dependence on other people is a very real part of him. If someone lets him down, as Nina does later, he is defenceless.

Kostya is scornful of the established theatre which his mother personifies. He singles out for special contempt the routine naturalism and banal moralizing of the contemporary repertoire. When Nina comments on Kostya's own play that it has too little action and no love interest, and that there are no 'real people' in it, this is a cue for Kostya to state his own artistic credo. 'Real people!' he snorts contemptuously. 'Life must be shown neither as it is, nor as it ought to be, but as it appears to us in dreams.' His play has been written to illustrate this idea, and we are left in no doubt that the play's success or failure is of vital concern to Kostya. There is a certain childish self-importance about the way in which he sends Masha and Medvye-dyenko off to the house because they have arrived too early, and keeps looking at his watch, wondering if Nina will appear in time. Nor is there much doubt at whom the play is primarily directed; but is he trying to impress or to provoke Arkadina? He does not know. After Arkadina's first interruption—'This is something decadent'—Kostya's ambiguous feelings are revealed by his tone of voice, which is both imploring *and* reproachful. And when, after the frivolous remark that Arkadina cannot resist, Kostya rings down the curtain, his action is not entirely unpremeditated. One part of him knew that Arkadina would dislike the play, and this idea of how he might pay her out had already crossed his mind.

Kostya's personality, then, is built up by Chekhov very largely in the course of Act I; and as we shall see later, this careful portrait is necessary if Kostya's subsequent behaviour in the play is to make sense. The portrait is built up through what he says about himself, his past life and his mother; even the contents of his play can, if one chooses, be analysed to see what light they shed on its author's personality.[9] Essential to Chekhov's technique is that Kostya should be made to reveal more about himself than he is consciously aware of.

Indeed, Chekhov offers so many clues of this nature that it would be easy to compile a very detailed psychological dossier, or case history, for Kostya. All these clues point towards the unusual importance of his mother as a shaping influence in his life. Here another valuable piece in the jigsaw of Kostya's personality is added by his remarks in Act III, just after he has asked Arkadina to change his bandage for him:

KOSTYA. I remember, a very long time ago, when you were still working in the state theatre—I must have been quite small then—there was a fight in our courtyard, and one of the tenants, a washerwoman, was badly hurt. Do you remember? They picked her up unconscious . . . and you kept going to see her, and took her medicine, and bathed her children in a tub. Don't you remember?
ARKADINA. No.

This reminiscence of Arkadina as a tender young mother at the start of her career reinforces the idea of a duality in Kostya's behaviour. One part of him has rebelled strongly against what Arkadina has now become, striving to assert his artistic independence; but another part has remained permanently attached to the tender young mother that Arkadina once was. This explains the childish element in Kostya, the part of him that has not grown up: his dependence on other people, inability to stand on his own feet and general instability. When he stamps on the ground in temper, orders the curtain of his theatre to be lowered and then stalks off, does he not remind us of a petulant child saying that he's not going to play with us any more and abandoning himself to a fit of sulks?

Unconscious self-revelation, the abnormal influence exerted since childhood by the mother (which an outsider can soon detect but which cannot be seen objectively by the person concerned), the urge to rebel, neurotic traits arising out of the persistence into adult life of elements from childhood: all this sounds very familiar, very Western, very much of the twentieth century. In Kostya Chekhov seems to anticipate the psychoanalytical approach. But this is only one way in which the main characters are presented in *The Seagull*—as we shall see in turning now to Trigorin.

Chekhov's outsiders are middle-aged, highly successful in the world of art, and at the peak of their artistic powers; but here the similarity between them ends. Arkadina worships Trigorin because she worships

success, and because his attentions are flattering to her self-image. It
is ironical that Trigorin himself is not interested in success at all, and
is genuinely perplexed when Nina asks him what it feels like to be
famous. Still more ironical is that when Arkadina is trying to win him
back from Nina, her final weapon is to flatter him outrageously as a
writer: 'You're so talented and clever, you're the best of all the modern
writers, you're Russia's one and only hope . . .' To this Trigorin
might have replied, in the words that he had used earlier to Nina,
that 'to me all these fine words . . . are just like sweets, which I never
touch'. It is obvious that Arkadina has no appreciation of Trigorin's
self-doubts; to her his melancholy moods are just a part of his 'genius'.
When he does try to explain his feelings to her, she is incapable of
understanding. Trigorin is only able to unburden himself so fully to
Nina at the end of Act II because he thinks that Nina is about to pass
from his life immediately and for good. What he says is almost like
talking to himself; though the knowledge that he has revealed his
innermost feelings to her may be one reason that attracts him to Nina.
He tells her of the torment of his early years as a young writer struggling for recognition, and of how writing has now become an obsessive
compulsion, which preys upon every other aspect of his life. But what
is the point, he asks, in 'eating away' his own life in such a fashion?
Is it just to hear himself described as a charming and talented writer,
but not as good as Turgenev? That he knows is painfully inadequate:
a writer of his ability should have a clear purpose in writing, should
be pursuing aims of real seriousness and importance. But this is where
the difficulty lies. He has no aims or purposes. 'The *worst* thing is
that I live in a kind of daze and often don't understand what I'm
writing . . .' The subjects that he writes about are those which society
expects him to write about. Foisted on him from outside, these subjects
present themselves in such alarming profusion that he feels unable to
keep up with them all, like the peasant vainly chasing after the departed
train.

How are we to explain Trigorin's plight? The explanation seems to
be that his lack of aim as a writer is a reflection of his lack of aim as
a person—of what Kostya uncharitably refers to in Act IV as his
beskharaktyernost' ('lack of character' or 'spinelessness'). If Trigorin
really knew what was important to him, he would not feel such a sense
of inadequacy in writing about important human issues; but unfortunately he does not know. He has always been so busy observing life
round him that he has never had time to experience it at first hand,

to discover what kind of person he is himself, and to make up his mind on what is and is not important to him in life. Writing has become a substitute for living. He pursues it with quite abnormal compulsive energy—nothing can be allowed to slip past in case it might come in useful—because he hopes that in some way it will solve his problem for him: through his writings it will become clear to him and to the rest of the world what kind of person he is and where he stands in life. So he is caught in a vicious circle: he seeks a solution to the problem of his personal identity through his writing, but his writings only reflect his failure to find such an identity. Trigorin has drifted into a liaison with Arkadina in the hope that she will 'place' him, give him an identity that he can believe in, but all Arkadina does is to confirm him even more hopelessly in his existing role of the 'famous writer'. He switches his attention to Nina because he is excited by the possibility that in a relationship with her he might discover something new about himself, that with her he might actually start to live life instead of observing it. But he is not seriously convinced that this could happen. It only needs a display of forcefulness by Arkadina (the words that she uses are not important—as we saw, they are in fact highly inappropriate) to push him back to where he was before. 'I have no will of my own,' Trigorin comments; and we might revise his words to read: 'I do not know my own mind.' Such a person is a prey to those who feel that they do know their own minds. When, after agreeing to leave with Arkadina, he promptly takes out his writer's notebook to record an interesting expression, Trigorin seems to be saying: 'If you're so convinced that I am to play the role of the famous writer, then I suppose I might as well make a good job of it!'

Scarcely has Arkadina turned her back, however, than he is arranging to meet Nina in Moscow. Nina proves unable to help him; her adulation of him as the brilliant writer differed little from that of Arkadina, and she was too spellbound to pay close attention to what he was saying in Act II. Trigorin's corrosive disillusion, on the other hand, was bound to have an unhealthy effect on Nina. When we learn of the shabby way in which Trigorin has treated her, we wonder how it was possible for Kostya in Act I to describe him as a 'very decent fellow'. The explanation must be that Trigorin is never consciously immoral—he is not the middle-aged man 'trifling with a young girl's affections'—but he is absorbed in himself to such an exceptional degree that what happens to other people is considered by him only in relation to his own problem. This self-absorption explains why he fails to guess the thoughts that are passing through Nina's mind when he tells her his 'plot for a short story'; and why he is so curiously frank and even unworldly in asking Arkadina to release him. His self-absorption is revealed again in Act IV when Kostya observes that 'he's read his own story right through, but he hasn't even cut the pages of mine'. From the final act it becomes clear that Trigorin is unchanged, and that his problem has been indefinitely shelved. He does still say that he would like to conquer his passion for writing and spend all his time fishing, but this is a very light-hearted echo of his remarks in Act II. On the contrary, he now appears to be even more firmly in the grip of the professional writer's routine:

TREPLYOV. Will you be staying with us for long?
TRIGORIN. No, I think I'll go back to Moscow tomorrow. I've got to. There's a story I'm in a hurry to finish, and on top of that, I've promised something for an anthology. Life as usual, in other words.

The final impression of Trigorin is of a dangerous drifter through life, a man of considerable talent who does not know his own mind, a man whose brilliance involuntarily attracts other people to him but who can only cause them harm. His 'plot for a short story' remained permanently in his notebook and was forgotten; and when on his return to the estate after an interval of two years he is presented with the stuffed seagull, he is very puzzled—priding himself as he does on his retentive writer's memory—by his inability to remember anything at all about the incident. The ironical comment is implied that just as the seagull story was a brief moment in his literary career which never came to anything, so in his own life Nina was only an episode which soon passed and left no trace behind it.

Trigorin's personality, then, is built up by Chekhov very largely via his introspective speeches at the end of Act II. Though the above account has considered him as he appears throughout the play, it is clear that, just as Kostya can only be understood from Act I, so it is those long speeches in Act II that must hold the key to Trigorin. In contrast to Kostya, he does not describe any aspect of his parental background or past life, other than the torments which he had to undergo as a young writer struggling for recognition. He does not reveal himself unconsciously; and there is no point in compiling a psychological dossier for him, since the psychological traits that he exhibits—his ineffectuality, for example—can all be seen as arising out of the one problem of which he is consciously aware. There is no jigsaw with pieces here, but a single problem from which everything else radiates: the problem of why he feels this terrible compulsion to go on writing, when he does not even think much of what he writes anyway. This is the point to which Trigorin's own introspection can take us; he himself can go no further. It is then left to the audience to take over, and to seek whatever explanation of Trigorin's problem seems to them most appropriate. This is a much more enigmatic, open-ended way of presenting a character than the way in which Kostya is presented. Kostya is *circumscribed* by all the information that is given about him and by his relationship to Arkadina; any interpretation of him can, as it were, be checked against his psychological file. But Trigorin is presented in a way which poses the audience an intellectual problem, and demands a speculative answer.

Kostya's recollection of Arkadina as a tender young mother at the start of her career is very far removed from the Arkadina whom we now see, at the height of her fame, some twenty years later. The self-image that she has been perfecting during this time—as the celebrated actress serving the sacred cause of art, and as the woman of irresistible fascination—is constantly and clearly before her, dictating the role that she assumes in life. It is an image that needs to be repeatedly confirmed from outside: by the devotion of those round her and by the applause of her audiences. She needs to be the centre of attention, to feel all eyes turned admiringly in her direction, and she does not tire of regaling others with the details of her artistic triumphs:

ARKADINA. What a reception they gave me in Kharkov! My goodness, I still haven't quite got over it! . . . The students gave me a standing ovation . . . I had three baskets of flowers, two garlands, and this . . . (*Takes a brooch from her breast and throws it on the table.*)
SHAMRAYEV. Yes, that's really something . . .

But to live up to this demanding image requires determination and constant vigilance; and this has made her hard, self-seeking and competitive. 'You must praise no one but her,' Kostya remarks. Arkadina is jealous of Nina from the start—because Nina is young, because she will be the centre of attention in Kostya's play, and because she may attract Trigorin, the brilliant and successful writer whose attachment to her provides so fitting a confirmation of Arkadina's self-image.

E

Arkadina is involved in a number of emotional scenes throughout *The Seagull*; and in each case the reason why her emotions are so strongly aroused is that her self-image is being threatened. Shamrayev angers her, not because she was really very anxious to visit town with Polina, but because his attitude shows a lack of respect for her famous position. She is upset by Sorin's diffident request that she should give Kostya a little money—for she recognizes that the request is reasonable, yet is convinced that she must hang on to her last copeck if she is to maintain an appropriately expensive wardrobe and way of life. The possible defection of Trigorin is a particularly serious challenge. When he asks for his release, it is characteristic of the role-playing Arkadina that she should switch rapidly from genuine emotions of fear and anger to emotions that are entirely assumed. Chekhov cannot help poking fun at her 'performance' as the passionate lover brought to her knees by grief:

> ARKADINA. My handsome, splendid man. . . . You are the last page in my life! (*Kneels down.*) My joy, my pride, my happiness . . . (*Embraces his knees.*) If you leave me even for a single hour, I shall never survive, I shall go out of my mind—my wonderful, magnificent man, my master. . . .
> TRIGORIN. Someone may come in. (*Helps her to her feet.*)
> ARKADINA. Let them, I'm not ashamed of my love for you.

Of course, she gets her way in the end—not because Trigorin is in the least swayed by the words she uses, but because he senses the determination that lies behind them.

It is Kostya however who provokes Arkadina most sharply. He is the one who knows her best, the one who knows just what goes on behind the scenes of the image that she projects to the outside world. And Arkadina knows that he knows. Mother and son have too much in common—self-centredness, jealousy, preoccupation with success—not to be able to read one another's minds and to be susceptible to one another's emotions. If there is an element of premeditation in Kostya's action when he rings down the curtain in Act I, there is certainly an element of premeditation in Arkadina's reaction to her son's 'decadent' play. She had been half expecting a play like that, and sees quickly enough the challenge that it contains to her own artistic position. Does he expect her to sit there and just let him get away with it? The strength of his reaction to her facetious comments may take her by surprise; but when Kostya rings down the curtain, he has played his only card and stalks off in a childish temper, leaving the field clear. Out comes Arkadina's justification for her facetiousness—'he told us himself that it was going to be a *joke*'; and out come the arguments that had been building up inside her against the pretentiousness of modern drama. Kostya's challenge has been repelled, and with a certain ruthlessness; Arkadina switches the conversation to the sounds coming from the other side of the lake; yet there was another feeling—of affection for Kostya—struggling for survival against the demands of her self-image, and which prompts her belated show of remorse.

Perhaps this expression of remorse was just another of her assumed emotions? Her rhetorical question—'Why did I hurt my poor boy's feelings?'—does not *sound* very sincere. But if the 'bandage' scene in Act III is to be convincing, it must convey that the obvious friction between them is coloured, if not intensified, by a mutual bond of affection. They taunt one another like children squabbling, and who know very well which remarks will hurt the other most. He scoffs at her beloved theatre and calls her a miser; she tells him that he has no talent, cannot even support himself, and—most hurtful of all—is a complete nonentity. It is the knowledge of what each has said to the other that makes them burst into tears and that leads to their reconciliation. 'My darling child, forgive me . . .,' says Arkadina. 'Forgive your sinful mother. Forgive me, I am so unhappy.' This too sounds theatrical; but then Arkadina has lost the ability to give natural expression to her more tender feelings. She is at this moment genuinely moved, and her remarks seem to come out involuntarily. The self-image and the role-playing briefly drop away from her; behind them we glimpse another Arkadina—superstitious, hoarding her money in the bank, scared of growing old and of dying. 'I could play a girl of fifteen', she had said at the beginning of Act II; and in retrospect, her remark seems not so much conceited or ludicrous, as full of a certain defiance and desperation.

After the neurotic complexities of Kostya and Trigorin's obsessive problem, Arkadina may seem at first a straightforward character. Her jealousy, her stinginess, her desire for the limelight—personal qualities such as these are sharply defined and unambiguous. But as I have tried to show, this is not quite a portrait in the orthodox tradition. Her self-image, her role-playing, especially the briefly glimpsed contrasts between the role that she plays in public and the concealed feelings that lie behind it: all these features of the way in which Chekhov presents Arkadina strike just as modern a note as the way in which he presents her son.

iv. NINA, KOSTYA AND THE FINAL ACT

There is nothing neurotic about Nina, the fourth member of Chekhov's inner quartet. Like Kostya, she is in revolt against parental values; but unlike him, her rebellion against the tyrannical supervision of her father and stepmother strikes us as a healthy, vigorous and uncomplicated response. There is no obsessive problem gnawing away at her; nor is her life dominated by the need to live up to a clearly defined image of herself. Nina can be defined in terms of an emotional aspiration: her desire to become a famous actress.[10] That aspiration may be modified during the play (the youthful romantic aura—the thirst for glory—disappears), but basically it remains unchanged; so that the interest in Nina's portrayal is focussed not so much on what she feels, as on whether or not her ambition will be fulfilled—in other words, on what she *does*. There is a sense of movement about the characterization of Nina which is entirely lacking from the other three. It is no coincidence that she literally comes galloping into the play, and when last seen is running off into the garden. This element of suspense—will she achieve her ambition? are the obstacles going to prove too great?—makes Nina into the most conventionally *dramatic* of the four main characters.

Nina is drawn to the house near the lake not so much by Kostya's devotion as by the glamour and excitement of famous names. Kostya's play does not interest her; but she welcomes the opportunity of acting in it, because she knows that Arkadina and Trigorin will be present. Her performance is immature, but this does not put her off. Trigorin, the writer of genius, has fascinated her in a way that Kostya never could, and in Act II she refers even more scathingly to Kostya's play as 'so uninteresting'. When he lays at Nina's feet the seagull that he has shot, and threatens to take his own life in the same way, Kostya unwittingly casts a spell on himself—even though, with the passage of time, the seagull disappears entirely from his mind. Nina is unimpressed, though Trigorin's 'plot for a short story' does impress her greatly. When Nina decides to leave home she sees ahead of her only the bright lights of the theatre, and Trigorin's genius; she does not see the difficulties that face an inexperienced actress, or the disillusion that has eaten into Trigorin. Our impression of her at this stage is of someone who is moving forward all the time (however rashly), un-deterred by setbacks, looking only to the future, able to act indepen-dently but at the same time willing to sacrifice herself completely to someone like Trigorin, whom she admires as a real genius of art. Kostya, meanwhile, whose fate is continually compared to hers, creates exactly the opposite impression. He has forgotten Dorn's words of encouragement and convinced himself that his play 'was a stupid flop'. His self-esteem cannot withstand this setback, Nina is unsym-pathetic, and rather than contemplate the future, he tries to shoot himself.

When Kostya and Nina are next seen together, two years later, personal happiness has eluded both of them, though far more dramatic-ally in the case of Nina. Kostya is still hopelessly self-centred and dependent—'I'm lonely, I've no one's devotion to warm me, I'm so cold it's like being in a dungeon'—and he is still living in the past: he sees no reason why he and Nina should not start all over again and recapture the feelings of two years earlier. Nina is acutely aware that she has wronged Kostya, but she knows that going back on the past is quite impossible: a great deal has happened to her during these two years, she is now a very different person, and in any case she is still —for reasons that are not made clear in view of past events—'desper-ately in love' with Trigorin.

But it is on the artistic rather than on the personal level that Chekhov works out the fates of his two characters. Kostya seems to have made some progress; at least his stories are published now. We see him at work on one of these stories, and coming to certain conclusions about his own writing. He realizes that he is as prone to literary clichés as any other writer, that no writer can hope to succeed unless he has worked out for himself certain basic techniques, and that what is important is not old or new forms, but 'that a person should write without thinking about forms at all, but because it just comes pouring freely from his soul'. This is ironical, when one remembers Kostya's outspoken championing of 'new forms' in Act I; but should it be taken to imply that Chekhov intended to deflate Kostya completely as a writer? This young man with his defiant claim to Arkadina that he was 'more talented than the lot of you' and his grandiose plans to revolutionize the theatre—is he after all far more pretentious than talented? This 'ironic reversal' does not seem to me quite what Chekhov had in mind. Is he not suggesting that Kostya's discoveries are ones that every serious writer *needs* to make, and that had it been anyone but Kostya, they might in the long run have proved beneficial and helped him to realize the talents he undoubtedly possessed? Doctor Dorn again seems to speak for Chekhov when he praises Kostya's stories for their imaginative power, but regrets their lack of any definite purpose. This echoes his remarks in Act I, when he had warned Kostya that 'if you follow the picturesque path of your imagination without a definite aim in mind, you'll lose your way and your talent will destroy you'—and had expressed his conviction that 'a work of art should express a clear definite idea'.

Our final impression of Kostya as a writer comes from Nina's last speech of all, when she repeats the opening lines of Kostya's play, in which he sets the scene:

> Men, lions, eagles and partridges, horned deer, geese, spiders, silent fishes living in the deep, starfishes and creatures not seen by the human eye—in short, all life, all life, all life, having completed its melancholy cycle, has been extinguished. For thousands of centuries earth has not borne a single living creature, and this poor moon now lights her lamp in vain. In the meadows cranes no longer wake with a cry, and the droning of May beetles is heard no more in the lime-groves.

It seems obvious that Chekhov inserted these lines here so as to give Nina her one opportunity of convincing the audience that she really has made a genuine advance as an actress. This speech, if not the rest of the play (with its heavy-handed use of triple repetitions, so reminiscent of Kostya's over-emphatic way of talking), must provide a vehicle for the demonstration of her talents. It does of course have strong nostalgic associations: Nina is recalling the earlier, innocent period of her friendship with Kostya. But what Nina also realizes now is that these lines do have a haunting poetic quality of their own. The last sentence in particular has many pleasing sound effects which cannot be reproduced in translation. It can be read as a poetic couplet:

> *Na lugú uzhé nye prosypáyutsya s kríkom zhuravlí*
> *i maískikh zhukóv nye byváyet slýshno v lípovykh róshchakh.*

The first line builds up quietly to a climax on its subject, *zhuravlí*, while the second starts with its subject, *máiskikh zhukóv*, and then slowly 'unwinds'. There is concentrated assonance at the end of the first and beginning of the second lines: most obviously, of the musical *ʒh* (*jh*) sound, in *ʒhuravlí, ʒhukóv,* and of *sk, k, kh,* in *s kríkom, máiskikh ʒhukóv.* Though Chekhov would have been embarrassed by such a compliment to his poetic abilities, it is not entirely out of place to compare these lines with the haunting first couplet of Pushkin's *Ruslan and Lyudmila,* which Chekhov uses, to very similar effect, in Acts I and IV of *Three Sisters.* The speech as a whole is a good illustration of Kostya as a writer. It is not untalented, and it has a certain poetic imaginative force; but although its subject matter appears to be 'significant', it is not clear whether the author has any serious purpose in mind or is merely concerned to produce an immediate effect.

If Chekhov is suggesting that a serious artist needs to make mistakes, there has certainly been no lack of them in Nina's artistic career. Her failures during the past two years have been numerous and public. 'You can't imagine what it feels like to know that you're acting abominably,' she tells Kostya. But though she has plunged so much lower in her artistic career, she is now beginning to climb slowly upwards—realizing that failures can and must be lived with, and that personal suffering need not deflect one from an artistic vocation:

> NINA. I know now, Kostya, I've come to see, that what matters in our work—whether we're actors or writers—is not the fame or the glamour, not all the things I used to dream about, but just learning how to keep going. Learn how to bear your cross and have faith. I have faith, and I don't suffer so much now, and when I think of my vocation, I'm not afraid of life.
> TREPLYOV (*sadly*). You've found your right path, you know which way you're going, but I'm still drifting about in a chaotic world of dreams and images, without knowing what it's all for or who needs my work. I have no faith and I don't know what my vocation is.

This moving exchange is the climax of the play, and it sets the seal on Kostya's fate. The overwhelming sense of failure, both personal and artistic, is too much for him. In reality, the prospects for his life are not so bleak, but Kostya does not have the resources with which to fight against adversity. Whereas Nina has reconciled herself to the disappointments of life and can turn her back on the lake by accepting a degrading job in a provincial theatre, Kostya cannot break its magic spell. He cannot plunge boldly into life as Nina has done, but remains turned in on himself, attracted to the unreal, fairy-tale world of the lake, where success is a vivid dream that can be realized overnight. Kostya's last thought before he goes off to shoot himself is of Arkadina. It was his failure to detach himself from her influence that was ultimately responsible for his 'imprisonment' beside the lake. Literally and metaphorically Kostya had become stuck in the same place in life, never able to move forward properly, until at last he came to a complete halt and saw no alternative but to destroy himself —so falling a victim to the seagull spell of two years earlier.

In discussing the final act of *The Seagull*, it becomes clear that Nina detaches herself from the quartet, standing out in contrast to the other three main characters, and one begins to see why Chekhov regarded her role as so vital to the play. Nina is Chekhov's seagull, and the seagull represents an object of beauty that is wantonly destroyed by a thoughtless and selfish act. Full of naive idealism, Nina is drawn like a seagull to the lake and to the house on its shores; but the people that she meets there are all in their own ways intensely self-absorbed and self-seeking. Arkadina is absorbed by her own success, Kostya by his lack of it, and Trigorin by his lack of purpose. Between them they very nearly destroy the seagull. Arkadina sees in her only a potential rival, while Kostya and Trigorin try to exploit her for their own ends. The self-centred Kostya could only take from her, never give; and Trigorin too was so preoccupied with his own problem that he scarcely noticed what was happening to the people round him. There was nothing wrong with Nina's decision to leave home and to break with her past; on the contrary, it was very much to be applauded. How often Chekhov portrays characters who never have the courage to take such a step! Nor was there anything wrong with her decision to give herself entirely to Trigorin, for she acted in the belief that she would be contributing to the sacred cause of Art. She was not to know that the man whom she so greatly admired was simply not worthy of this self-sacrifice. Her idealism has disastrous consequences; but Nina survives, and breaks the spell of the lake and the seagull, because she is in the long run spiritually much healthier than the other three. Whatever her talents, Arkadina's pursuit of self-glorification is little short of grotesque. The lives of Kostya and Trigorin are disfigured by their failure to find any definite aims in art, which in turn reflects a failure to resolve their inner problems; and this leads in the one case to a considerable talent being frittered away, and in the other to an unnecessary act of self-destruction. It is not enough that an individual should be talented: this we might regard as the 'clear, definite idea' of *The Seagull*. If the personal qualities of the talented individual are not on the same high level as his talent, then the talent itself can easily be distorted. Nina may or may not become successful (though the indications are that she may well be a great actress one day). What is more important is that such talents as she has are not flawed by any personal defects. Talent is appropriate to her, and this is the real beauty of the seagull.

In his own life Chekhov strove to achieve the same consistency between his artistic talents and his personal qualities. A rural school-teacher befriended by Chekhov in the Yalta period was later to write of him: 'It is hard to say what was uppermost in Chekhov—the man or the artist. His warm personality represented an entirely harmonious whole, in which it was impossible to separate the human being from the artist or the artist from the man.'[11]

v. 'THE SEAGULL' AND THE CHEKHOV PLAY

A deep breath will be in order at this point: for we need to stand well back from *The Seagull* in order to see it once more in its overall relation to the Chekhov play.

Earlier on I described *The Seagull* as a testing ground; and by this I meant that Chekhov was trying out new ideas and new approaches, seeing how they worked and whether he liked them. The most important testing area concerned his main characters. Here he chose to portray four very dissimilar individuals and to present them, using four very dissimilar methods.

What is striking from the point of view of the Chekhov play is that so far as these main characters are concerned—but not the minor characters—*The Seagull* must ultimately be regarded as a 'blind alley'. None of the methods used to present the main characters occurs again in the later plays. As for the characters themselves, two of them—Kostya and Nina—strike me as quite distinct figures in the gallery of Chekhov's dramatic portraits. Trigorin and Arkadina, on the other hand, do have successors—we shall argue that the Professor and his wife in *Uncle Vanya* have quite a lot in common with them; but what is significant is that in *Uncle Vanya* these characters no longer domin-ate. Other characters, of a very different kind, have been moved to the centre of the stage. In *Three Sisters* the 'line' is perpetuated by Natasha, a figure who contrasts with all those round her; while in *The Cherry Orchard* it dies out completely.

Why were the main characters of *The Seagull* 'non-productive' in this way?

The answer, I think, is that Chekhov has chosen to portray four characters who could only be presented as individuals—not as members of a group constantly responding to one another on the emotional level; and this would be the main reason for not regarding *The Seagull* as an example of the Chekhov play.

For a start, three of his characters are exceptional individuals, extreme cases: the unusually celebrated actress; her son, faced with the untypical psychological problem of having a famous mother; and the unusually distinguished writer. Moreover these three are all intensely wrapped up in themselves. The fourth character, though her situation is not exceptional and she is not self-absorbed, is selflessly dedicated to Art; and this means that she too is seen in individual terms.

It is because of this emphasis on the characters as individuals that Chekhov, untypically, had to present them one by one, and not together: the large dose of unconscious self-revelation used for Kostya, Trigorin's introspection, Arkadina striving to preserve her self-image, and Nina finally winning through. Quite apart from the narrowing of focus that results from this individual treatment, Chekhov's approach does seem to have other limitations. It is doubtful whether from one hearing in the theatre it would be possible to grasp all the psychological implications in Chekhov's portrayal of his three more complex characters. An audience needs to be very alert to spot how Kostya 'gives himself away'. As for Trigorin, Tolstoy—otherwise very scathing about *The Seagull*—admired his introspective speeches, but added that they did not belong in a play.[12] This criticism seems justified. These long and psychologically puzzling speeches (they have no counterpart in the later plays) need to be read at leisure and pondered over; they would be more at home on the pages of a work of fiction or an autobiography. Arkadina too—because Chekhov gives only a slight indication of psychological complexities beyond what is immediately apparent in her character—is always in danger of being reduced to a very one-dimensional, if not farcical, figure.

Because they are such special people and have such special problems, the emotions which they feel do not have the Chekhovian quality of being widely appreciable. 'I know just how that character must be feeling' is not a frequent response to *The Seagull*. They bring to the play not a set of emotional preoccupations, but a psychological problem, a self-image, a lack of identity, to which their emotions take second place—as in the case of Arkadina, who only experiences genuine emotion when her self-image is being threatened. The single emotion that is perhaps most in evidence in *The Seagull* is in fact dramatically conventional and largely disappears from the later plays. This is the emotion of jealousy, which is clearly demonstrated in Arkadina, Kostya and Polina. Nina, it is true, brings to the play an emotional aspiration, and of an unusual kind; but during the play that aspiration is very much taken for granted, and the qualities that she displays in pursuing her goal—her dedication, her recklessness, her fortitude—are dramatically more conventional. Nina is one of those unpretentious people who reveal an unsuspected strength of character in their ability to overcome obstacles and to survive ordeals; and as such, she may be regarded as a traditional, *action*-based heroine. Was it for this reason that Nina had no successors?

In the current reinterpretation of *The Seagull* by the Moscow Art Theatre—almost a rewriting, since whole scenes from the last act have been cut or transposed—one scene that has survived intact and makes a deep impression is the 'bandage' scene between Arkadina and Kostya. The reason may well be that this is one of the few moments in the play, apart from the group scenes, when the emphasis is not on particular individuals, so much as on the way in which emotions flow between individuals. But—and this is important for the evolution of the Chekhov play—the complex emotional network between Arkadina and Kostya is very exceptional in *The Seagull*. Chekhov at this stage seems to have felt that the flow of emotion between individuals could only plausibly be shown within the context of an intensely personal— from Kostya's point of view, suffocatingly personal—relationship between two people. They are moreover susceptible to one another's emotions, rather than emotionally responsive: they rub one another up the wrong way. To find emotional responsiveness in *The Seagull*, one has to look beyond the central characters. Sorin, because he is rather old, infirm and endearing, is able to inspire a tenderness of feeling in all those round him; if he could not persuade Arkadina to part with a little of her money, then no one could!

It goes without saying that the self-absorbed central characters are incapable of looking beyond their private fortunes to the significance of their lives within the scheme of human life as a whole. But what of Nina? Does she impart a more centrifugal quality to *The Seagull*? The steadfastness of her aspirations, her willingness to dedicate her life to an outside cause—these do strike a more general note. But they are always seen within the limited context of Art, and not, as in the later plays, of life itself. Sadly perhaps, it is difficult for us now to feel ourselves into a situation where literature and the theatre appear as powerful spiritual forces capable of regenerating mankind. Nina's bold affirmation that, come what may, she will continue her career in the theatre, is very touching; but can we say with honesty that it *matters* very much to us whether or not she becomes a great actress? The final impression of *The Seagull* is of a beautiful and moving play, memorable, very Chekhovian in manner—if less so in emotional content—but somewhat dated and distant from us in a way that is not true of its successors.

A Study in Evolution
From 'The Wood Demon' to 'Uncle Vanya'

i. 'THE WOOD DEMON'

W HEN *The Seagull*, to quote its author, 'came down with a crash'[1] in October 1896, this was not Chekhov's first experience of failure in the theatre; his second full-length play, *The Wood Demon*, had been almost universally condemned after its première in Moscow on December 27th, 1889. Unlike *The Seagull*, *The Wood Demon* was never resurrected. Chekhov was adamant that the play should not be staged again or even reprinted, and did not include it in his *Collected Works*. His feelings were justified—*The Wood Demon* did not deserve to be rescued—but this artistic failure is nonetheless very significant if one wishes to follow through the evolution of the Chekhov play.

Imagine a piece of music, left unfinished by a composer of originality, and later completed, hastily and in an entirely conventional style, by an uncomprehending amateur—and you will have some idea of the curious impression created by a first reading of *The Wood Demon*.

The start is promising. A rich young landowner, Zheltukhin (from *zheltukha*, meaning 'jaundice', which suggests his disposition) is celebrating his birthday by throwing a luncheon party, to which a number of friends and neighbours have been invited. All the play's characters make their appearance during Act I. Apart from Zheltukhin there is his sister Julia, small in stature but mightily efficient; Orlovsky, Julia's godfather, a landowner, who led a riotous life until the age of forty and was then seized by a Dostoyevskian urge to make public confession; his son, Fyodor Ivanovich, a kind of comic parody of such early nineteenth-century Romantic heroes as Lermontov's Pechorin; Khrushchov, a wealthy landowner and medical graduate, nicknamed the Wood Demon because he spends more time preserving forests than practising medicine; Dyadin, an impoverished landowner who now lives in a water-mill which he leases from the Wood Demon; and the largest contingent of all, the Serebryakov family. This household consists of the Professor, recently retired from the university; his beautiful young second wife, Yelyena; Sonya, his daughter by his late first wife, and another of Orlovsky's goddaughters; his first wife's mother, Maria

Vasil'yevna; and her son, Yegor Petrovich, otherwise known as Uncle George, who has been responsible during the past twenty-five years for running the family estate.

Within the typical Chekhovian atmosphere of a domestic occasion, all these characters in Act I are given the same amount of attention—in contrast to the lack of decentralization in *Ivanov*. Chekhov quickly establishes the atmosphere of an intimate group, deformalizing the dialogue and relying very largely on small talk, of which this extract is a good example:

> SONYA. Come on then, Godfather, tell us all about it. Where did you spend the winter? Where did you run off to?
> ORLOVSKY. Well, my dear, I was in Gmunden and in Paris, I was in Nice, London. . . .
> SONYA. You lucky man!
> ORLOVSKY. Why not come with me this autumn? How about it?
> SONYA (*sings*). 'Only tempt me if you must' . . .
> FYODOR IVANOVICH. And if you must sing at lunch, your husband's going to have a fool for a wife.
> DYADIN. Wouldn't it be interesting now to have a bird's eye view of this table? What an entrancing posy! A union of grace and beauty, of profound scholarship and . . .
> FYODOR IVANOVICH. What an entrancing mouthful! I've never heard anything like it! You talk as if someone were tickling your nose with a feather. . . .
>
> (*Laughter.*)
>
> ORLOVSKY (*to Sonya*). So you're still not married, my dear . . .
> VOINITSKY. I ask you, who can she marry? Humboldt's dead, Edison's in America, Lassalle's dead too . . .

With its life-like spontaneity, banter between old friends and rapid jumping from one subject to another, this passage already has several of the distinctive features of Chekhov's dialogue. The conviviality of the act as a whole—in which the scene becomes more and more animated with each new arrival, toasts are proposed, and many of the characters become slightly tipsy—looks forward to the atmosphere of Irina's name-day party at the beginning of *Three Sisters*; and even Act I of *The Cherry Orchard* is anticipated by the use that Chekhov makes of reunions between characters who have not seen one another for some time. If the first act of *The Wood Demon* has a defect, though, it is a certain superficiality. The characters seem one-dimensional and what they say, as in the passage quoted, is close to the surface; Chekhov has not yet mastered the art of writing dialogue that is both trivial *and* revealing—able to suggest the emotions that lie beyond the words.

The second act, though entirely different in character, also makes a strong impression. The setting is the house of the Serebryakovs. Frustration is the keynote of this act, and Chekhov makes skilful use of the weather and of sounds from off-stage to intensify the psychological mood. It is some time between one and two in the morning. The air is close. A storm is approaching. The Professor and his wife, who has been sitting up with him, have both been dozing; he is in some pain and keeps asking what time it is. Serebryakov feels an acute sense of frustration; no one around him seems to appreciate the awful change that has taken place in his life since he retired from the university. He vents his bitterness on the unfortunate Yelyena. As they are talking, the watchman in the garden begins to sing; and a contrast is evoked between the freedom outside and the oppressive atmosphere of illness and frustration indoors, where the characters are cooped up together, playing on one another's nerves. When Uncle George (Voinitsky) comes in, there is a flash of lightning, which seems to underline the tension between him and the Professor. Voinitsky's subsequent conversation with Yelyena deepens the mood of frustration. 'Things are all wrong in this household,' Yelyena twice repeats, gloomily. The storm, says Voinitsky, will soon pass by, and nature will be refreshed; but he will continue to be tormented by the thought that he has wasted his life, that his love for Yelyena is not returned and that she is stifling her youth unnecessarily.

At this point, the Wood Demon, who has been attending Serebryakov in his professional capacity, enters unexpectedly, sees Voinitsky apparently kissing Yelyena's hand, and with her departure proceeds to lecture him on the impropriety of his behaviour—displaying some of the moral rigidity of Dr. L'vov, the insufferably 'honest man' of *Ivanov*. In a soliloquy Voinitsky regrets that he is not like other men who never know 'this wretched, poisonous irony'; and in a brief scene Sonya reproaches her uncle for neglecting his work on the estate. Then follows a long talk between Sonya and the Wood Demon, characteristic of Chekhov in that it takes place while they are helping themselves to a snack from the sideboard. They are in love, but the intellectual Sonya simply cannot make up her mind whether the Wood Demon is 'genuine' or not, and accuses him of inverted snobbery and of being a fake. He lectures her on the need to 'look people straight in the eye', tells her that she is too suspicious ever to fall in love, and eventually the pair of them part angrily. By now the storm has passed; and for a brief period the storm-clouds lift over relations between the characters. Sonya and Yelyena, who have not been on speaking terms, are reconciled, and Sonya goes to ask her father if Yelyena may play the piano. Outside the watchman is whistling cheerfully to his dogs. But Sonya comes back with a curt refusal, and on this final repressive note the curtain descends.

It is during the course of the third act that *The Wood Demon* begins to go off the rails. It does so because Chekhov has apparently decided that now is the time to 'hot up' the action of his play. There is a crude moment in scene II when Fyodor Ivanovich says that if he *were* going to marry, he'd marry Julia . . . and then claps his hand to his head, saying: 'That gives me an idea!' Unconvincing too are Yelyena's remarks in the third scene that if she were to be unfaithful, 'then wives everywhere would take their example from me and desert their husbands, and I would be punished by God and tormented by my conscience . . .' But it is in scene VI that we move out of Chekhov's world into a world of very conventional drama. It seems that by chance a letter from Voinitsky to Yelyena has been left lying around the garden (though why he should be writing to her when they live in the same house is not made clear); and that Sonya has come upon this letter and presumably read it. When Yelyena comes in, Sonya hands the letter to her, saying that her soul 'feels too pure today for me to go on talking to you and pretending'. Scarcely has Yelyena had time to feel properly insulted before Fyodor comes in and she is having to give him a slap in the face. The big scene in the act, when the Professor proposes to sell the estate, arousing feelings of hatred and despair in Voinitsky, is much more convincing; but Chekhov follows it up by piling one dramatic sensation upon another. To describe in detail how the characters all fall out with one another would be tedious, and rather like rubbing Chekhov's nose in the dirt—as it is, we have already ignored his wish to see *The Wood Demon* decently buried! Suffice it to say that the act concludes with a shot off-stage, the reappearance of Maria Vasil'yevna who promptly faints, and Sonya's voice shouting from the next room that Uncle George has shot himself. Everyone rushes out except Yelyena, who is left moaning: 'Why? Why?'; and when Dyadin appears in the doorway, she beseeches him to take her away from the house that very moment.

The final act takes place against the Arcadian setting of Dyadin's water-mill, where Yelyena, unknown to the other characters, has been living for the past fortnight. Voinitsky's suicide and Yelyena's disappearance have had a sobering effect on everyone. The Wood Demon arrives at the mill to work on his maps which illustrate the deforestation of the district during the past half-century, and explains that after Voinitsky's death, his diary was found, from which it is clear that the rumours of an affair between him and Yelyena were totally unfounded. All the characters except Maria Vasil'yevna, and Yelyena who remains indoors, now assemble for a picnic—another domestic occasion which balances the birthday party of Act I. But although there is some lively Chekhovian dialogue, the parallel is more between the final act and Act III. After the rapid series of violent rifts between the characters, the final act presents an equally rapid series of reconciliations. While the Wood Demon is lecturing the company on the need for real heroes to lead Russia out of its 'dark wood', Yelyena appears, amid 'general consternation'—but her husband's reaction is at first decidedly cool. Then everything begins to happen very quickly, as in Act III. The upshot of it all is that Yelyena and the Professor go off together on rather less distant terms, Sonya is happily paired off with the Wood Demon, Julia with Fyodor Ivanovich who promises to reform, and only Zheltukhin, who had had designs on Sonya, is left out in the cold —which jolly well serves him right because he was the one who first spread the slander about Yelyena and Voinitsky. The play ends with Dyadin's catch-phrase: 'Entrancing! Absolutely entrancing!'

ii. TRANSFORMING THE NATURE OF THE PLAY

Chekhov's first reference to *Uncle Vanya* was in a letter to Suvorin on December 2nd, 1896, when he spoke of '*The Seagull* which is known to you already and *Uncle Vanya*, which is not known to a single soul'.[2] It is impossible to say at what period between the beginning of 1890 and December 1896 Chekhov converted *The Wood Demon* into *Uncle Vanya*. There is some documentary evidence that it might have been as early as March or April 1890,[3] but all the internal evidence suggests that a considerable interval separates *The Wood Demon* from *Uncle Vanya*, and that the latter might well have been written after *The Seagull*.

Of the characters from *The Wood Demon* who survived into *Uncle*

F

Vanya the most important were the Serebryakovs, who were transferred *in toto*—the only change being that in the later play Voinitsky is Ivan Petrovich (Uncle Vanya, which is homely and Russian) and not Yegor Petrovich (the more sophisticated and cosmopolitan Uncle George—or more accurately, Georges, in the French spelling). The Wood Demon also survived, though his surname is no longer Khrushchov, which has comic associations with *khrushch*, 'a cockchafer', but Astrov, suggesting stars; and he is described in the *dramatis personae* as a doctor, not a landowner. Four characters—Zheltukhin, his sister and the Orlovskys—disappeared altogether, though a few of their lines were given to other characters. Dyadin lost his name and his water-mill, becoming Telyegin, a permanent hanger-on in the Serebryakov household; and a new character, the old nurse Marina, was introduced to supplement him, the two of them forming a kind of chorus which comments on the behaviour of the main figures.

Of the four acts in *The Wood Demon*, practically nothing survived of Act IV, except the Wood Demon's maps, which were to acquire much greater importance in Act III of *Uncle Vanya*. The longish sequence in which the Professor proposes to sell the estate is almost all that survives from Act III; and from Act I Chekhov only made use of those scenes which concerned the Serebryakovs and the Wood Demon. The second act of *Uncle Vanya*, on the other hand, does follow the second act of *The Wood Demon* very closely.

Yet although these two plays share a number of characters and a certain amount of content, they are fundamentally quite dissimilar; and Chekhov always referred to *Uncle Vanya* as a new play. What is it that makes them so dissimilar? What were the different stages by which Chekhov transformed an artistic failure into an artistic success?

Writing to the editor of a literary journal on January 8th, 1890, Chekhov implored him to return the text of *The Wood Demon* and not to publish it, as this would deprive him of the possibility of doing some more work on the play.[4] He obviously felt that there was something in *The Wood Demon* that deserved a better chance, and *Uncle Vanya* makes it clear that this something must have been the second act. The characters involved here were the Serebryakov family and the Wood Demon. Why not concentrate attention on these characters and eliminate entirely the other four, who in any case were all light-weight figures? But how then would the action of the play develop? Chekhov had probably conceived a strong dislike for the last act—it had caused him a great deal of trouble at the time—and was eager to try something quite different. So far as the Serebryakovs were concerned, the high-light of the action had been Voinitsky's suicide at the end of Act III. But supposing that Voinitsky did not shoot himself? From a psychological point of view this suicide was not entirely convincing, and it had the further disadvantage of removing one of the best characters! What if he were to shoot the Professor instead of himself? No, that would be very melodramatic, and would still leave the problem of what happened next. But supposing that Voinitsky were to shoot at the Professor and to miss? That would create a very different kind of effect—less theatrical, more true to life. Nothing at all would be resolved by it; on the contrary, Voinitsky would be frustrated in this attempt, just as his whole life up to that point had been one long frustration.

This alternative would immediately have 'clicked' with the second act of *The Wood Demon*, in which frustration had been the keynote throughout. Now what if *frustration* were to be made the central theme and everything else built round it? There was already a considerable element of frustration in the depiction of the Professor—loathing retirement in the country—and of his young wife, realizing that her marriage had been a mistake; this was the one part of the plot in *The Wood Demon* that did not end up in joyful reconciliation, but in a more doubtful compromise. Sonya and the Wood Demon, however, were in a different category; the young lovers romantically destined for one another from the start, they had been separated by nothing more serious than mutual misunderstandings, dramatically swept aside in the course of the final act.

At this point, a new 'character' comes on the scene: provincial Russian life itself. Chekhov's awareness of how much frustration was to be found at every level of rural Russian society must, I feel, have influenced him greatly when he was converting *The Wood Demon* into *Uncle Vanya*. One is by no means convinced that the author of *The Wood Demon* had a first-hand acquaintance with life in rural Russia. The rambling old house is plausible enough, with its twenty-six rooms which resemble a labyrinth; but the environment as a whole remains shadowy (based more on an acquaintance with stories about country life than with country life itself?), and Dyadin's water-mill is never convincing. There are details however in *Uncle Vanya* which could only have been known to a writer who had for some time been part of life in the country, not just a temporary visitor: Astrov's description, for example, of the unbelievably squalid conditions in a Russian village affected by an outbreak of typhus, or the little detail in the stage directions for the last act of the mat placed by the door of Voinitsky's estate office, so that the peasants shall not dirty the floor with their muddy boots. Details such as these support 1896 as the date of composition, when Chekhov had already been living in Melikhovo for five years. By then he would certainly have been very familiar with the life of a rural doctor, and he might well have come across the kind of plain, sensitive girl of marriageable age, who cannot find a suitable match in the district. And so in *Uncle Vanya* Sonya's love for Astrov is not returned; while the Wood Demon ceases to be the well-to-do landowner who practises medicine when he feels like it, and becomes instead the grossly overworked provincial doctor whose life is hemmed in by frustrations. In *The Wood Demon* Khrushchov can tell Sonya that when you're walking at night through a wood, you don't mind the darkness and the branches that strike you in the face so long as you can see a light in the distance; and that whatever the difficulties he may encounter in his campaign to save Russia's forests, he can see that light ahead—in his love for Sonya. The same image, of walking through a wood on a dark night, is used in *Uncle Vanya*, but here Astrov goes on:

> ... As you know, I work harder than anyone in the district, fate strikes me one blow after another and there are times when I suffer unbearably—but for me there is no light shining in the distance.

'No light shining in the distance': this illustrates very exactly the contrast between the generally light-hearted, gay character of *The Wood Demon* (Voinitsky's suicide notwithstanding) and the much deeper and darker emotional tones of *Uncle Vanya*.

This new 'character' did not only influence Chekhov's approach to Sonya and Astrov, but was also to play a vital role in establishing the atmosphere of the later play. There is nothing specifically Russian about the lakeside setting in *The Seagull*, and the characters portrayed belong to the relatively rootless community of writers and actors. But in *Uncle Vanya* we feel trapped, just as the characters themselves do, within the humdrum life of a landowning family, whose estate is deeply embedded somewhere in the heart of rural Russia and encircled by the primitive life of the Russian villages. The Professor feels as if he'd 'dropped on to some foreign planet', so powerful is the sense of isolation. In *The Seagull* we are at least aware of other estates around the lake; but in *Uncle Vanya* some twenty miles of wretched roads separate the family's estate from that of their closest friend, Doctor Astrov.

Chekhov's idea for the plot of *Uncle Vanya* was now simple. The two characters who felt most imprisoned by their humdrum life should try to make a run for freedom: Vanya striving to break out to Yelyena, and Sonya to Astrov. Astrov too tries to break out to Yelyena, though Chekhov stopped short of suggesting that he wanted to break with his old life completely. The function of the opening act would be to establish the mood of provincial boredom, and to show different characters voicing their frustrations. It was in the middle two acts that the action of the play was to develop. The outcome of this action would be that Vanya, Sonya and Astrov failed in their attempts to break free—for it turns out that there is nowhere for them to run to. This would be confirmed in the final act, when it becomes obvious that the lives of these three characters have not changed, and that an old pattern of life has re-established itself.

This outline sketch of *Uncle Vanya* makes it clear that in the course of elaborating his theme of frustration, Chekhov had chanced upon many of the features of his dramatic formula, as described in Chapter I. Here we have the intimate group without a central character (it would be hard to argue that Uncle Vanya is of greater importance than Sonya or Astrov, any more than the Wood Demon is the central character of the earlier play)—members of the upper class, cultured, leading introspective lives within their own self-contained world and seen against the background of a carefully suggested environment. If, as seems likely, Chekhov was writing *Uncle Vanya* soon after he had finished revising *The Seagull*, this might explain the inclusion of other features which complete the formula. In *The Seagull* Chekhov had made effective use of a contrast between outsiders and residents. Such a contrast had been potentially present in *The Wood Demon*, since the Professor and his wife had only recently retired to the estate, but was not developed, and at the end of the play they were still very much in residence. Chekhov took this contrast and pointed it much more sharply in *Uncle Vanya*. It was moreover not difficult to see that the return of the residents' life to normal in Act IV might be made to coincide with the departure of the outsiders—so creating a much more satisfying pattern than in *The Seagull*, where the outsiders' departure had taken place at the end of Act III.

To return now to the original question of why the conversion of

The Wood Demon into *Uncle Vanya* resulted in such an entirely different kind of play.

In *The Wood Demon* Chekhov takes the characters' personal preoccupations and emotional involvements, and uses them as a means of setting in motion a complex series of dramatic events, at the end of which these preoccupations and involvements have been almost entirely resolved. Voinitsky's frustration is 'resolved' dramatically by his suicide. This has an effect on the other characters, and the earlier series of rifts among them is followed by a series of reconciliations. But these rifts and reconciliations follow one another in such rapid and improbable succession that the emotional impact of each is progressively dissipated, and by the end of the play the audience is likely to be in that detached frame of mind which results from an awareness of how plot and characters are being manipulated to produce a happy ending. In the later play, Voinitsky sees it through to the bitter end. Nothing at all is resolved by the two shots that he fires at the Professor; on the contrary, his sense of frustration is heightened, and the emotional tension, which in *The Wood Demon* is released too early, is sustained right through to the final curtain.

What Chekhov has in fact done is to replace a play of action by a play of emotional content; and this is why the two are so fundamentally dissimilar. The new play is built entirely round an emotion—the emotion of frustration; that, and that alone, is the play's subject matter. It is no longer the actions that arise out of emotional processes, but the emotional processes themselves that are important; 'a shot, after all, is not a drama, but an incident'.

One is reminded here of that curious feature of natural evolution, whereby it may sometimes be advantageous for a species not to proceed to its adult stage of development, but to remain permanently in the pre-adult stage, thereby giving rise to an entirely new species. A similar process seems to have occurred in the evolution of the Chekhov play. *Uncle Vanya* never reaches the 'adult' phase of dramatic action and intrigue, but remains permanently in the 'pre-adult' phase of emotional processes; and in this way a new species of drama came into being.

iii. TRANSFORMING THE DIALOGUE

This new type of drama was bound to involve considerable changes both in the nature of the dialogue and in the treatment of the characters in *Uncle Vanya*.

The earlier play, it might be argued, was *bound* to be somewhat superficial, because Chekhov had not yet mastered the art of writing dialogue that conveyed emotional depth. To see how Chekhov transformed the dialogue in *Uncle Vanya*, and to measure the difference in depth between the two plays, let us compare a passage from *The Wood Demon* with its counterpart in *Uncle Vanya*. Voinitsky in *The Wood Demon* has been complaining about his wasted life, and the conversation continues:

SEREBRYAKOV. Wait a moment. You seem to be blaming your former principles for something. But they're not to blame, you are. You're forgetting that convictions mean nothing without deeds. You should have done something *positive*.

VOINITSKY. Something positive? We can't all be perpetual writing-machines.

SEREBRYAKOV. And what do you mean by that?

VOINITSKY. Nothing. Let's stop this conversation. We're not at home now.

(Act I, scene VII.)

In *Uncle Vanya*, the Professor's lines are given to Maria Vasil'yevna (Serebryakov had gone into the house to work immediately after his walk—Chekhov perhaps wishing to avoid a direct clash so early on between him and Voinitsky). The passage has also been considerably extended:

MARIA VASIL'YEVNA (*to her son*). You seem to be blaming your former principles for something. . . . But they're not to blame, you are. You're forgetting that convictions by themselves are nothing, just empty phrases. . . . You should have done something *positive*.

VOINITSKY. Something positive? We can't all be perpetual writing-machines, like your Herr Professor.

MARIA VASIL'YEVNA. And what do you mean by that?

SONYA (*beseechingly*). Grandmother! Uncle Vanya! Please!

VOINITSKY. I'm sorry. . . . I'll say no more.

(*Pause.*)

YELYENA ANDREYEVNA. The weather's nice today. . . . Not too hot. . . .

(*Pause.*)

VOINITSKY. Yes, nice weather for hanging oneself. . . .

(*Telyegin tunes the guitar. Marina walks about near the house, calling the hens.*)

MARINA. Chook, chook, chook. . . .

SONYA. Nanny, what did the villagers come for?

MARINA. The same old thing, they're still on about that piece of waste land. Chook, chook, chook. . . .

SONYA. Which one are you calling?

MARINA. The speckledy's gone off with her chicks. . . . Must see the crows don't get them. . . . (*Walks away.*)

(*Telyegin plays a polka; they all listen in silence; a workman comes in.*)

WORKMAN. Is the doctor here? (*To Astrov.*) If you please, Mikhail L'vovich, you've been sent for.

In her first remarks, Maria Vasil'yevna is repeating what sounds like a well-prepared lesson. These sentiments are ones that her beloved son-in-law is no doubt fond of expressing (the audience is not to know that in the earlier play he actually did express them!) and she even uses a catch-phrase of his: 'You should have done something *positive*.' Vanya recognizes the catch-phrase only too well. He seethes, and is openly rude to his mother about her 'Herr Professor'—conveying by this Germanic title a Russian contempt for dull pedantry.

It was at this point that Chekhov decided to extend the original scene. The disjointedness of the dialogue that follows, with its long and uneasy silences—three at least in the course of this short passage—is not only in the interests of deformalization, but also suggests the tension and brooding uneasiness in relations between the characters. Sonya is seen in the characteristic role of peacemaker; as at the end of the play, she is the only one who still has any influence with her uncle. The tense silence which follows Vanya's rather truculent apology might well be thought of as a good example of what George Calderon had in mind when he suggested that an almost electric field exists in the air among all the persons in a group. Yelyena tries to break the tension with her trivial remark about the weather being 'not too hot'. Is it just for something to say, and not even true? (After all, Astrov had been complaining earlier to Marina about how close the weather was!) If so, it is characteristic of the lack of conviction that Yelyena brings to what she says. Vanya does not let her get away with it. He does not wish to shock. It is just that as we mentioned earlier, he cannot stop this emotion welling up in him and finding expression; and the other characters at least respect the strength of his emotion. His bitter rejoinder only makes the atmosphere more tense. Then it is Sonya who seems to be trying to break this atmosphere when, speaking more loudly perhaps than usual so as not to betray any tension in her voice, she turns and addresses a question to Marina, who is busy near the house calling the hens; but when Marina disappears from sight, the uneasy silence returns. Telyegin's guitar-playing (an innovation—Dyadin in *The Wood Demon* has no guitar) is an example of the way in which Chekhov uses sounds, rather than words, as a means of deepening the emotional atmosphere. The device is used sparingly in *The Seagull*, but becomes more important as the plays progress. Here the inappropriately cheerful sounds of the polka seem intended to contrast with the decidedly uncheerful mood of the characters. Finally, the magic circle of silence has to be broken from outside—by the arrival of the workman, who has come to call the doctor away from his unaccustomed relaxation.

The passage from *The Wood Demon* may be said to make its psychological point; but in *Uncle Vanya* Chekhov has transformed the dialogue by giving it a new dimension of emotional depth and suggestivity.

iv. TRANSFORMING THE CHARACTERS: THE 'MORAL' APPROACH

The most immediate reaction to the question of how Chekhov transformed the characters in *Uncle Vanya* may well be to say that in the later play the residents are presented in a much more admirable light, and the outsiders in an even less admirable light, than in *The Wood Demon*.

It is true that the overt and rhetorical moralizing of *The Wood Demon*, influenced perhaps by Tolstoy, has largely disappeared from the later play; but Chekhov, it may be argued, did not need to point any moral in *Uncle Vanya*, because it is obvious from how the characters behave, and especially from the contrast between outsiders and residents. Having done the residents a disservice in *The Wood Demon* by failing to realize how difficult their lives were, Chekhov was now making amends. Voinitsky is no longer the cynical, sharp-tongued Uncle George of *The Wood Demon*, whose suicide barely moves us, but has become the straightforward, hardworking Uncle Vanya—'a great little man', to use the Soviet critic, Yermilov's, phrase.[5] Sonya has lost the aggressive, hypercritical streak which repels sympathy in

The Wood Demon, and is characterized instead by hard work, patience and courage. Astrov, like Vanya, has also undergone a pointed change of name—ceasing to be Khrushchov, the Wood Demon, a dilettante doctor with a bee in his bonnet about preserving trees, and becoming Astrov, a man whose gaze is fixed on the stars, whose idealism is sincere beyond question and who does not spare himself in his medical practice. This upgrading of the residents is moreover accompanied by a corresponding demotion of the outsiders. The Professor, who as Blagosvyetlov had been a boring but praiseworthy figure in Chekhov's original plan for *The Wood Demon*, was steadily downgraded until in *Uncle Vanya* he appears entirely self-centred and self-seeking. His wife, whose positive sense of virtue was one of the moralizing themes in *The Wood Demon*, remains virtuous in *Uncle Vanya*, but in a nega- tive kind of way, and the part that she plays in relations between Sonya and Astrov is morally dubious. The contrast between the residents and the outsiders, it has been suggested, represents the contrast between good and evil (Magarshack), and between true and false beauty (Yer- milov); and it is in the tragic clash between Vanya and the Professor that the contrast is most clearly highlighted.

This moral approach to *Uncle Vanya* is very widespread, not only in the Soviet Union. Certainly, the general proposition—that the residents in *Uncle Vanya* are more and the outsiders less sympathetic than in *The Wood Demon*—cannot be disputed. Our argument how- ever will be that when Chekhov was converting *The Wood Demon* into *Uncle Vanya* he did not *set out* to point a moral contrast between his characters, but that this happened incidentally. In particular, the moral approach breaks down precisely when one considers the rela- tionship between Vanya and the Professor; for the view that Chekhov wished to represent here a contrast between 'virtuous victim' and 'evil exploiter' is very superficial.

It is usual to agree with Voinitsky when he claims that Serebryakov has been reading and writing about art for twenty-five years without understanding the first thing about it, and to accept his judgement when he tells the Professor in *Uncle Vanya*: 'You've hoaxed us.' For Magarshack, Serebryakov is a 'brainless pedant',[6] for Yermilov 'just a pompous mediocrity, cram-full of vanity and pretensions'.[7] The worthy Uncle Vanya has been tricked by this academic impostor.

But is that quite the situation which Chekhov is presenting, in either play? No doubt the Professor was extremely third-rate, with a much higher opinion of his own importance than the rest of the world; but no doubt Voinitsky too was exaggerating. For why is it only *now*, after twenty-five years, that he has 'seen through' the Professor? During all those years he studied every word that the Professor wrote, and yet it never occurred to him then to question his brother-in-law's brilliance; though there was nothing to stop him from forming his own judgements. Either Voinitsky is a man of considerably less intelligence than we have been led to believe; or else it was not the Professor who hoaxed him, but Voinitsky who was hoaxing himself. He did not want to see through the Professor, but refused to notice something that ought to have been staring him in the face.

First remarks and first appearances are often of special importance in the Chekhov play; and when Voinitsky first appears in *Uncle Vanya*, though not in *The Wood Demon*, he is described as 'adjusting his smart tie'. Strangely out of keeping, one may feel, with a middle-aged man who looks after a remote country estate—Vanya is not exactly a youngster eager to create an impression. Was Chekhov making the point that Voinitsky is not a boorish landowner, but a man of culture and refinement? Or was he also hinting that Vanya has *stood still* spiritually for the past twenty-five years, that he has continued to see himself in the role of the idealistic young man, and failed to modify that role with the passage of time? When Serebryakov comes to live on the estate—a pathetic, gouty old man who has not made any mark at all in the world—Voinitsky is daily confronted by the *reality* of the ideals he has been serving. The doubts which had belatedly begun to trouble him are amply confirmed. And the presence of Yelyena does something else. It makes him constantly aware of the other possibilities that had once been open to him, of the alternatives in his life that have simply gone by default. That Yelyena is very beautiful only intensifies the pain of what might have been.

Voinitsky, then, was not 'hoaxed'; he has made a foolish, if well-intentioned mistake, which it is now too late to rectify. Reluctant to accept that he alone must bear full responsibility for what he has made of his life, he seeks to turn the Professor into a scapegoat. His plight is real enough; but in his anguish he ceases to be entirely honest with himself emotionally, and begins to dramatize his situation. This self-dramatization reaches its height in the scene of the family conclave. To say that Voinitsky is justly incensed by the Professor's illegal proposal to sell the estate is to miss the point. The intensity of his emotion has nothing to do with whether Serebryakov is acting legally, whether his scheme is good or bad, but derives from a quite different source. The

Professor's blunt proposal makes it inescapably plain that those things by which Voinitsky had always set so much emotional store—the running of the estate, and the work involved in providing an income for the Professor—had never had the *slightest* emotional significance for Serebryakov. The truth of the situation is sadly simple: Voinitsky had wrongly imagined in the past that his brother-in-law genuinely appreciated the work that he was doing. Voinitsky is too stunned to be able to reconcile himself to this ordinary little truth. In his confusion he does not say to himself: 'What a fool I was to imagine he was *grateful*!', but instead dramatizes the situation, working himself up into a great rage as he paints a lurid picture of the Professor as his 'worst enemy'.

This, to put it crudely, is a pretty silly remark; but then Chekhov realized that in moments of great emotional intensity, what people say ceases to be very rational. The Professor is genuinely baffled: how could he possibly know that Voinitsky had invested all his emotional capital in the task of serving him, and through him, Culture? Voinitsky's self-dramatization reaches a climax when he declares that 'if I'd lived a normal life I might have been a Schopenhauer or a Dostoyevsky'. These words, Yermilov writes, 'do not evoke an incredulous smile'.[8] But surely they *were* meant to be absurd—however pathetic at the same time? Voinitsky is an intelligent man, not a brilliant one. And in his impulsive decision to take his revenge on the Professor, he is still refusing to accept the ordinary little truth. How much easier to think of himself as a victim than as a fool!

How much easier, it seems, for critics also to see him as a victim pure and simple! But this anxiety to draw a moral lesson from *Uncle Vanya* obscures the true nature of Voinitsky's predicament. It was Chekhov's intention in both plays to show the plight of a man who is not only frustrated, but who really has no one but himself to blame for the mess that he has made of his life. This gives Voinitsky's frustration much greater depth than if he were simply the innocent victim of a cunning exploiter; it is the inner state itself that Chekhov wishes to explore, not the rights and wrongs of what has caused it.

There is one further objection to the view that in *Uncle Vanya* the happiness of the 'evil' characters is bought at the expense of the 'good' ones. If frustration were to be made the subject matter of the play, it needed to be extended to all the characters. The Professor may be selfish and unsympathetic, but we should not lose sight of the fact that he is no less frustrated than anyone else. A significant comparison can be made here between the scene from Act II of *The Wood Demon* in which the Professor is helped off to bed, and its counterpart in *Uncle Vanya*. In the earlier play the Wood Demon's sudden access of tenderness towards the Professor is unexpected, the latter does not respond, and the scene as a whole seems intended only to clear the stage for Voinitsky and Yelyena. In replacing the Wood Demon by Marina, Chekhov gave the scene in *Uncle Vanya* both more plausibility and emotional depth. She is the only one to recognize that the Professor is actually in pain; and what is more interesting, the Professor does respond to her immediate concern for him. It is sufficient to remind us that Serebryakov is not a complete ogre, and that behind all his selfishness there is a genuinely frustrated human being. In *Uncle Vanya* there are no winners, only losers.

V. TRANSFORMING THE CHARACTERS: THE EMOTIONAL APPROACH

Rather than jump to hasty conclusions about Chekhov's moral intentions in *Uncle Vanya*, let us go back to that point in the conversion of *The Wood Demon* where Chekhov saw the possibility of making not only Voinitsky's life a frustrated one, but also the lives of Khrushchov and Sonya: by making Khrushchov into an overworked provincial doctor and Sonya into a girl whose love is not returned.

Frustration is by its nature one of the long-term pervasive emotions referred to in Chapter I. It may persist for a lifetime; it may or may not reach a point of crisis; but it is always bound to build up over a considerable period. To extend his characters' frustrations backwards in time was therefore an obvious first step for Chekhov. Nothing needed to be done in the case of Voinitsky; at the age of forty-seven he had already been slaving away in *The Wood Demon* for the past twenty-five years to extract from the estate the maximum income to be sent to the Professor. The Wood Demon's age is not, so far as I am aware, ever specified in the earlier play, but he may be presumed to be in his late twenties. In *Uncle Vanya*, however, Astrov is in his late thirties, and the opening scene of the play informs us that he has been working in the district as a doctor for at least eleven years. During that time he has not had a single free day; no wonder then that he feels dragged down by the 'boring, stupid, dirty life' all around him. As for Sonya, she was a young girl of twenty in *The Wood Demon*. In order to extend her frustration backwards, Chekhov makes her twenty-four in *Uncle Vanya*, and it transpires that she has been in love with Astrov for the past six years without ever receiving the slightest encouragement. Her age, it might be added, is never explicitly stated, and unless one is very familiar with the play, one may easily draw the conclusion that she is meant to be several years older.

The frustrations of these three characters were to be seen against the background of their routine working lives. Again, Voinitsky's capacity for hard work had already been stressed in *The Wood Demon*, and Astrov's was immediately established by his conversion into a rural doctor. Sonya in *The Wood Demon* is not associated with work, though Chekhov may well have had in mind that she too helped to run the estate, in view of the way that she reproaches her uncle for neglecting the harvest. It was not in any case difficult to bring Sonya into line with the other two hard workers, and she may also have acquired from *The Wood Demon* some of Julia's practicality. But it would be a simplification to suggest that in associating his three central characters so closely with the theme of work, Chekhov's primary aim was to make them more *sympathetic*, to point a moral contrast. He wanted rather to give them an extra emotional dimension. Masha in *The Seagull* is also preoccupied with her unrequited love, but because this is the only important thing about her, she is a much more one-dimensional figure than Sonya. Work and routine were an essential part of Chekhov's scheme for *Uncle Vanya* because they provided something for the characters to fall back on emotionally, once they had been frustrated in the fulfilment of their personal desires. Work, individual frustration, and more work is the fundamental pattern of *Uncle Vanya*.

Now if the three central characters were to be presented in this way in terms of emotional preoccupations seen against the background of their working lives—a consequence follows that is of considerable importance for the evolution of the Chekhov play. It is that these characters' individual *qualities* are no longer relevant—indeed, they could only interfere, confuse the issue. The trouble with Voinitsky in *The Wood Demon* is that he has two centres of interest. On the one hand, there is the psychological portrait of a cynical man with a low opinion of his fellow men—on the other, there is an emotional portrait of a man who has wasted his life on an unworthy cause; and Chekhov falls neatly between the two. It is hard to accept that the cynic would commit such a desperate act as suicide; while at the same time the suicide of the emotional man is much less moving than it might be, because Voinitsky has revealed so many unpleasant traits. In the later play, the psychological portrait has almost entirely disappeared—all that survives is Vanya's scepticism (as opposed to cynical mockery in *The Wood Demon*) towards Astrov's forestry schemes. Gone is his caustic turn of phrase, and gone the complacency which makes him say that with his 'powers of observation' he could write a novel about the Professor's life. The best illustration of how Chekhov transformed the character of Voinitsky is provided by his soliloquy in Act II, immediately after Yelyena has gone out. The first part of this soliloquy—in which Voinitsky recalls how he first met Yelyena, and thinks how wonderful it would be if she were now his wife—is identical in both plays. In *The Wood Demon* he then continues:

> Why was I made this way? How I envy that crazy Fyodor or that stupid Wood Demon! They're just straightforward, honest, stupid. . . . They've never known this wretched, poisonous irony.
>
> (Act II, scene VI)

In *Uncle Vanya* this is replaced by the following:

> Oh, how I've been fooled! I used to worship that pitiful old gout-ridden professor, I worked like a slave for him! Sonya and I squeezed every drop out of this estate. We traded in linseed oil and peas and cream cheese—just as if we were miserly peasants. We went short on food ourselves so as to save copecks and send him thousands of roubles. I was proud of him and his learning, he was the breath of life for me! I thought that everything he wrote and said was the product of genius . . . but now? My God! Here he is in retirement and you can see what his life amounts to. Not a page of his writing will survive, he's completely unknown, he's nothing! A soap-bubble! And I've been fooled. . . . I can see I've been completely fooled.

Voinitsky's remarks in *The Wood Demon* were almost certainly intended to be the psychological key to his character. Like Ivanov before him, and like Trigorin later, Voinitsky is analysing his own character. He has been struck down by the psychological curse of 'irony', which distinguishes him from all the other mediocre people—just as the talented Ivanov was struck down by the curse of over-exertion, and the gifted Trigorin by the more obscure psychological malaise of not knowing who he was. This element of self-analysis has been removed from *Uncle Vanya*: the continuation of Vanya's soliloquy does not tell us anything about his individual qualities, but it does considerably deepen our awareness of his emotional preoccupation.

Sonya and Astrov likewise lose their distinctive individual qualities. The Wood Demon's righteousness (self-righteousness?) is eliminated, and Sonya loses that aggressive, hypercritical streak from the earlier play. Moreover, she and her uncle have both been deprived of those intellectual qualities which enabled Yelyena in *The Wood Demon* to refer to the Serebryakov household as 'a nest of the intelligentsia'. The Sonya of *Uncle Vanya* is still described by Yelyena as having 'clever, suspicious eyes', which had always seemed to me a worryingly inconsistent detail until I realized that it had been left over, not at all aptly, from *The Wood Demon*.

Chekhov's focussing on his characters' emotional preoccupations, rather than on their individual qualities, had a further consequence of great importance for the evolution of the Chekhov play. It meant that his characters acquired a much more general, universal relevance. Voinitsky is no longer the unusual man with an unusual problem. Rather we feel for him as we might for any middle-aged man, looking back critically at his past life and overwhelmed by feelings of futility and disillusionment. In Sonya there is personified something no less universal—the collapse of a long and dearly cherished hope; while Astrov represents a man struggling to maintain a philosophical outlook on life in the face of life's exhausting everyday demands.

Tolstoy was scathing (once more!) about *Uncle Vanya*, which he saw performed by the Moscow Art Theatre on January 24th, 1900. He noted in particular Astrov's remark to Vanya near the end that 'in the whole of the district there were only two decent, intelligent men: you and I'. Chekhov, Tolstoy claimed, had done nothing to show why the audience should accept such a high opinion of the two characters, and so there was no reason why we should feel pity for them. And he threw in for good measure his own opinion that Vanya and Astrov 'had always been bad and mediocre, and that is why their sufferings cannot be worthy of interest'.[9]

'Bad and mediocre' was a perversely harsh judgement on Chekhov's heroes. One might have expected that at least Astrov's plans for saving the countryside would appeal to Tolstoy. But perhaps Tolstoy had more of a point in the case of Vanya? Vanya tells us bitterly that he used to be considered 'an enlightened personality'; but what his ideals were and how this enlightenment revealed itself (other than in the altruistic renunciation of his share of the estate)—here Chekhov remains decidedly vague. And yet Tolstoy's comments seem to involve a basic misunderstanding, a refusal to see that Chekhov had conceived his play exclusively on the emotional plane. Chekhov was not concerned with whether Vanya's ideals *as such* were barren; he wanted to show, and make his audience respond to, the painful emotional consequences which may arise when ideals are no longer able to inspire a man's life. This is a very broad concept. It is something that may happen to many different people in many different situations; and to particularize it, by giving Vanya specific ideals, would be to sacrifice this whole breadth of relevance.

In the last chapter it was suggested that an audience is likely to remain somewhat detached from the artistic aspirations of Kostya and Nina in *The Seagull*. Only a tiny minority will have had first-hand experience of such feelings; and it may even be difficult to imagine why Nina's vocation as an actress should be presented as a matter of such vital importance. These criticisms cannot be levelled at *Uncle Vanya*, where everyone is likely to have had some experience of the feelings presented. Whatever he may have said in public, it seems unlikely that Tolstoy—a pioneer in conveying the emotional states of his fictional characters—could have remained indifferent to this. And indeed, as Sophie Laffitte points out in her article on Chekhov and Tolstoy, it was on returning from his visit to *Uncle Vanya* that Tolstoy sketched out the plan for his own play, *The Living Corpse* (1900)—a work in which, as she writes, there is 'a kind of Chekhovian atmosphere', and which is exceptional among Tolstoy's works for its 'note of human sympathy, free of all moralizing dogma', and its pity for man's 'weaknesses and sufferings'.[10]

Although Tolstoy, the rational thinker, could not help finding Chekhov's play inadequate, Tolstoy, the man of feeling, seems to have responded more positively to *Uncle Vanya* than he was willing to admit.

vi. THE TAKERS

In *Uncle Vanya* the contrast between residents and outsiders is twofold. First, there is the way in which Chekhov presents these characters: the residents being presented in terms of emotional preoccupations, and the outsiders, as in *The Seagull*, in terms of their individual qualities. Secondly, there is the relation of the characters to the 'work' theme. The residents' involvement with work, we argued, arose incidentally, in the course of their emotional transformation; it was not

G

Chekhov's starting-point. In rejecting the 'good and evil'/'true and false beauty' kind of approach to *Uncle Vanya*, we were rejecting its simplistic moralizing and its distorting emphasis on the moral, as opposed to the emotional, content of the play. That there is an implied moral distinction between outsiders and residents in relation to work is however clear enough; but it is a much quieter contrast than is generally made out, not morally strident at all. It is a simple contrast—following on from the way in which Nina differentiated herself from the other three main characters in *The Seagull*—between *takers* and *givers*: between those who are absorbed in themselves to the exclusion of other people and those who are not; and between those who find it natural and those who find it unnatural, to work for the benefit of others. The following exchange between Yelyena and Sonya shows that it is predominantly a question of attitude:

> YELYENA ANDREYEVNA. . . . I'm dying of boredom, I don't know what to do with myself.
> SONYA (*shrugging her shoulders*). But there's so much to do if you wanted to.
> YELYENA ANDREYEVNA. What, for example?
> SONYA. Helping to run the estate, teaching, looking after the sick. There are lots of things. Why, before you and Papa came, Uncle Vanya and I used to go to market and sell our own flour.
> YELYENA ANDREYEVNA. I'd be no good at that kind of thing, and anyway it doesn't interest me. It's all right for people in novels with a message to go round teaching and nursing peasants—but how could I suddenly rush off just like that and start nursing or teaching people?
> SONYA. And I just don't understand how you can help wanting to go off and teach them.

It is not, one should emphasize, merely a contrast between those who work and those who do not. No one will deny that the Professor has worked hard in his own fashion. But work may mean one of two things: it may mean work as a contribution to solving the common human predicament of needing to keep body and soul together, and of trying to relieve human suffering (the kind of work in which the givers are involved); or it may mean work aimed at trying to satisfy a thirst for glory and self-advertisement. That thirst still drives the Professor on.

The takers in *Uncle Vanya* are the Professor, Yelyena and, to some extent, Mariya Vasil'yevna. All the other characters are givers—an interesting reversal of the balance between givers and takers in *The Seagull*. The similarities between the takers in the two plays are not however confined to Chekhov's emphasis on their individual qualities, for there are also striking affinities between the characters themselves.

A parallel may be drawn between the two most obvious takers in *The Seagull* and *Uncle Vanya*: Arkadina and Serebryakov. Their lives are dictated by their self-image. Just as Arkadina sees herself as the celebrated actress, serving the sacred cause of Art, so the Professor must look upon himself as one of Culture's leading representatives. It is the desire to preserve this self-image that has made them materialistic. The audience is not deceived when the Professor makes out that he is not a practical man and has no head for financial matters—his plans for selling the estate sound practical enough! They both crave the limelight, and cannot adjust themselves to the obscurity of life in the country. By the time she reaches the Professor's age, we can well imagine Arkadina exclaiming, as he does:

> ... I want to live, I want to be successful and well known and talked about—but this is just like being in exile. To spend every moment longing for the past, watching other people succeed, being afraid of death ... It's too much! It's more than I can stand!

Both are self-important, the Professor perhaps rather more so. Arkadina may exaggerate her triumphs, but at least they are real; whereas the importance which Serebryakov gives himself in his own eyes seems like a way of obscuring the uncomfortable truth of his own insignificance. 'Excellent, excellent ... splendid views,' says the Professor when he first appears, returning from a walk; and it is as if the residents were receiving a little pat on the back because they have succeeded in giving him pleasure. 'My friends,' he continues pompously, 'would you be so kind as to send my tea to the study. There is something else that I have to do today.' This first impression—of illusory self-importance—is one that lasts throughout the play.

To label Maria Vasil'yevna as a taker would be unfair, since she, like Vanya, has devoted so much of her life to the Professor—only to be described by him, in the course of the play, as 'that old idiot'! But she shares certain qualities which are closely associated with the takers: self-importance, and a complete absorption in her own affairs. At her first appearance, she comes in with a book, 'sits down and reads; tea is put before her and she drinks it without looking up'. This 'without looking up' is one of those tiny details of behaviour which Chekhov used so effectively in his short stories to suggest some underlying feature of a person. It is reminiscent of Lida, the self-important elder sister in *The House with a Mezzanine*, which Chekhov wrote in the winter of 1895–96. Lida is full of 'good works', but the narrator notices that when she is collecting subscriptions for the victims of a fire and explaining everything in great detail, she does so without even bothering to look up at the people she is addressing.[11] Maria Vasil'yevna sits quietly for a while, and then makes a comic intervention into the dialogue:

> SONYA. Il'ya Il'ich is our helper, he's our right hand man. (*Tenderly.*) Let me pour you some more tea, Godfather.
> MARIA VASIL'YEVNA. Oops!
> SONYA. Whatever is it, Grandmother?
> MARIA VASIL'YEVNA. I forgot to tell Alexander ... My memory's going ... I had a letter today from Pavel Alekseyevich, in Kharkov. He sent his new pamphlet ...

These pamphlets accompany her throughout the play, a symbol of her self-absorption and devotion to the world of Culture personified by the Professor. Everyone is used to them. The dots at the end of her speech suggest that no one is very anxious to pursue the subject of her latest pamphlet.

Yelyena is a more complex taker than her husband; and the scene of her reconciliation with Sonya shows that she is not entirely self-absorbed but capable of emotional responsiveness. The trouble with characters like Yelyena, and her counterpart in *The Seagull*, Trigorin, is that their outward brilliance attracts other people, who are fascinated by their beauty or their fame—but that they can give little in return. This outward brilliance conceals an inner void. Without fully realizing what they are doing, they can cause havoc in the lives of others: Trigorin all but destroys Nina, and Yelyena deprives Sonya of her one slight chance of happiness.

My impression is that Chekhov did not manage the transition of Yelyena from *The Wood Demon* to *Uncle Vanya* altogether successfully—failing to make a clean enough break with the earlier play—and that there are inconsistencies about her characterization in *Uncle Vanya*; but it would be tedious to pursue this in detail. Chekhov's intentions seem reasonably clear. In *The Wood Demon* Yelyena's virtue is presented as something sincere and positive, whereas in *Uncle Vanya*, this virtue has become much more shallow and passive. Yelyena in *The Wood Demon* seems to speak with full conviction when she says to Voinitsky: 'Give me your help in reconciling everyone! I'm not strong enough to do it alone'; but in *Uncle Vanya* the remark has been changed to read: 'Your job is not to complain, but to reconcile everyone'—which is spineless and shuffles off responsibility. Similar comments intended in the earlier play to convey a moral message ('you must have faith in everyone, it's impossible to live in any other way', for example), in *Uncle Vanya* sound merely platitudinous. 'It seems to me that whatever the truth may be, it can't be as terrible as not knowing,' she says, after persuading Sonya to let her speak to Astrov; eminently sensible and yet it has a strangely hollow ring. Sonya pauses for a moment and then murmurs: 'No, not knowing's better ... At least there's still hope'—which may be shortsighted, but is much more human and convincing.

Yelyena in *Uncle Vanya* plays the role of the virtuous wife rather in the way that Trigorin plays the role of the famous writer—because they don't know what else to do. They both lack a sense of inner identity. It would be as wrong to suppose that Yelyena deliberately attracts Astrov towards herself, thereby destroying Sonya's chance of happiness, as it would be to imagine that Trigorin deliberately sets out to turn Nina's head by revealing his most secret thoughts to her. Yelyena reminds us of those characters in Turgenev (like the hero of *Asya*), who have to wait for something to happen to them from outside before they can make up their minds about the nature of their own feelings. Astrov was wrong when he said that Yelyena was 'absolutely delighted' because he'd been pursuing her so diligently; she had never been so clear about her feelings as that. Even when she volunteers to 'interrogate' Astrov, she still consciously believes that she is acting with the best of intentions. She receives a great deal more than she bargained for from this interview. The scene recalls the one in Turgenev's *Fathers and Sons*, between the heroine, Odintsova, who is not unlike Chekhov's character, and the hero, Bazarov, who describes Odintsova in the same terms—as a 'luxurious woman' (*roskoshnaya zhenshchina*)—that Astrov uses of Yelyena. When Odintsova encourages Bazarov to talk about his emotions, she elicits an alarmingly passionate declaration of love. Her reaction is not altogether unambiguous—'she did not free herself from his embraces straight away'—but it is less ambiguous than that of Yelyena to Astrov. Had Vanya not come in with that bouquet of autumn roses, who knows what might have happened?

In the final act, Yelyena shows the same kind of defeatism that Trigorin displays when he agrees to be marched off on a lead by Arkadina in the course of Act III. Just as Trigorin is reconciled to playing out the role of the famous writer once again, so Yelyena has resigned herself to playing out the role of the faithful wife. She can allow herself to kiss Astrov, because she knows she would never be able to find the energy to reverse her decision.

vii. THE GIVERS

The givers in *Uncle Vanya* are quite ordinary people. It is impossible to regard them as figures of heroic stature. Vanya is intelligent and hard-working, Sonya is hard-working also and sensitive to what others are feeling, while Astrov has a more original, philosophical turn of mind (very much highlighted by the mediocrity of all those round him); but they are none of them exceptional. Unlike the takers, who are trapped within their self-centred preoccupations, they find it natural to make some contribution to the welfare of other people; and they feel (or in Astrov's case, have felt) that there is no reason why they should not obtain a modest amount of happiness in life. But, Chekhov suggests, so inimical are the conditions prevailing in provincial Russia—where the atmosphere of 'desperate boredom' closes in on an individual, 'dim grey shapes' engulf him, and 'vulgar trivialities' become the accepted norm of conversation—that even such ordinarily human qualities and aspirations as these are threatened with extinction.

A symbolic parallel to this human situation was to be found in the world of nature, in the threatened destruction of Russia's forests; and this symbol of the forests in *Uncle Vanya* is both less artificial and less obtrusive than the symbol of the seagull, with its restricted application to particular individuals. In *The Wood Demon* the forests had also been used symbolically—the devil of destruction that makes people unthinkingly chop down trees being equated with the same devil that makes them behave inhumanly towards one another. But this symbol was tangled up with the question of the Wood Demon's 'genuineness'; and when the preservation of the trees is first mentioned, Voinitsky makes cynical suggestions about Khrushchov's underlying motives, and gives a mocking take-off of his declamatory style. ('Human beings! You are destroying the forests which adorn the earth, which

teach man to appreciate beauty and which inspire in him lofty emotions
...', etc.) With one ingenious stroke, Chekhov in *Uncle Vanya*
transformed the theme of the forests entirely. Voinitsky's mocking
words were transferred, almost without alteration, to Sonya. This
immediately lifted the theme out of the realm of the personal—for
Sonya's sincerity was beyond question; and the same words in her
mouth gave the simple idea of afforestation an unexpectedly poetic
and visionary dimension. The planting of new forests becomes
associated with the constructive behaviour of the characters in *Uncle
Vanya*, and symbolizes the possibility of a better future for mankind;
just as their destruction is linked to the destructive characters, and
points towards human as well as natural degeneration.[12] It is no
coincidence that the Professor should casually suggest that one way
of raising money would be to chop down a forest or two; nor that
Yelyena should be unable to raise any interest in Astrov's maps.

Because they are not self-centred but are more concerned with
other people, it is among the givers that the most subtle vibrations
of the emotional network are to be found in *Uncle Vanya*.

Astrov is not in love with Sonya, and when he leaves at the end of
the play, she knows that he will never again be more than an in-
frequent visitor. This relationship is a failure: Sonya is unable to make
him understand her feelings, and he only learns about them later
through Yelyena. Yet the big scene which the pair play together—the
'snack' scene in Act II—is one of the emotional highlights of *Uncle
Vanya*, making a deeper impact than any number of more 'successful'
love scenes; and I would not hesitate to claim that this is one of the
occasions when the emotional network is vibrating with special intensity. But does this not involve a contradiction? The idea of the
emotional network implies that there should be some flow of emotion
between individuals; yet Astrov throughout the scene remains quite
unmoved. But there is a sense in which Sonya and Astrov are not the
only people involved here; for in any scene the emotional network can
only be completed by the presence of another party, also responding
on the emotional level—the audience itself. Sonya's emotions may not
reach Astrov, but they do reach the audience. When Astrov, philosophizing, tells her that he no longer expects anything from life,
is not fond of people and has not been in love with anyone for ages,
and Sonya asks him: 'No one at all?'—the audience is placed in the
position of the middle party, sharing Sonya's secret, aware of her
emotions and anxious to pass them on to Astrov, to make him see

and respond to what she is feeling. It is the audience's inability to do this which gives the scene its special emotional tension.

Astrov then goes on to speak of the suspicion that he arouses because he is unconventional, and again, his philosophizing is followed by an emotional interruption from Sonya. As Astrov is about to raise his glass of vodka, Sonya intervenes:

SONYA (*preventing him*). Please, I beg you, I implore you, don't drink any more.
ASTROV. But why?
SONYA. It's so out of keeping with you. You're a man of taste, your voice is so gentle . . . And then again, you're not like all the other people I know. You're a fine person. So why should you want to be like ordinary people, who drink and play cards? Oh, don't be like that, I implore you! You're always saying that men never create anything, they only destroy what God's given them. So why then, why do you destroy yourself? You mustn't do it, you mustn't, I implore you, I beseech you.
ASTROV (*holds out his hand to her*). I'll not touch another drop.
SONYA. Give me your word.
ASTROV. My word of honour.
SONYA (*presses his hand warmly*). Thank you!
ASTROV. So that's settled and I'm sober again. You can see I'm quite sober now, and so I shall remain till the end of my days. (*Looks at his watch.*) But to resume . . .

Here at least there seems to have been some communication between Sonya and Astrov, some flow of emotion between them; but has there? The final act will confirm that what had seemed to Sonya like a serious undertaking on Astrov's part was really little more than a light-hearted gesture of the moment, a brief diversion in the course of his philosophizing. There is one thing in life, he goes on, which does still move him, and that is beauty; and at this point the audience must feel tempted to pitch in to Astrov, and to tell him just how much pain this offhanded remark is bound to cause the unattractive Sonya. The conversation pauses; and Sonya, summoning up her courage, puts to Astrov the question that she must have thought out long before their present encounter:

Tell me, Mikhail L'vovich . . . Supposing that I had a friend or a younger sister, and supposing you found out that she . . . well, let's say that she was in love with you—what would your reaction be?

The halting delivery, the naively self-revealing nature of the question —surely Astrov cannot fail to notice something now? But Astrov's thoughts during this conversation have been very self-centred; and taking the question at its face value, he just shrugs his shoulders, tells Sonya that he is incapable of falling in love, and announces that it is time for him to be off. Left alone, Sonya's immediate reaction, in spite of Astrov's complete indifference, is to 'laugh with happiness'. This is quite unexpected, yet psychologically it is so obviously right, for in telling Astrov for the first time what a fine person she thinks he is, Sonya has broken through a barrier in her own mind.

If the relationship between Sonya and Astrov is characterized by a failure in communication, then that between Sonya and her uncle reveals a high degree of emotional responsiveness—more so indeed than any previous relationship that we have encountered in the Chekhov play.

In *The Wood Demon* Sonya and Voinitsky had been two of a kind: intellectually rather high-powered, and critical—often aggressively so—towards the people round them, including one another. But there was a brief moment in the earlier play when a different kind of relationship seemed apparent:

SONYA. Our hay hasn't been gathered, Gerasim told me today it was going rotten from the rain—and all you do is spend your time on illusions. (*Alarmed.*) Uncle, there are tears in your eyes!
VOINITSKY. Tears, what tears? Nonsense . . . don't be silly . . . The way you looked at me then was just like your poor mother. My darling . . . (*Eagerly kisses her hands and face.*) My sister . . . my darling sister . . . Where is she now? If only she knew! Oh, if only she knew!
SONYA. Knew what, Uncle? Knew what?

Here Sonya reveals, as well as practical sense, a tender side to her nature, which is not developed elsewhere in *The Wood Demon*; while Voinitsky too appears without any of his habitual irony. It is at this moment indeed that the two plays, so widely different in other respects, seem to be closest together; for the scene from *The Wood Demon* precisely anticipates what is most striking about Sonya and her uncle in the later play—their deeply emotional natures, and their degree of emotional responsiveness towards one another. Vanya sees in Sonya the sister whom he once idolized, and perhaps because of this, the relationship between him and Sonya seems more like one between brother and sister than between uncle and niece. Sonya alone of the characters can understand her uncle and feel for him. She sees through his outward bitterness to the vulnerable, emotional person beneath, and she realizes how much he is lacerating himself by his bitter tirades. When Vanya complains that he cannot sleep for frustration at the stupid way in which he has wasted his life, Sonya remonstrates with him: 'Uncle Vanya, that's boring!' But it would be wrong to imagine that Sonya is just ticking her uncle off; rather, she is feeling with him, trying to make him see that he is only making matters worse for himself by this indulgence in self-pity.

Chekhov extended the closeness between these two characters by making their fates run along parallel courses, switching the audience's attention from one to the other as they each try to break away from their frustrating lives—until for both a period of crisis is reached in Act III. Although Vanya occupies the centre of the stage with his bitter, self-dramatizing attack on Serebryakov, the audience must not be allowed to forget about Sonya, whose silent grief on learning of Astrov's reply is quite devoid of self-dramatization. When finally she can remain silent no longer, her despairing plea for help is made to parallel that of Vanya:

VOINITSKY. ... I'm talking rubbish, I'm going mad.... Mother, I'm in despair! Mother!
MARIA VASIL'YEVNA (*sternly*). Do as Alexander tells you.
SONYA (*kneeling down in front of Marina and pressing close to her*). Nanny! Nanny!
VOINITSKY. Mother! What am I to do? Never mind, don't say anything! I've got my own answer! (*To Serebryakov.*) You'll not forget me in a hurry! (*Goes out through the middle door.*)

In their moment of need, both residents turn unthinkingly to the figures who meant most to them in their childhood. With Vanya's departure, it is left to Sonya, in one of the play's most moving speeches, to appeal to her father for understanding:

SONYA (*kneeling, turning towards her father; in an agitated, tearful voice*). You must be charitable, Papa! Uncle Vanya and I are so unhappy! (*Restraining her despair.*) You must be charitable!

Remember when you were younger and how at night-time
Uncle Vanya and Grandmother would translate books for you
and copy out your papers ... night after night after night!
Uncle Vanya and I worked without rest, we were afraid of
spending a thing on ourselves and sent all the money to you.
... Our life wasn't an easy one! I'm not putting it properly, not
properly at all, but you must understand us, Papa. You must be
charitable!

The grief that is really uppermost in Sonya's mind is bound of course
to remain unexpressed here; but it is characteristic of her as a giver
that she is not preoccupied by her own grief, but tries to intercede
with her father on Vanya's behalf. Sonya is fully aware of why her
uncle has been so deeply shocked by the Professor's proposal, and
tries to explain this to him. But she realizes that words are very inadequate—'I'm not putting it properly, not properly at all'—to
express how one person may invest the whole of his emotional capital
in another, as Vanya has done in the Professor. Serebryakov is incapable of seeing all the emotional implications of what his daughter is
saying; he cannot supply the extra emotional element which can only
be hinted at, not stated in words. Sensing this, Sonya has to fall back
on a more general emotional appeal ('You must understand us, Papa.
You must be charitable!'), showing here the same emotional directness
with which she had implored Astrov to give up drinking.

Astrov, the third important giver in the play, is no less frustrated
than Sonya and Vanya. His medical practice exhausts him, physically
and emotionally. But there is a crucial difference between Astrov and
the other two givers. Until very recently Vanya may have consoled
himself with an illusion, while Sonya still cherishes a vain hope of
happiness; whereas Astrov has long since passed those points. He has
neither hope, nor illusion; for him 'there is no light shining in the
distance'.

This does not mean that Astrov has become bitter or cynical, though
there is a certain hardness in his character, and a streak of coarseness,
which no doubt were not present when he first arrived in the district as
an enthusiastic young doctor some eleven years earlier. He is by nature a
giver—why else should he have remained in such a thankless job?—and
the loss of hope for any improvement in his own life has had the effect
not of making him bitterly introspective, but of directing his attention
outward, to areas beyond the realm of his own immediate happiness.
The idea of planting new forests appeals to him, partly because it is a

way of being in closer touch with nature—for Astrov refuses to see man
as the unique product of creation—but more as a means of contributing
to the happiness of future generations. This is the main area to which
his attention has been directed: that of speculation about the significance
of his life, not to himself, but within the wider context of human evolution. Sonya and Vanya, when hope and illusion fail, are plunged into
personal grief; but Astrov has passed beyond that point also. He is not
content to think of his fate as something uniquely individual to him. In
the opening speeches of the play he places his life within the context of
life in provincial Russia generally; and he speculates even more widely
when he thinks about 'the people who'll be alive in a hundred or two
hundred years' time, the people we're preparing the way for', and
wonders whether 'they'll have a good word to say for us'.

It is clear from the above that in this character, who has passed
beyond the point of hope for himself and whose mind is therefore free
to wander in much wider areas, Chekhov has opened up, perhaps quite
inadvertently, a rich new emotional seam; for the emotions presented
through Astrov are not those which arise in response to the behaviour
of other people, nor those relating to states of happiness or unhappiness,
but stem from what we feel about our position within the scheme of
human life as a whole. This creates the centrifugal effect, which Calderon
was the first to comment on; and it marks an important milestone in the
evolution of the Chekhov play.

When Chekhov decided that Astrov should be attracted to Yelyena,
he may well have been influenced in the first place by the demands of
his plot. Sonya might be frustrated because Astrov does not love her,
but there was no reason, as Yelyena points out, why she should not
make Astrov a perfectly suitable wife. For Astrov to become infatuated with Yelyena's physical attractions, which contrast so sharply
with Sonya's unattractiveness, would effectively block such a development.

At the same time, it introduced an element of movement into the
character of Astrov. Like Vanya, he temporarily kicks over the traces
of his frustrating life—abandoning both trees and medical practice
in order to pursue the glamorous Yelyena. Psychologically, too, this
sensuality acted as a plausible foil to the highmindedness of his philosophy of life. Astrov's sensuality contrasts with the more old-fashioned,
romantic approach to love of Uncle Vanya, symbolized in the bouquet
of autumn roses that he has gathered for Yelyena. Astrov makes fun of
this poetic approach. Sooner or later, he tells Yelyena in Act IV, she'll

give way to her feelings—how much more poetic if it were to happen here, 'in the bosom of nature' (not in unromantic Kursk or Kharkov), against an idyllic background of trees and crumbling old estates like those in Turgenev's novels! And he asks Yelyena for a farewell kiss, while there's nobody about, and before 'Uncle Vanya comes in with one of his bouquets'.

Astrov himself pursues Yelyena with fatalistic determination. When he first refers to his feelings for her (speaking to Sonya about beauty in Act II), he says that if she wished, Yelyena could turn his head in a single day, and he goes on:

> . . . But that wouldn't be love of course, not a lasting attachment. (*Covers his eyes with his hand and shudders.*)
> SONYA. What's the matter?
> ASTROV. Nothing. . . . During Lent a patient of mine died under chloroform.
> SONYA. It's time you forgot about that.

Why should Astrov recall the incident at this particular moment? We know already that he feels guilty about his patient's death, though he was in no way to blame. His inability to suppress his growing desire for Yelyena sets up a conflict in him, and activates these feelings of guilt and conscience. Astrov gives way to his desires—with grim acquiescence rather than romantic yearning. Vanya sees his love for Yelyena in terms of holding her in his arms and protecting her from the storm; but the image that comes to predominate in Astrov's mind is of Yelyena as a 'beautiful, fluffy marten', which needs victims—the marten, significantly, being a destructive force in nature. Whereas Vanya pursues Yelyena in the hope of attaining happiness, Astrov is under no such illusion. It is for this reason that one feels at the end of the play that the memory of Yelyena will disappear from Astrov's mind almost at once, whereas it will leave a lasting impression on Vanya. Vanya would be willing to pursue Yelyena to the ends of the earth if he felt that anything would come of it; but it is hard to envisage Astrov abandoning his trees and his medical practice for good. His pursuit of Yelyena is on a level with his vodka-drinking: it is tempting—irresistibly tempting—because it holds out the possibility of release, at least temporarily, from the unbearable tensions of life; but it offers nothing in the way of a permanent solution.

In the first three acts, Astrov is not really drawn into the emotional network of *Uncle Vanya*. He is very much the non-reacting partner in the 'snack' scene with Sonya; and even in the 'map' scene of Act III with Yelyena, though he is far from emotionally passive, he does not stand revealed in his emotional entirety in the way that Sonya is in the earlier scene. It is only in Act IV that Astrov becomes fully involved in the play's emotional network.

viii. THE FINAL ACT

Chekhov's closing stage direction before the curtain slowly descends at the end of *Uncle Vanya* informs us that 'Telyegin is tuning his guitar softly, Maria Vasil'yevna making notes in the margin of her pamphlet, and Marina knitting a stocking'. The poses are characteristic. It is a little tableau scene in the background, making it clear beyond doubt that the old way of life has taken over once again. 'It only needed you and your husband to turn up,' Astrov tells Yelyena, 'and all of us here who were working away busily and creating something, had to drop what we were doing and spend the whole summer attending to you and your husband's gout. You two infected us all with your idleness.' But now the circle of work, of frustration brought to a climax by the outsiders' arrival, and of more work, has been closed once and for all.

This conclusion is already anticipated in the opening scene of Act IV. The setting is no longer the garden on a summer's afternoon, nor the lounge which was only ever used on grand occasions, but Vanya's room—a functional, lived-in room—on an autumn evening; and it comes as a surprise to learn that Vanya had identified himself with his job so closely that he was in the habit of sleeping in the same room where he worked during the day. It was round this room that Vanya's life centred before the outsiders' arrival, and it is from here that the estate will be run in future. As in *The Seagull*, the curtain rises on two minor characters: Marina and Telyegin. They are both hard at work—even though their work consists only of winding a ball of wool as quickly as possible. The two of them are perhaps the estate's most permanent fixtures; and Marina in particular would have opposed the Professor's plans with more intransigence than anyone. They make little secret of their satisfaction at being able to say that the Professor and his wife were simply 'not fated' to live on the estate, and that everything will at last return to normal. In the first act Marina was complaining that they had dinner at seven instead of one, and Chekhov now makes her echo these remarks:

We'll have morning tea by eight, lunch before one, and we'll sit down to supper in the evening. We'll do everything properly, like other people . . . like good Christians.

Their sense of relief is beautifully captured in the exchange that follows:

> MARINA (*with a sigh*). It's a long time since I had noodle soup, old sinner that I am.
> TELYEGIN. You're right, it *is* a long time since we had noodle soup.

Noodle soup could never have been offered to the Professor and his wife! It is to Marina that Chekhov gives the first explicit statement of the 'work' theme. Telyegin is depressed because a shopkeeper in the village has called him 'a hanger-on', but Marina replies:

> We're all hangers-on in God's eyes. Whether it's you, or Sonya, or Ivan Petrovich—we none of us sit around and do nothing, we all of us work hard. All of us. . . .

Ivan Petrovich (Uncle Vanya) is not however psychologically prepared yet for this return to the working routine. Sonya sees that there is no alternative; but when the last act begins, Vanya is still playing out a drama, with himself in the role of tragic hero. His scene with Astrov, early in Act IV, is one of the most striking scenes in the play; and it is here that Astrov, for the first and only time, becomes fully involved in the play's emotional network. After seeing *Uncle Vanya* performed by the Moscow Art Theatre in Sevastopol during their tour of the Crimea in the spring of 1900, Chekhov surprised Stanislavsky by recommending that in this very sombre scene Astrov should *whistle*.[13] The suggestion becomes easier to understand in the light of Chekhov's letter (January 2nd, 1901) to Olga Knipper, who was then rehearsing the part of Masha in *Three Sisters*, in which he says that 'people who have long borne grief inside them and have grown used to it, merely whistle from time to time and often become lost in thought'.[14]

Astrov refuses obstinately—at first sight, even callously—to play any role in Vanya's drama:

> VOINITSKY. What a fool I've made of myself—firing twice and missing both times! I'll never forgive myself for that.

ASTROV. If you were so keen on shooting someone, why didn't you put a bullet through your own head?

VOINITSKY (*shrugging his shoulders*). It's a funny business. I've just tried to murder somebody, but I've not been arrested or charged with anything. So they must reckon I'm mad. (*With an unpleasant laugh.*) Oh yes, I'm mad, but people who pass themselves off as professors and learned oracles so that you don't see how dull and dim-witted they are, how completely heartless—they're not mad. And women who marry old men and promptly deceive them in front of everyone—they're not mad either. I saw you, I saw you kissing her!

ASTROV. That's right, kissing her . . . and so much for you, sir. (*Thumbs his nose.*)

The 'unpleasant laugh' is Chekhov's way of indicating an unnatural element in Vanya's words. He is still exaggerating the Professor's failings, and he tries to make a great drama out of the incident between Astrov and Yelyena, in the hope that Astrov will be completely thrown off balance by his sudden revelation. But Astrov's reaction is cheekily unperturbed, and quite takes the wind out of Vanya's sails. Vanya has to harp back again to the Professor:

VOINITSKY (*looking at the door*). No, it's the earth that's mad for still keeping you.

ASTROV. Now you're being stupid.

VOINITSKY. Well, if I'm mad and not responsible, I've the right to say stupid things.

ASTROV. That's an old line. You're not mad, you're just a crank. A comic turn. I used to think every crank was ill or abnormal, but now I reckon that being a crank is man's normal state. You're perfectly normal.

At this point in the conversation a change occurs. Vanya has so far been striking attitudes; and Astrov has been deliberately refusing to play along with him. But now Vanya begins to express his feelings with much more sincerity; and a greater degree of complexity also begins to enter into Astrov's reactions:

VOINITSKY (*covers his face with his hands*). I feel so ashamed! If only you knew how ashamed I feel! The feeling's so acute, it's worse than any pain. (*With anguish.*) It's unbearable. (*Leans over the table.*) What am I to do? What am I to do?

ASTROV. There's nothing you can do.

VOINITSKY. You'll have to give me something. Oh, my God! I'm forty-seven. If I live to be sixty, that'll mean another thirteen years. It's too long! How can I live through thirteen more years? What can I do? How can I fill them? Oh, if only.... (*squeezing Astrov's hand convulsively*) if only one could live the rest of one's life in some new kind of way. To wake up on a fine, clear morning and to feel that you'd made a new start in life, that the past had all been written off, had vanished like a puff of smoke. (*Weeps.*) To begin a new life.... Tell me how to begin ... where to begin....

ASTROV (*with annoyance*). Oh, get along with you. Whatever sort of new life is there? Our position's hopeless, yours and mine.

VOINITSKY. Are you sure?

ASTROV. I'm convinced of it.

Astrov's 'annoyance' is the first time that he has shown any kind of emotion during the conversation. His seemingly callous attitude to Vanya is not the result of indifference, for he realizes that Vanya's only hope is to overcome his tendency towards self-pity; but what really lies behind Astrov's 'hard line' is an extreme reluctance to let his own deeper emotions become involved in Vanya's plight. While Vanya is so obviously dramatizing his situation, it is not difficult for Astrov to remain quite detached. When Vanya becomes more sincere and begins talking of 'a new life', Astrov's earlier composure is threatened. He is quite sure that there can be no way out, no fresh start, and that Vanya is just harbouring an optimistic illusion; but at the same time his own rejection of these alternatives is not so very distant, and it would not take much for him to fall into the same kind of mood as Vanya. Hence the note of tension which enters into Astrov's response. But Vanya's next appeal is even more difficult to resist. It contains neither self-dramatization nor illusion. It is simply a desperate plea for help, as from one human being to another:

VOINITSKY. You must give me something ... (*Indicating his heart.*) I've a burning sensation here.

Astrov's immediate reaction is one of anger. This is essentially defensive, for he is still resisting the need to become emotionally involved; but he realizes that short of complete callousness he has no alternative

H

but to reveal his own deepest philosophy of life. Previously in the conversation Vanya had been leading and Astrov responding; now Astrov takes the lead:

> ASTROV (*shouts angrily*). Stop it! (*More gently.*) The people who'll be living in a hundred or two hundred years from now and who'll despise us for leading such tasteless and unintelligent lives—maybe they'll find a way to be happy, but as for us. . . . There's only one hope for you and me, the hope that when we're lying in our graves, visions may come to us—maybe even pleasant visions. (*With a sigh.*) Yes, my friend. In the whole of this district there were only two decent, cultured people—you and I. But ten years or so of this pettiness, this contemptible life, dragged us down—it poisoned our blood with its foul vapours until we became just as coarse as the rest of them. (*Energetically.*) But don't you go trying to put me off. You give me back what you took from me.

As these last remarks show, Astrov has reverted once again to the role of the hard-headed doctor determined to recover his bottle of morphia; but not before he has become emotionally involved in Vanya's situation, and has at the same time himself stood emotionally more fully revealed than ever before. He has been drawn into the play's emotional network—briefly but very deeply. The effect of this upon Vanya is not apparent straight away. It needs the direct emotionality of Sonya to persuade him to hand over the morphia, and to adopt an attitude of greater resignation. But Astrov's words will have a long-term effect upon Vanya. The 'drama' of his life is at an end. The self-dramatization, and the proneness to fall back on comforting illusions, have been exploded; and this helps him to reach the point where he can say to Sonya that they must get down to work, must start doing something, at the earliest opportunity.

The farewell scenes which conclude *Uncle Vanya* do not add anything to the psychological action of the play, but provide instead an outward demonstration of processes that have already been completed on the psychological level. The first of these farewells is between Yelyena and Astrov. When Olga Knipper, who was to play the part of Yelyena, wrote to Chekhov that Stanislavsky interpreted Astrov's behaviour here as that of the most passionate lover, 'clutching at his feeling like a drowning man clutching at a straw', Chekhov was quick to reply that 'this was wrong, absolutely wrong':

Yelyena appeals to Astrov, he is captivated by her beauty, but in the last act he already knows that nothing will come of it, that Yelyena is disappearing from his life forever—and he talks to her in this scene in the same tone as he talks of the heat in Africa, and kisses her quite simply, just for something to do. If Astrov plays this scene very passionately, then the whole atmosphere of Act IV— which is quiet and subdued—will be lost.[15]

Astrov is merely going through the motions, knowing full well that, as he says himself, 'the comedy is over'. (*Finita la commedia!*)

The Professor now comes in to say goodbye to Vanya. Vanya tells him that everything will be as it was before, and that the Professor will continue to receive exactly the same amount of money. Vanya no longer has any illusions about the Professor's worth, but he knows that this is the best way in which he can help himself; his offer provides the outward demonstration of a process that has already been completed in his mind. Serebryakov leaves the play with words of advice for everyone. If the 'work' theme in Act IV may be likened to a musical motif which is passed round from one member of Chekhov's dramatic orchestra to another, then the Professor's contribution can only be described as a mockingly grotesque variation:

Permit an old man to introduce into his farewell greetings just this one observation. You should do something positive, gentlemen! Something positive!

Following the departure of the two outsiders, Serebryakov and Yelyena, there is a short interval before the departure of Astrov— formerly the semi-resident with his own working corner in Vanya's room, but now to become an almost complete outsider. Astrov gives Marina a goodbye kiss, and she says to him:

MARINA. Are you off without any tea then?
ASTROV. I don't want any, Nanny.
MARINA. What about a drop of vodka?
ASTROV (*uncertainly*). Well, perhaps . . .

(*Marina goes out.*)

This exchange echoes the very opening lines of the play:

MARINA (*pours out a glass of tea*). Here you are, Doctor.
ASTROV (*accepting the glass reluctantly*). I don't really feel like it.

MARINA. What about a drop of vodka?

ASTROV. No, I don't drink vodka every day. Besides, the weather's so close.

There is a certain painful irony in Astrov's acceptance of the vodka in Act IV. In Act II he had of course given his word to Sonya that he would stop drinking altogether. It seems most unlikely that he had kept his word, but now, in her presence, he recalls the earlier promise and hesitates. Only, however, very briefly. It is a further demonstration of a psychological process already completed, of an old pattern re-established.

The cumulative effect of these farewell scenes may well be to make us feel that nothing has changed—moreover, that nothing could have changed. They intensify the feeling of circularity, the awareness in the audience's mind that the main characters have tried, and failed, to escape from the dull routine of their working lives. Indeed it is not even true to say that the central figures are 'back at square one'; for both Sonya and Vanya have passed well beyond that point. The emptiness of their lives is no longer to be offset by the consolation of hopes or illusions. If there is further imposed upon such impressions the effect of Sonya's final speech, with its implication that she and Vanya will only find release from their present misery in life beyond the grave, it is easy to see why *Uncle Vanya* has been widely regarded not only as a sad play, but also as one which is permeated by a spirit of defeatism. A British audience, with its strongly developed notion of individual justice, finds particular difficulty in reconciling itself to the apparent defeatism with which Vanya meekly offers to pay the Professor the same as before; surely he could at the very least have insisted on a larger allowance for himself, so that one improvement, however slight, would have emerged from all the play's upheavals? There is too a sense of inevitability, of hopeless resignation, about the way in which, after the departure of the Professor and Yelyena, the remaining characters file slowly back into the house one after the other, each in turn repeating the same phrase: 'They've gone' (an effect that is repeated after Astrov's departure)—as if Chekhov were suggesting that human relations are always bound to be insecure, and human beings constantly fated to part company, to go their separate ways. As for Astrov's 'pleasant visions' and Sonya's 'angels' and 'diamond-studded sky', these posthumous rewards may seem a very doubtful consolation for the sufferings to be undergone in the here-and-now.

The sadness of *Uncle Vanya* is beyond dispute. It is the sadness of lives that will remain unfulfilled; and the sadness of separation—whether in the literal sense of characters parting company, probably never to meet again, or in the psychological sense of characters failing to relate harmoniously to one another. But the presentation on stage of sad lives does not tell us anything about the spirit in which these sad lives are presented; and I very much doubt whether Chekhov would have approved of an interpretation of his play in which the keynote was one of defeatism, of pessimistic resignation.

For a start, it is a misreading of the 'work' theme in *Uncle Vanya* to assume that Chekhov regarded a life of hard-working routine as a kind of hell on earth. Work itself is not denigrated in *Uncle Vanya*. On the contrary, work that helps to satisfy man's most basic needs is presented as something which automatically places those involved in it on a higher level than those who only take from life. There is every reason to think that Chekhov believed that in life, work should occupy the central position. What is wrong is a situation in which dedication to work is called upon to act as an emotional *substitute* for harmonious relations between people—when ideally the two should go hand in hand. But work itself is not the culprit; and it is not possible to argue that *Uncle Vanya* is a pessimistic play just because it shows its main characters having to return to their working lives.

Nor is it fair to say that Vanya's offer to the Professor is an indication of emotional apathy or resignation. The weak course of action here would have been to hang on to the bottle of morphia; it requires an element of courage to dedicate himself again to a life of hard work. But perhaps we should not be viewing his situation so much in 'action' terms of weakness and courage. Vanya realizes that to resume the old life is the only answer emotionally to his predicament. Sonya's devotion may sustain him, but it cannot fill his life. He has to turn back to the one emotional force that is still available to him. It is, if you like, an emotional emergency measure, utilized in response to an extreme situation.

This idea of the emotional emergency measure also seems to me to offer the best description both of Astrov's faith in a better future for mankind—a secular faith in which the 'pleasant visions' are presumably no more than a figure of speech; and also of Sonya's religious—and no doubt literal—faith in a glorious life after death. When the play ends, Astrov will return to his practice and his plantations. He will continue to remain loyal to his philosophical outlook on life, in spite of the total incomprehension of all those round him. The faith in a better future is the emotional emergency measure adopted in response to the apparent hopelessness of the present; it is the equivalent, on the mental level, of the vodka-drinking which helps to relieve the physical tensions of his life.

The religious tone of Sonya's final remark is not, as is sometimes suggested, a complete surprise: we know that she is a churchgoer, and has been 'praying all night' about her love for Astrov. But the question of belief is not really important here. It would have been cynical if Chekhov, whom Tolstoy described as a perfect atheist, had deliberately tried to play upon his audience's religious feelings; and there is no reason to think that Chekhov expected his audience either to share or to reject Sonya's belief in an after-life. Just as she turned to the childhood figure of Marina for consolation at the end of Act III, so here Sonya is drawing on a poetic and child-like vision of life after death with which to combat present misery. The vision is primarily important as a way of bringing out the intensity of her feeling about the present. Vanya is moved, not because he shares her belief—it is very unlikely that the vision of life after death has any meaning at all for him—but because he can share her feeling: he knows that she feels as intensely as he does.

The simple criticism, therefore, of the 'defeatist' approach to *Uncle Vanya* is that it is too static. It makes a critical assessment of the characters' lives, and since these are sad and offer no hope of improvement, it concludes that the spirit informing the play is also one of sadness and resignation. We have argued in favour of a more dynamic view—one in which the characters are seen as adopting emotional emergency measures in response to an extreme situation. But it may be argued that this does not at all affect the essential sadness of *Uncle Vanya*—and may even intensify it, by pointing up the extreme nature of the characters' plight. This is quite true. On the other hand, what the dynamic view also does is to underline the extent to which these emotional emergency measures have been *forced* upon the characters from outside, through no fault of their own. The spectacle of human suffering is always liable to evoke feelings of sadness. The spectacle of suffering when those who suffer are blameless and suffer unjustly, will evoke sorrow likewise, but in the wake of that sorrow there may follow other feelings—feelings of injustice and indignation. This seems to be very much the case with *Uncle Vanya*. Chekhov's three main characters may not be exceptional people, but they embody certain very vital human properties—the capacity for deep affection, a willingness to co-operate and to work hard for the benefit of others, man's urge to understand more about his place within the overall scheme of things—and they deserve better from life. Why should human beings of this quality be forced into such desperate emotional corners? This seems to me to be the underlying tone of the last act of *Uncle Vanya*—with the emphasis on quiet indignation rather than on quiet resignation; and once the initial impact of the sadness of the characters' lives has been absorbed, it is this kind of reaction that begins to take shape.

Indignation, and perhaps also a certain admiration: admiration that the three of them will continue to soldier on with courage but without melodrama, not becoming bitter or cynical, but continuing to believe that a better life is possible, if not for them. Much comment has centred round Astrov's remark near the end of the play when he goes up to the forgotten map of Africa which is hanging on the wall of Vanya's study and observes that 'the heat in Africa must be really quite something now'. Chekhov had included the map in the stage props for the final act solely for the sake of this remark, and when he wanted to explain to Olga Knipper about the 'quiet and subdued' quality of Act IV, it was to this remark that he drew her attention, so there is reason to think that Chekhov did attach special importance to it. It is one of the most striking examples in the Chekhov play of 'surface' words which are very simple, whereas the emotional state giving rise to them is complex and hard to define. The comment in Chekhov's letter makes it clear that Astrov's tone of voice is reflective and even absent-minded, so that it is unlikely that they were intended to convey a note of bravura and challenge, as Stanislavsky thought. But neither is it likely that they are quite unrelated to the general context of the play—they seem too strategically placed for that. How very odd, Astrov seems to be musing, that there really does exist a place called 'Africa', a vast unpopulated mysterious continent where the sun beats down—when our own world (for Astrov, the world of nineteenth-century provincial Russia, for us, our everyday world wherever it may be) seems so circumscribed and inescapable!

But Africa does exist; just as the possibility of a different life exists; and Astrov, through his plantations and his faith in a better future for mankind, pledges his allegiance to the possibility of that different life.

If I had to choose one quotation, however, to convey the spirit of *Uncle Vanya*, I would be tempted to settle rather for Astrov's remark to Sonya in Act II, when he says: 'I'm fond of life as a whole, but this petty, provincial life of ours in Russia—that I can't stand, I despise it utterly.' Chekhov's play can of course be very plausibly regarded as an indictment of the situation in provincial Russia which could give rise to the sadness of the lives he portrayed. But because his characters are not exceptional, because they have such general human relevance, Chekhov's indignation is likely to strike us as more open-ended than this: it is an indignation on behalf of people anywhere who through no fault of their own are forced to lead lives of sadness and frustration. Yet Astrov can still say, in spite of all his dissatisfaction, that he is 'fond of life as a whole'; and this combination—of profound dissatisfaction, together with an absence of bitterness—seems to me very characteristic of *Uncle Vanya*. Man himself, Chekhov implies, cannot be held responsible for all the suffering that exists in the world; he is only the victim of circumstance. Telyegin remarks in Act II that 'we're all living together in peace and harmony'. In their context these words are deeply ironical. But I am inclined to suspect that Chekhov, just like Telyegin, always harboured a stubborn underlying belief that there was no reason why men should not ultimately live in peace and harmony, no reason why they should be condemned indefinitely to lives of sadness and frustration.

4

'Man Needs a Life Like That'
An Appreciation of 'Three Sisters'

i. TECHNIQUES OLD AND NEW

IT was only after much persuasion that Chekhov began to write *Three Sisters*. The humiliating first night of *The Seagull* seems to have wounded him deeply.[1] Two months later he wrote to Suvorin: 'On October 17th it was not the play that failed, it was myself as an individual . . . I'm calm now, my mood is back to normal, but all the same I can't forget what happened any more than I could forget, for example, if I'd been struck by someone.'[2] Perhaps it was not coincidental that only a short time after, in March 1897, he suffered a haemorrhage of the lung, brought on by his tubercular condition. Although he recovered, he now knew for certain that he could not expect a normal life span (a knowledge which may well have made itself felt in *Three Sisters*, where the outcome of the lives of *individuals* seems of less importance than the emotional attitudes which are evolved towards life in general). Not even the successful revival of *The Seagull* by the Moscow Art Theatre in 1898 was enough to make Chekhov alter his opinion that he should stick to writing short stories. Only the patient cajoling of Nemirovich-Danchenko, to whom Chekhov felt a particular obligation—for it was he who had consistently championed *The Seagull* in the face of great opposition, including that of Stanislavsky—made Chekhov change his mind. The first mention of a new play occurs in a letter to Nemirovich of November 24th, 1899.[3] Writing the play itself was spread over the year 1900.

An interval of almost four years thus separates Chekhov's two final plays—*Three Sisters* and *The Cherry Orchard*—from *The Seagull* and *Uncle Vanya*. In the evolution of the Chekhov play, this interval is significant; and I hope to suggest, in this chapter and the one which follows, that Chekhov achieved a much greater emotional depth in his last two plays than in the two earlier works.

From a technical point of view also, *Three Sisters* seems a considerable advance on the earlier plays, both in its elaboration of previous techniques and its introduction of new ones. To begin with, deformalization of the dialogue, especially in the first two acts, is carried to much greater lengths than before. I have translated below a short passage from Act II, in which many of these deformalizing features are illustrated. It is a typical Chekhovian domestic occasion: the stage is crowded, people are moving to and fro, and doing various other things as well as talking to one another; while the dialogue itself darts unpredictably from person to person and from subject to subject—at times inconsequential (Chebutykin), at times outrageous (Solyony's reply to Natasha), at times referring back to something much earlier in the conversation (Masha):

(*The samovar is brought in and Anfisa attends to it. Shortly afterwards Natasha comes in and also busies herself round the table. Solyony enters, greets everyone, and sits down at the table.*)

VERSHININ. What a wind there is, though!

MASHA. Yes, I'm sick and tired of winter. Can't even remember what summer's like.

IRINA (*playing patience*). It's coming out, I can see it is. So we *shall* be in Moscow.

FEDOTIK. No, it isn't. You've got that eight on the two of spades. (*Laughs.*) Which means you won't be in Moscow.

CHEBUTYKIN (*reads his newspaper*). Tsitsihar. They've got a smallpox epidemic there . . .

ANFISA (*going up to Masha*). Masha, the tea's ready, dear. (*To Vershinin.*) If you'd like to go through, sir. . . . I'm sorry, I can't remember your name.

MASHA. Bring it out here, nanny. I'm not going in.

IRINA. Nanny!

ANFISA. Coming, coming.

NATASHA (*to Solyony*). Tiny babies understand very well. 'Good morning, Bobik,' I said to him, 'Good morning, precious!' And he gave me a special sort of look. You may think it's only a mother's partiality, but you'd be wrong, quite wrong. He's an exceptional child.

SOLYONY. If that child were mine, I'd fry him up in a frying-pan and eat him.

(*Takes his glass of tea into the drawing-room and sits down in a corner.*)

NATASHA (*covering her face with her hands*). What a rude, ill-bred person!

MASHA. How nice not to bother about it being winter or summer. If I lived in Moscow, I don't think I'd mind at all about the weather.

VERSHININ. The other day I was reading a diary written in prison by a French cabinet minister—he'd been sentenced over the Panama affair. . . .

Chekhov's technique of varying the emotional key is likewise much in evidence in *Three Sisters*. In Act I, after his eloquent speech about life in two or three hundred years' time, Vershinin himself varies the emotional key by changing the subject to flowers and the Prozorovs' wonderful flat; while in the second act a serious and untypically sustained discussion is undermined when Chebutykin announces that 'Balzac was married in Berdichev'.[4] Perhaps the most daring and effective use of this technique in *Three Sisters*, if not in the whole of Chekhov, comes in Act IV. Vershinin has just left. Masha is distraught, and her sisters are trying to console her. Then Kulygin produces the false beard and moustache that he has confiscated from one of the boys, pops them on his face and pretends to be the German master. For a brief moment Masha manages to smile.

The dialogue of *Three Sisters* strikes one in general as more varied and subtle than in the earlier plays, elaborating the distinctively Chekhovian combination of words that are very simple in themselves, yet full of emotional and psychological implication. But Chekhov also introduced into *Three Sisters* a new technique: that of revealing his characters not so much *through* their words, as in spite of them. When Andrei, for example, is trying to persuade his sisters—and himself—of his love for Natasha, his meaning seems perfectly clear; yet the audience is made to sense that his words are a mask which conceals feelings of a very different kind. One small instance where tone of voice explicitly contradicts meaning occurs in Act I:

IRINA. . . . And if I don't get up early and work hard, promise you won't be friends with me any more, Ivan Romanych.
CHEBUTYKIN (*tenderly*). I promise, I promise.

From here it is but a short jump to the very remarkable language of love which Chekhov invented for *Three Sisters*—a language in which Masha and Vershinin converse with one another not through words at all, but through short snatches of tune.

Alone of the major plays, *Three Sisters* is set in the town; and this opened up for Chekhov much wider possibilities in the realm of sound effects. Although certain sounds do occur on stage—the sound of the humming top, for example, in Act I, can make a deep impression —most of the important sound effects are in the background. In Act II the cheerful hubbub of the revellers down below in the street contrasts with the cheerless atmosphere that has descended on the Prozorov household; while the soul-searing noise of the fire-bell and the fire engines both helps to induce, and then to reinforce, the emotional disturbances of Act III. But it was in the final act that Chekhov exploited the use of sound most fully. The echoing voices in the garden and across the river, which so startle Irina; Natasha incongruously picking out the notes of 'The Maiden's Prayer' on the piano inside the house; the travelling musicians; the sound of the migrating birds as they pass overhead; Natasha again, flinging open a window and ticking off Andrei for talking; 'the muffled sound of a distant shot'; all these effects culminate in one of the most emotive sounds in Chekhov—the cheerful strains of the military band which slowly die away as the play approaches its final curtain.

ii. 'NOTHING EVER HAPPENS AS WE'D LIKE IT TO'

In his new play Chekhov dispensed with the inner quartet of characters which he had used in *The Seagull* and *Uncle Vanya*. *Three Sisters* can be described as the most democratic of Chekhov's plays, in that it contains no less than ten characters whose contributions are all of roughly equal importance. Chekhov further dispensed with the complex interlocking love relations that are a feature of the earlier plays. Although the characters are on close terms with one another, their individual stories develop separately. What happens to Masha and Irina may move us more deeply than the undramatic fates of Andrei and Olga, but we are unlikely to feel that any one of the four stories is to be regarded as central; Chekhov strikes a balance between them. It was this feature that prompted the American critic, Valency, to describe *Three Sisters* as a 'polyphonic' play.[5]

There is however one very important link between the Prozorovs' stories, and that is their common desire to return to Moscow, their native city. However much else may be forgotten about Chekhov's play, nobody will forget that 'it's the one about the three sisters who wanted to go to Moscow'. In tracing the occurrence of the Moscow motif one is following the development of the play itself: from the high hopes of Act I, when Moscow seems so near and attainable, through the restless yearning of Irina's exclamation at the end of Act II and her desperate plea at the end of Act III, to the final act where Irina has decided that if she's 'not destined to live in Moscow, that's all there is to it. That's fate.' This symbol for all the Prozorovs of the life that might have been has far more poignancy than the symbol of the forests in *Uncle Vanya*—especially when one remembers that Chekhov himself, for health reasons, was cut off in distant Yalta from all the people and places in Moscow that meant most to him. But Moscow is also, like the forests, emotionally a very open-ended symbol. It is not only the dreams of particular individuals that are important here; nor is it the particular city of Moscow, for as Vershinin tells the sisters: 'You won't notice Moscow once you're living there.' The craving for Moscow symbolizes in a more general way the widespread human desire for a better life than the life one has, for the better life that people dream of.

The emotional subject matter of *Three Sisters* can be described very simply. It is the disappointment of human hopes and expectations. This can be distinguished from the frustration of *Uncle Vanya* by saying that it is one stage further back, that frustration is the long-term condition arising out of disappointment. Here Sonya provides a link between the earlier play and the characters of *Three Sisters*, for her hope of marrying Astrov is disappointed in the course of *Uncle Vanya*. And this leads us on to a very basic feature of *Three Sisters*: that it is a play about young people. When Rodé teasingly asks Chebutykin how old he is, and the doctor replies, knocking off the odd thirty years or so, that he is thirty-two, this seems somehow very fitting, for he finds himself surrounded by young people. At the beginning of the play, almost all the play's important characters are still in their twenties; only Chebutykin and Vershinin, who is forty-two, do not belong to the younger generation.

For all these young people, the routine, the fixed patterns of childhood are in the past; but the routine of adulthood has yet to be established. In the first act, many different possibilities are open for all of them, and they appear to be creating their own futures; but by the end of the play, these possibilities have been drastically reduced, and for each character the future has been finally settled. By spreading the action over four years, Chekhov was able to show his young characters passing through this period of transition—when all their hopes are still in the balance, and chance events may tip their lives in one direction or another. Throughout the play, Chekhov touches many emotional nerves in his audience, but the ones that he touches on

most subtly and acutely are concerned either with the lost opportuni-
ties of the recent past (the 'if onlys' and 'might have beens' of life),
or with deep yearnings for a better future; though these might be
regarded as two sides of the same coin. Nostalgia for the more distant
past, in contrast to *The Cherry Orchard,* is of little importance in
Three Sisters; the passing of time is important only to the extent that
it smothers and rules out happier possibilities for the characters.
'Nothing ever happens as we'd like it to' (*Vsyo dyelayetsya nye po-
nashemu*), says Olga in Act IV; and perhaps her simple words, with
their calm but slightly puzzled tone, their avoidance of any suggestion
of *blame,* are the clearest expression of the subject matter of *Three
Sisters.*

Whereas *Uncle Vanya* operates only within the narrow emotional
band from frustration to despair, *Three Sisters* passes through a much
wider range of moods, from extreme high spirits to profound sadness,
and this gives each act a distinctive emotional quality of its own. The
first act, Irina's name-day party, is perhaps the most delightful act that
Chekhov ever wrote. Gone is the claustrophobic atmosphere of *Uncle
Vanya.* Visually, an impression of spring and lightness is always before
us. As in *The Wood Demon* and his vaudevilles, Chekhov starts with a
relatively empty stage, and then introduces one new character after
another, which creates an effect of growing noise and animation, so
that by the time all the guests have arrived, there is considerable
disorder and hubbub. It is a cheerful disorder though. Chekhov succeeds in generating an atmosphere of such easy warmth and intimacy that the discordant notes—Masha's depression, Chebutykin's
embarrassing gift, Solyony's painful jokes and Natasha's unfortunate
choice of sash—are quickly absorbed by it. The opportunity of
welcoming to their midst a sympathetic newcomer from Moscow—
even if *he* isn't very enthusiastic about their native city—provides
the final touch that makes the sisters' day complete. Their unspoken
closeness and their gaiety are infectious, and all the guests, apart
from Natasha, are affected by a mood of childish high spirits. Vershinin
already feels like one of the family, and when he asks if he can return
in the evening, it is an excellent touch (first used in Nemirovich-
Danchenko's 1940 production) that he should hold up his hand like
an eager schoolboy.[6]

Act II starts with a sharp visual contrast. The set is still the same;
but the clear light of midday in early spring has been replaced by the
gloom of a winter's evening. So too the characters' hopes have been

dimmed by contact with reality. The second act can be seen as a distorted reflection of Act I. Guests are arriving once again for a party, but we know in advance that Natasha has no intention of allowing the party to take place. Instead of being drawn in towards the warm emotional atmosphere of the Prozorov household, the characters are now all in a hurry to depart. But Act II is not altogether gloomy. Tuzenbach remains persistently happy in his devotion to Irina, and Vershinin tells Masha how much he loves her. It is not the first time that he has done so; but it may well be the first occasion on which she has told him that she has no objections.

The importance of the fire in Act III is primarily psychological. The atmosphere of panic and disturbance plays on the nerves of the characters; matters which have been allowed to fester beneath the surface for months or years are brought to a head on this terrible night. This is the most dramatic act in *Three Sisters*, the one in which Chekhov springs a series of surprises on his audience. Yet here too, not everything is gloomy. We are drawn into complicity with Masha and Vershinin in their love affair, and are delighted by their unique language of love, though the rumour of the regiment's departure casts a heavy shadow. Tuzenbach is *still* happy; and there is some hope that Irina's decision to marry him will lead to contentment, even though it is painfully clear that she is not acting from love but from desperation. Yet even here there is a shadow—for the audience remembers Solyony's threat to kill a successful rival.

In the final act, every remaining hope is overtaken by disappointment. Ties of friendship are permanently broken; the sisters' dream of Moscow is quietly abandoned; Vershinin and Masha have to part; and the last outstanding hope, that of Irina and Tuzenbach, which has been under sentence from the start of the act, is dashed when Tuzenbach is shot by Solyony. All hopes are thwarted; and in looking closely at the final act, one has the frequent sensation that Chekhov has taken his opening act and somehow inverted everything, as if one were looking at a mirror image. It is midday once again, but now in autumn, not spring. We come on the scene not as preparations for a party are being made, but just as a party is breaking up; the young officers, Fedotik (still taking photographs and giving presents) and Rodé, who were the last to arrive in Act I, are now the first to depart. At the beginning of the play, Irina tells Chebutykin that she feels as if she were 'sailing along, with a great blue sky above me and huge white birds soaring about'; and this bird imagery is used again to different effect in Act IV, when Chebutykin compares Irina and Tuzenbach to migrating birds who will leave him behind, and when Masha too follows the flock of birds as they pass overhead and is reminded of her inability to escape. Vershinin, who had arrived in the course of Act I, takes his leave in the course of Act IV; and after he has gone, Masha calls to mind the haunting opening lines of Pushkin's *Ruslan and Lyudmila*, which she had been saying to herself before she first met Vershinin. Natasha, the diffident visitor at Irina's party, is now in complete control of the house; the beautiful rooms have been vulgarized by the presence of Protopopov, and the sound of 'The Maiden's Prayer'; and even the flowers of Act I have been 'inverted', when Natasha talks of cutting down the beautiful trees and planting instead 'lots and lots of pretty little flowers'. A clear echo of Olga's remark to Natasha in Act I about her wrong-coloured sash is Natasha's remark to Irina: 'My dear, that sash doesn't suit you at all . . . It's in very bad taste . . .'; has Natasha perhaps been waiting over the years for just such an opportunity? And finally, our attention is drawn at the end of the play to the three sisters—seen together as a group, just as they were when the curtain first rose.

iii. STANISLAVSKY'S APPROACH

Why *were* the hopes of the Prozorovs so cruelly disappointed?

One answer might be that they were living in such uncongenial surroundings. Here were four sensitive, cultured young Russians, stranded in a backward provincial capital, which, as Andrei tells us, had existed for two hundred years and never produced anyone of the slightest distinction, and where people 'eat, drink, sleep, and so as not to die of boredom, add variety to their lives by their loathsome gossip, vodka, card-playing and lawsuits'. If we are to judge from an article by the Soviet scholar, Stroeva, based on the director's prompt book, it was this aspect of the play that Stanislavsky seized upon and made central in his original production.[7] Stanislavsky saw *Three Sisters* primarily in terms of conflict: as a representation of man's struggle with the power of banal, everyday life, which, in contrast to *The Seagull* and *Uncle Vanya*, here 'becomes an active, aggressive, far more dangerous force' (Stroeva). It is noticeable that whenever Stanislavsky appears to take the most questionable liberties with Chekhov's text, he is always accentuating some element of conflict. Thus the antagonism between Natasha and the other characters is made unduly explicit: in Act II, after Natasha's French phrases, the director introduced a whole 'laughing scene' ('Some hiss; others rock with laughter,' Stanislavsky noted; though surely the sisters are far too well bred to laugh openly in Natasha's face?); and in Act III, in her argument with Olga, Natasha is made to end up 'with a squealing hysterical scream. She squeals with tears in her voice.' (But can one reconcile this with Chekhov's indication that Olga and Natasha then walk off and leave the room together, apparently quite peaceably?) Stanislavsky even toyed with the idea of strengthening the forces of banality by bringing the unseen character of Protopopov on to the stage in Act IV:

> Just imagine: suddenly a fat man with a cigar between his teeth would unexpectedly leap from the balcony; he would run after the ball, bending over several times since he could not catch it at once. Then he disappears forever with the ball.

A vivid impression of Protopopov, but not part of Chekhov's play.

But it is in the treatment of the surroundings—in Stanislavsky's desire to emphasize their hopeless banality and crudity—that we are most likely to feel that the director was adding his own commentary to Chekhov's play. Simov, the stage designer, was instructed to prepare for Act I 'a very ordinary apartment, cheaply furnished', and to regard the sisters as the daughters of a captain, not a general; Chekhov's 'drawing-room with columns, beyond which a large ball-room can be seen' was ignored. In Act II the stage was filled with toys, baby clothes, and all the paraphernalia of Bobik's existence, while from time to time a mouse was heard scratching. Olga's remark in Act III that 'it's quiet in this room, you can't see the fire from here' made little impression on Stanislavsky; instead, in his production, the 'ever-intensifying heavy-sounding bell of the fire-alarm' clangs through the entire act, 'the firemen thunder past the house, across the yard'; and 'a red light falls in patches on the floor'. Chekhov himself was moved to complain of the excessive noise in Act III: 'Why noise? The noise is only in the distance, dull and confused . . .'[8] For the final act, Simov was given the task of embodying in his set the whole spirit of provincial Russia, in all its inimical greyness: a typical provincial house in a provincial street, with washing hanging out, a wretched little garden, surrounded by a dilapidated fence with a pile of bricks beside it . . . As in the opening act, Chekhov's own stage directions—'a long avenue of fir-trees, with a river at the end, and on the far bank of the

I

river a forest'—were largely ignored; so too were the 'beautiful trees' from which Tuzenbach was so loath to part.

The Soviet critic, Roskin, neatly summarizes the relations between Chekhov and the Moscow Art Theatre at the time of the first production when he writes that 'while the theatre was moving away from conventional pathos towards concrete everydayness, Chekhov had long since been moving back from concrete everydayness towards poetry and a freer handling of material from life'.[9] Concrete everydayness does not seem to be at all important in *Three Sisters*. Chekhov was very anxious that the details of military uniform and bearing should be life-like, but this was only because he was so afraid that his characters would be turned into 'stage officers'. There are not however any naturalistic details to compare with the starling in the cage, or the mat placed by the door for the peasants to wipe their feet on, which Chekhov included in the stage directions for Act IV of *Uncle Vanya*. The atmosphere of the provincial town is suggested only fleetingly and indirectly—through what people say about it. In emphasizing one element, the suffocating atmosphere, so strongly, Stanislavsky can be criticized for upsetting the balance of *Three Sisters*. It is not surprising that after the hopeless gloom of what had gone before, critics of the original production found it hard to accept the optimistic notes in Olga's final speech, and felt that to introduce hopeful talk about the need to 'live' and to 'work' showed a heartless cynicism on Chekhov's part.[10] More fundamentally, Stanislavsky can be criticized for trying too hard to fit *Three Sisters* into existing dramatic patterns. In seizing upon the greyness of provincial life, Stanislavsky was falling back on a theme which had been familiar in Russian fiction and drama at least since the time of Gogol'. In seeing Chekhov's play as a dramatic conflict between the characters and their environment, he was relating it to the traditions of action-based drama—failing to see the full extent to which the drama of *Three Sisters* was contained within the inner lives of its characters.

iv. THE MORE ORTHODOX APPROACH

Stanislavsky's approach to *Three Sisters* was personal and is by no means typical. The more orthodox approach to *Three Sisters* may be formulated along these lines: Chekhov's play is to be regarded as a tragic victory for the forces of evil as represented by Natasha, and passes judgement on the sisters and their like, who, however charming and dignified they may be in defeat, and however much they may excite our sympathy and pity, were nevertheless too weak to stand up to Natasha, or to show the determination necessary to take them to Moscow.

Such an approach is comparable to the 'moral' approach to *Uncle Vanya*, in that it invites an audience to take sides, and to see the sisters as victims and Natasha as the evil exploiter. But it also incorporates what may be called a sociological element: for Chekhov, it is suggested, was commenting on the fates of the Prozorovs not so much as individuals but as representatives of a certain class, the Russian nobility. In the characters of Natasha and the unseen, but not unimportant Protopopov, Chekhov was introducing representatives of a new and rising urban middle class; and it is impossible not to contrast what these two achieve in the play with what the Prozorovs fail to achieve.

It will of course be generally agreed that Chekhov ascribed to Andrei Prozorov and his sisters many of the more attractive features of the Russian upper classes. The Prozorovs have been well educated: they all speak French, German and English, and Irina speaks Italian as well. They wear their culture lightly; though refined, they are never affected or pretentious. Emotionally the sisters are unusually sensitive and fastidious. This is not an aristocratic pose; it is simply how they are. 'Coarseness upsets me,' says Masha to Vershinin in Act II, 'it makes me feel insulted. When I see that someone lacks delicacy, or gentleness and good manners, I really suffer.' Olga echoes her words in Act III, after Natasha has told the aged Anfisa to stand up in her presence:

OLGA. Try to understand me, my dear . . . We may have been brought up oddly, but I can't stand that kind of attitude. It depresses me, makes me feel ill . . . I just can't bear it.
NATASHA. Forgive me, do forgive me. (*Kisses her.*)
OLGA. Any coarse remark, however slight, any jarring word upsets me.

There is nothing mean or possessive about the three sisters: Olga has no hesitation about taking clothes from her own wardrobe to be handed out to the fire victims, while Masha and Irina find it a great joke that Chebutykin has not paid his rent for eight months. In their spontaneous generosity of spirit the sisters belong to the same tradition as Natasha Rostova in *War and Peace*, unloading the family possessions from the carts to make room for wounded prisoners-of-war.

Olga shows a similar kind of compassion when she defends the right of Anfisa to sit around and sleep, and later, to Anfisa's huge delight, gives her a room of her own in the flat attached to the school.

Sooner or later, however, one is bound to come up against a very simple question in relation to the sisters. Why was it that Olga and Irina, who were free agents and financially independent, did not simply pack their bags and leave for Moscow? There were never any insuperable difficulties, after all.

This question may perhaps best be answered by introducing Andrei Prozorov into the discussion. Of brother Andrei's attractive qualities we see less, since they tend to recede into the background after his marriage to Natasha. In the first act, his manner is engagingly modest, his love for Natasha is deep and poetic (even though the object of that love may not be), and he still intends to translate a book from English; but he has grown fat, an ominous sign of incipient spiritual degeneration. There is however an inescapable spinelessness, a spiritual flabbiness about the way in which he later abandons his academic career without any apparent struggle, allows himself to be so thoroughly dominated by his wife, and consoles himself by gambling with Chebutykin, running up debts that can only be paid off by mortgaging the house that belongs to all four of them (an echo of the Professor's plan in *Uncle Vanya*). To some extent, an explanation of his weakness can be found in personal circumstances. General Prozorov was obviously a dominating character, and with the disappearance of his paternal influence and strict regime, Andrei quickly collapsed. 'Thousands of people were raising up a bell,' says Masha in Act IV. 'A great deal of effort and money had been spent on it. Then suddenly it fell and was smashed to pieces. Suddenly, for no reason at all. It's been like that with Andrei . . .' But Chekhov also seems to be making a comment through Andrei on weaknesses in the Russian upper classes as a whole. The sheltered life of families like the Prozorovs, who were conscious of their social and cultural superiority, and whose house had until recently been full of orderlies ready to carry out their slightest wish, may tend to sap all personal initiative and to produce a charming but ineffectual breed. *Three Sisters* shows clearly how the upper classes could no longer rely on this position of unchallenged superiority, and how their authority might rapidly pass to more vigorous elements from classes below: Andrei has to take orders from Protopopov, just as Natasha assumes the position of authority in the sisters' household.

None of the sisters can be described as weak characters, yet neither do they seem entirely free of the negative qualities which are made so obvious in their brother. The outspoken Masha contemptuously describes Natasha in Act II as a *meshchanka*—a cross between bourgeoise and philistine—and this epithet illustrates the sisters' conviction that they are superior to Natasha both socially and culturally. But against Natasha's purposeful attacks and increasing temerity, they have little defence. They would never dream of playing her at her own game; though they continue to despise her inwardly, in practice they simply have to accommodate themselves to Natasha's wishes. And we can be quite sure that had Natasha suddenly taken it into her head to move to Moscow, she would have allowed nothing and no one to stand in her way. The inability of the sisters to make up their minds once and for all about Moscow, and to keep to their decision, suggests a lack of nerve, a reluctance to assume responsibility for one's own fate, that might be regarded as typical of their class.

A similar comment suggests itself at this point to the one which is so often made about *The Cherry Orchard*. The sisters have an undeniable spiritual beauty, but they belong to a class which is dying on its feet; just as the orchard, which symbolizes that same class, is very beautiful to look at, but ripe for the axe.

Chekhov does not of course present the sisters' lives in isolation. They become involved with the outsiders of the play, and these contacts might well lead to important changes in the sisters' lives. Irina in particular must be constantly dreaming of the handsome, intelligent young officer who would fall in love with her, resign his commission and whisk her off to Moscow.

But these outsiders, it may be argued, can offer the sisters nothing; for they too reflect in their various ways the deficiencies of the Russian upper class.

The rather decrepit old doctor, Chebutykin, offers the sisters only a sentimental and sometimes embarrassing devotion which has its origins in his past love for the sisters' mother. When, after his bout of drinking, he looks back in Act III on the course of his life, he realizes that it has been quite futile. His little medical knowledge disappeared long ago; as for cultural knowledge, he never had any in the first place:

> The other day at the club they were talking about Shakespeare and Voltaire. I'd never read either, not even a single line, but I managed to look as if I had. And the rest of them were doing just the same. . . .

Tuzenbach is a likeable and intelligent young man, even though he
falls far short of Irina's romantic ideal. But he suffers badly from the
aristocratic malaise of indecision: in Act II we learn that it has taken
him five years to make up his mind to resign his commission. And
although he has reacted strongly against the idleness of his privileged
class, his attitude to work remains aristocratically naive: when he
eventually decides in Act III to take a job at the brick factory, we
feel that he has reached much the same position as Irina in Act I, and
will have to face the same disillusionment. Yet Tuzenbach might
have been the means of giving Irina a life of modest contentment, had
not Solyony intervened. Solyony the person is not to be confused with
the grotesque mask that conceals him throughout the play. The person
is glimpsed only rarely—when he declares his love to Irina, or in his
remark to Tuzenbach in Act II:

> When I'm alone with someone, I'm all right, I'm just like other
> people, but in company I feel awkward and shy and—talk a lot of
> rubbish.

His shyness and dissatisfaction with the way life treats him express
themselves in a particular form of eccentricity—petulant and narcissis-
tic, with a strong colouring of violence—which is reminiscent, in a
somewhat debased form, of Pechorin, the Romantic hero of Lermontov's *Hero of Our Time* (1840). The completely self-centred Solyony
cannot bear to think of someone else achieving the happiness that is
being denied him.

Finally, there is Vershinin, who brings to the play a neurotic wife,
a mother-in-law, two small daughters and a penchant for eloquent
philosophizing. 'Lofty thoughts', he says to Masha in Act II, 'come so
naturally to a Russian, but tell me—why is his ordinary life so very
earthbound?' This observation is particularly relevant to his own case.
Vershinin's fine words and noble aspirations have never been matched
by any comparable achievements in his personal life; and this combination of noble sentiments with practical ineffectuality seems to
epitomize the well-meaning Russian liberal of the late nineteenth
century.

V. A REJOINDER

But how satisfactory are such views as an *overall* approach to *Three
Sisters*?

To begin with, is it entirely appropriate to see in the outcome of the play a victory for the forces of evil as represented by Natasha? In material terms she does of course triumph in the sense that she gains complete control of the Prozorov home. But the house and the garden were not beautiful in themselves; they were only made so by the sisters' presence. Once the sisters have gone, the whole place will be vulgarized by Natasha in no time at all. Her 'pretty' home and garden, a hen-pecked husband, the well-to-do lover close at hand: does Chekhov leave us in any doubt that Natasha is very welcome to all these?

Everyone has always agreed that Natasha is an odious character, and that to dislike her thoroughly is only right and proper. But there is such an impatient desire to find someone to blame in *Three Sisters*, such a gleeful rush to castigate Natasha for her most obvious failings, that comment on her has often been very superficial. When she disappears into the house for the last time, brandishing the fork and preparing to do battle with some inoffensive maid, it is not, as might have been expected, one of the sisters but Kulygin who passes the final comment on her: Kulygin, who makes it his business to be on good terms with everyone and who has so far shown no signs of antagonism towards Natasha. 'She's at it again!' he exclaims, with a mixture of amusement and contempt. It is clear from this remark, should confirmation still be needed, that so far as all the other characters are concerned, Natasha has become totally alien, emotionally quite unapproachable. Her life is devoted to the pursuit of certain selfish materialistic goals which she can see clearly ahead of her. In pursuing these goals so exclusively, she cannot help displaying a self-centredness and earthboundness which are more terrifying than her vulgarity or her materialism. People like Natasha are so preoccupied with their own affairs that they seem to have no awareness of the feelings of other people, and are quite oblivious to the existence of suffering around them. ('We rich people should always be ready to assist the poor,' observes Natasha sanctimoniously, and fails to lift a finger to help Olga look after the fire victims.) Moreover, they are so firmly entrenched in the world as we know it that they are quite unaware of the *possibilities* of human life, quite unaware of how much better life might be. It is as if, in their unawareness of human suffering and human potentialities, they are gazing at their own feet all the time—almost as if they have been deprived of some vital sense.

Natasha's victory, then, seems to me entirely hollow. The sisters yield nothing of their spiritual values, which would be the only true defeat. These are values which Natasha knows that she can never touch. Even Andrei, though he *is* absorbed into Natasha's way of life, is defeated only outwardly; he remains a Prozorov, in that he continues to despise inwardly everything that Natasha represents, and to long for a better life.

What of the sociological content in the orthodox approach to *Three Sisters*? That the characters do illustrate certain class features and that the play does show how power was passing from the nobility to more vigorous classes from below: about this there can be little dispute. But is that what really holds our attention in *Three Sisters*? Was it for their class representativeness that Chekhov chose the characters of the three sisters?

The point has already been made in the opening chapter that the theme of the spiritually bankrupt Russian gentry would have been very dated in Russian literature by 1900. It is difficult to imagine Chekhov choosing such a theme for its own sake. In his fiction the theme appears only to the extent that the body of Chekhov's fiction provides a remarkably comprehensive survey of the society of his time; but it is never singled out. The reasons for Chekhov's choice were much simpler. He was attracted to these characters because he wanted to explore their emotional world, because he felt that this emotional world would be well suited to his dramatic purposes. The class situation, in other words, is used as the *backcloth* for the emotional processes. It is the means to an end. Natasha too can be seen as a functional character: as someone who is action-oriented (Natasha never talks of her feelings, Natasha does not dream) she provides a contrast with all the other emotion-oriented characters; and she is used by Chekhov to bring about an extreme situation to which the emotion-oriented characters can be seen responding. The outsiders are primarily important because they bring to the play the 'philosophy of life' element: for it is in *Three Sisters*, to echo Chapter I again, that Chekhov explores most fully different ways of coming to terms with life emotionally.

But first to take up the remark that Chekhov was attracted to his characters' emotional world because he felt that it would be well suited to his dramatic purposes.

'I have a subject—*Three Sisters*,' Chekhov had written to Nemiro-vich-Danchenko in November 1899, when he first mentioned his new play.[11] This then was his starting-point. And it seems reasonable to guess that at a very early stage Chekhov decided that the sisters should be of noble birth, the daughters of a general, and living 'in a provincial town such as Perm in an army (artillery) milieu'.[12] Their brother, his romance, its consequences, the outsiders: these would all have been worked into the play later.

What was it then that attracted Chekhov to the sisters? Two features, I think: one was their emotional depth and sensitivity, the other—their emotional vulnerability.[13]

Chekhov saw that it was among very sheltered upper-class families that qualities of emotional depth and sensitivity were most likely to develop. To put it simply, members of other classes just did not have the time to be aware of their feelings in any depth. The emotional fastidiousness of the sisters has already been remarked upon; and their emotional self-awareness is perhaps best illustrated by the striking frequency with which on different occasions at the beginning of the play they each refer to their inner states:

OLGA. When I woke up this morning and saw all that light, when I saw the spring, I began to feel such joy inside me, I felt such a passionate longing to return home to Moscow. . . .

IRINA. I don't know why I'm so light-hearted! This morning I remembered that it was my name-day, and suddenly I felt so joyful, and I remembered when I was a child and Mother was still alive. . . . Tell me, why is it I'm so happy today? Just as if I were sailing along with a great blue sky above me and huge white birds soaring about. . . .

MASHA. I'm down in the dumps today, I feel miserable, so don't listen to me.

The sisters' emotional vulnerability requires more careful consideration. One might say that to be emotionally sensitive is also to be emotionally vulnerable, and that the sisters' environment, the coarse provincial town, was bound to affect them deeply. Of more fundamental importance, however, is the excellence of the Prozorovs' upbringing —its particular excellence, for it cannot necessarily be regarded as typical of their class. Everything suggests that their childhood and youth have been unusually harmonious. Their mother had died more than eleven years earlier, when they were still living in Moscow, but her presence continues to be felt in the family as a kind of benign influence, just as Vera Petrovna (Vanya's sister) is still remembered in the

Serebryakov family. General Prozorov is also recalled with affection, and enough is said about him to suggest that he was a man of wide culture and principle—Chekhov himself believing, according to Stanislavsky, that one of the tasks of a peace-time army was to act as cultural emissaries to the distant places where they were stationed.[14]

Paradoxically, it is the very excellence of the Prozorovs' upbringing which makes them emotionally so vulnerable. They enter upon adult life with the highest of expectations. Disappointment is inevitable. So too is the keenness with which they feel disappointment. The emotional preoccupation which they bring to the play is one that they all share, in contrast to the very individual preoccupations of the characters in *Uncle Vanya*. It is the longing for a better life, expressed as a yearning for Moscow—the longing for a life that would at least begin to match up to their high expectations.

The Prozorovs are vulnerable in one other respect, which becomes clear only gradually in the course of the play, and which is more directly related to their social situation. They are vulnerable because they are not adaptable people. Their upbringing has prepared them to participate in a much better world than the one which they actually have to encounter. When life shows its claws, they are quite defenceless. To imagine them scheming and plotting how best to reach Moscow, or how to outwit Natasha, is impossible (nor would one wish it otherwise). They can only hope, in Irina's words, that with God's help 'everything will work itself out', that they will be carried to Moscow on the crest of an emotional wave. This inflexibility, this defencelessness, render them emotionally highly vulnerable.

Why, finally, did it have to be three *sisters*? Partly, perhaps, because the lives of female members of the aristocracy were that much more sheltered, and thus emotionally richer, than those of their male counterparts. Or was Chekhov following that tradition whereby the female sex is regarded as the emotional half of mankind? He would have had before him the example of Tolstoy, in whose fiction such an assumption seems to be implicit. Tolstoy's heroines are never pursued by the restlessness of their thoughts in the way that his heroes are; on the contrary, their lives, like that of Anna Karenina, are centred exclusively on their emotions.

vi. ACT I: EMOTIONAL RESPONSIVENESS

Vershinin has just introduced himself. When he explains that he is from Moscow, the sisters can scarcely believe their ears. 'So you're from Moscow,' exclaims Irina in an ecstatic tone of voice. 'Well, what a surprise.' The dialogue continues:

OLGA. We're moving to Moscow, you see.

IRINA. We hope to be there by the autumn. It's our home town. We were born in Moscow, in Staraya Basmannaya Street.

(Both laugh joyfully.)

MASHA. Just fancy meeting someone from Moscow. (*Animatedly.*) Now I've got it. Olga, remember how we used to talk about 'the lovesick Major'. You were a lieutenant then and you'd fallen in love, and everyone teased you and called you 'Major' for some reason.

VERSHININ (*laughs*). Yes, yes, you're quite right—the lovesick Major.

MASHA. You only had a moustache then . . . And now you look so much older. (*Tearfully.*) So much older.

VERSHININ. Yes, when I was known as the lovesick Major, I was still young and in love. Things are different now.

OLGA. You haven't a single grey hair, though. You may have aged but you're not old.

VERSHININ. All the same, I'm getting on for forty-three. How long is it since you left Moscow?

IRINA. Eleven years. What are you crying about, Masha, you funny thing? (*Tearfully.*) You'll make me start.

MASHA. I'm all right. But tell me, which street did you live in?

VERSHININ. In the Staraya Basmannaya.

OLGA. That's where we lived!

I have chosen this passage as an illustration of the high degree of emotional responsiveness that exists among the Prozorovs, and which sets the tone for the whole of the play. In *Uncle Vanya* such responsiveness is only seen in the relations between Vanya and Sonya, whereas in *Three Sisters* it is present whenever there is more than one Prozorov on stage. There are times, as at the beginning of this extract, when the sisters seem to think and feel as one person, swiftly picking up and complementing one another's remarks. It is not that they consciously set out to conform to any kind of common standard, but rather that they cannot help being unconsciously involved with one another on an emotional level. When Masha characteristically says exactly what she feels and tells Vershinin how much he's aged, Olga cannot help feeling uncomfortable on her sister's behalf and softens the impact of Masha's remark by the tactful addition that Vershinin doesn't have a single grey hair. Their unconscious emotional involvement can also be seen in the way that Irina is infected by Masha's emotional state, and finds herself wanting to cry even though she cannot consciously see any reason for tears.

This emotional responsiveness is the product of a family relationship among four young people who have grown up together in a harmonious atmosphere. Childhood is not far behind them. When the play begins, Irina is already over twenty, but people still tend to think of her as a young girl, and although Irina herself has rather begun to resent this, she is nonetheless childishly delighted by Fedotik's present of a humming top. A family relationship, certainly, but with a difference—for only a year ago the one surviving parent had died. General Prozorov's word had undoubtedly been law in the family: he had stood firmly at the centre of the family's emotional network. His death has left a vacuum in more senses than one. The Prozorov house is no longer a focal point for the social life of the regiment; and whereas in the past, being the daughters of a general had provided the sisters with a way of life in itself, they must now seek some other *raison d'être*.

Most of all, however, the General's death has left an emotional gap. The mutual responsiveness of the Prozorovs remains, because that is something that can never be reversed. But with the General's death, the emotional relations between his four children were bound to move into a more fluid, unpredictable phase. Certain adjustments had to be made. When Chekhov opens his play, exactly a year later, these changes have already begun to make themselves felt, though the process of change is still continuing.

Olga, the eldest sister, who is twenty-eight when the curtain rises, is that much more bound up with the past than her younger sisters. 'Why recall old memories?' Irina asks her, as Olga reminisces about their father's death and funeral. But Olga seems also to have assumed a certain amount of parental responsibility towards the other members of the family. When Masha starts to whistle, Olga cannot help remonstrating with her (unless, of course, this is no more than an automatic reflex on Olga's part carried over from her school duties!) Masha takes no offence but neither does she pay much attention to her elder sister, and within a moment or two she is whistling again quite unselfconsciously. Olga's tone sounds definitely maternal when she says to Irina:

You're so radiant today, you're looking more beautiful than ever. And Masha's beautiful too. Andrei would be good-looking, only he's become so fat and it doesn't suit him.

For Irina, however, Olga's maternal attitude can be somewhat trying, especially when Irina has just finished an eloquent speech on the theme that everyone should work:

OLGA. Father taught us to get up at seven o'clock. Nowadays Irina is awake by seven and then lies in bed till at least nine thinking about something. And her expression's so serious! (*Laughs.*)
IRINA. You find it odd when I look serious because you're so used to thinking of me as a little girl. I am *twenty*, you know.

Masha is also affectionate towards Irina, though less protective than Olga. Having lived away from home ever since her marriage to Kulygin six years ago as a girl of eighteen, Masha recalls the time when their father was alive more as an outsider than Olga. She is upset by the contrast between Irina's party, with its pathetic handful of guests, and the parties of the past, when there were thirty or forty officers present (foreshadowing a theme from *The Cherry Orchard*). Olga is infected by Masha's mood. But now it is Masha's turn to move into the parental position—her forthrightness, one feels, may well derive from her father's example—when she rounds on the softer-hearted Olga and brusquely tells her to 'stop snivelling'.

It is however in the relations between the sisters and their brother that the most delicate adjustments seem to be taking place. Andrei's presence first makes itself felt as the sound of a violin coming from a nearby room:

MASHA. That's Andrei playing, our brother.
IRINA. He's the scholar of the family. He'll probably become a professor. Papa was a soldier, but his son chose an academic career.
MASHA. Which was what Papa wanted.
OLGA. We've been teasing him today. We think he's a bit in love.
IRINA. With a young lady from the town. She'll be calling in today, I expect.
MASHA. Oh, the way she dresses! Her clothes aren't so much

unattractive or unfashionable, they're simply pathetic. She wears an extraordinary skirt in a kind of bright yellow with the most awful fringe and a red blouse. And her cheeks are scrubbed, positively scrubbed! Andrei's not in love, he simply can't be— he does have some taste after all. I think he's just doing it to tease us, he's having us on. I heard yesterday that she's going to marry Protopopov, the chairman of the town council. And a good job too. (*Turning to a side door.*) Andrei, come and join us. Just for a moment, dear.

Andrei then is seen first through the sisters' eyes. Again, the impression is given of the sisters thinking and feeling as one person here, eager to expand one another's remarks; and Masha is no doubt speaking for all three of them when she criticizes Natasha, though her sisters might not have been quite so scathing and uncharitable. The sisters have a shared attitude towards 'our brother Andrei'. It is clear that they have transferred all their hopes for a better future, and probably much of their affection too, from their father to their brother. The General must have had strong ideas about what he wanted his son to become, and the sisters have not only inherited these ideas but built them up, since their own expectations from life are so dependent on Andrei's future. For Andrei to fall in love with Natasha is not part of the picture at all, and they are reluctant even to consider it seriously.

Andrei returns the sisters' affection. The ties of the past are very strong. There is a note of sympathetic indulgence about the way in which he tells Vershinin that his sisters—he uses the affectionate diminutive *sestritsy*—will give him no peace now that they know he is from Moscow. But he cannot feel entirely in sympathy with his sisters either. He wishes that Irina would not make *quite* such a fuss about the picture frames that he has carved for her. Then Olga spells out very explicitly and publicly the kind of person they see their brother as:

> He's the scholar of the family, he also plays the violin and he does all kinds of fretwork—so you can see he's a very talented person. Andrei, don't disappear! He has this habit of always disappearing. Come back!

Andrei's disappearing trick is very familiar to the sisters. They do not mind it at all, for a family relationship can easily accommodate such behaviour; and later, when Andrei, still missing, is impatiently called to the luncheon table by Olga and he replies: 'Just coming,' one feels that such an exchange has been repeated countless times before. But there is a suggestion also that Andrei's habit of disappearing has become a means of distancing himself from the sisters, of preventing himself from becoming too completely a part of their world. When the sisters enthuse about his brilliant future, does he not wonder whether he is entirely able or entirely willing to play the role that they so obviously have in mind for him? Andrei tells us that his body has grown flabby over the past year. How long will it be before his intellect follows suit? Does he see this already happening in himself?

Masha and Irina propel Andrei back into the room. The sisters begin to tease him again about Natasha. Their teasing is essentially childish, for sisters have always taken a peculiar pleasure in teasing their brothers, and Andrei is obviously used to it. But the sisters are less worried than they ought to be about their brother's feelings for Natasha.

It is against this background of relations among the Prozorovs as a whole that Andrei's mysterious infatuation with Natasha needs to be seen. For mysterious it certainly is, and at first sight, even somewhat implausible. When the gauche and tastelessly dressed Natasha makes her belated appearance, the audience is inclined to share the sisters' scepticism. Andrei himself says at the end of Act I that he doesn't understand how or when he fell in love with her. What can he possibly see in Natasha? No wonder the sisters are not taking the matter seriously. But perhaps it is precisely here that the key is to be found. Andrei's infatuation might best be explained by seeing in it an element of reaction against the sisters' standards, which he felt were over-refined and cliquish, and did not make enough concessions to the everyday world. In marrying Natasha he would be building a bridge to a more 'real' world, where people behaved more 'naturally' and 'ordinarily'. When Natasha, who has been feeling very much out of things at the Prozorov luncheon table, rushes in confusion into the other room, Andrei follows, and he consoles her by saying that 'they're all kind, good-hearted people and they're fond of me and of you'. He does not want to see that there might be any contradiction between the Prozorovs—himself as well as the sisters—and Natasha, but is inclined rather to believe that it will be possible for him to have the best of both worlds.

To return however to the luncheon party which immediately precedes that closing scene between Andrei and Natasha: for it is there that one sees how the emotional responsiveness of the Prozorovs can be extended to other people, how the mood which they engender can infect the people round them. Chebutykin and Tuzenbach are no strangers, of course, in the Prozorov home, but Vershinin is; and it is remarkable how quickly he responds to the Prozorov atmosphere. He contrasts the sisters' flower-filled apartment with the furnished rooms that he knows so well, where the stove never fails to smoke, but essentially it is the people that he is responding to. He needs no persuading to stay to lunch, and his remark to Olga—'How good it feels to be with you!'—shows that he too is very conscious of his emotional states. Kulygin is no stranger either, but it looks at first as if his pompous manner may isolate him from all the others. But the vodka and the Prozorov atmosphere soon thaw him out, and his schoolmasterish banter ('Take a black mark for conduct,' he tells the boisterous Masha) does not in any way strike a false note. Even Solyony seems to appreciate the Prozorov atmosphere; and his 'joke' about the liqueur being made from black beetles shows that in his peculiar way he is at least trying to become fully part of that atmosphere, though he is too inhibited to break out of his absurd Lermontov role. Natasha alone just cannot get the right mood at all, and strikes a note that is jarringly false. 'They're ever so informal here,' she confides to Vershinin. It is a remark that could only be made by someone who is outside the emotional atmosphere and cannot be spontaneous; to be inside it is to be living it and makes such an observation psychologically impossible.

The Soviet critic, Roskin, says of Tuzenbach that he does not love Irina alone, he loves everyone who possesses 'the Prozorov quality' (Roskin coins the adjective *prozorovskoye*).[15] What exactly do we mean by this quality? I would define it as possessing the sense of emotional harmony. Its origins are to be found in childhood. Though we do not see the Prozorovs as children, it is not hard to imagine what their childhood was like; indeed it is impossible to think of them as adults without wishing to supply this childhood element. During childhood an underlying emotional harmony has grown up between them, which is not consciously appreciated but has far-reaching implications. It means that in their behaviour towards one another the Prozorovs can be very uninhibited, for their emotional harmony is unlikely to be seriously threatened even when harsh words are spoken. It means that their intuitive reactions towards other people are likely to be very similar (Andrei's reaction to Natasha, as he later recognizes himself, having to be regarded as an unfortunate aberration). It means also that the spontaneity which characterizes relations among themselves is likely to be carried over to their relations with the people round them: there is an urge to communicate and participate with others on the emotional level. When things are running their way, as in the opening act, they experience a strong and swiftly communicated feeling that other people are bound to want to feel the same way as they do, to share their pleasure. It means finally, and this is where the problems arise, that they have a certain underlying confidence in life itself; but life unfortunately is not very good at returning this compliment.

The Prozorovs can be compared with an even more famous family in Russian literature: the Rostovs in *War and Peace*. Just as Tuzenbach was attracted to all the Prozorovs, so too the reader finds himself drawn towards the Rostovs as a family. Unlike Chekhov's play, Tolstoy in his novel is able to show us the early years of the Rostovs in some detail, thereby enriching our familiarity with these characters to a far greater extent than with any of the other characters in *War and Peace*. The Rostovs have that same lack of emotional inhibition among themselves, that same ability to communicate with one another without the need for words, that same capacity to be oneself towards all people—as when Count Rostov, for example, welcomes all his guests with equal affability, irrespective of their rank. There is also the implication that to become part of the Rostov atmosphere is something you are either born to, or not born to. Just as Natasha in *Three Sisters* is bound to remain on the outside, so too the elder daughter, Vera, though actually a Rostov, is almost a stranger to the others. When, in a famous passage, the thirteen-year-old Natasha Rostova senses that Boris Drubetskoy doesn't quite belong, she explains to her mother:

'There's something narrow about him, like a grandfather clock . . . yes, that's it, narrow, grey and pale.'
'What *are* you talking about?' said the Countess.
'Nicholas would know what I mean,' Natasha continued.

The Prozorovs too, one feels, would understand that kind of language. The difference between the two families is perhaps this: that the Rostovs' emotional confidence is not put to the test in quite the same way. Even when the fortunes of Natasha or Nicholas are at a very low ebb, the future will never seem to them so unchangeably bleak as it does for the Prozorovs.

K

vii. EMOTIONAL INVOLVEMENTS

Masha's emotional involvement with Vershinin is nothing like so enigmatic as that of Andrei with Natasha. Masha strikes us as the most wilful and unpredictable, and also the most original and talented, of the three sisters. She always speaks her mind, and her two references to Gogol' may not be just coincidental, for her language, like Gogol's, is vigorously down-to-earth, and she excels at the pithy, humorous phrase. Solyony is very much reduced to size by her tongue-in-cheek description of him as a 'horribly frightening man' (*uzhasno strashnyi chelovek*), and the picture of Natasha, stalking across the stage 'as if she'd started the fire herself' (*kak budto ona podozhgla*), is equally memorable. This forthrightness of speech reflects a forthrightness of behaviour. What distinguishes Masha is her willingness to give herself wholeheartedly to a man whose intellect she can respect. When she was eighteen, it was Kulygin, who then seemed to her the cleverest man in the world. Perhaps it is a Prozorov failing, which she shares with Andrei, to be inclined to put the most attractive interpretation on other people (in much the same way that Natasha Rostova becomes infatuated with Anatole Kuragin, or Nicholas forms such a high opinion of Dolokhov). As for Vershinin, her feelings for him were by no means love at first sight:

> I found him odd to begin with, then I felt sorry for him . . . and then I started to love him—to love his voice, the things he says, his misfortunes, the two little girls . . .

It is characteristic of Masha's generosity of spirit that she should love everything about Vershinin, the whole person—embracing the more than a trifle ridiculous aspects of Vershinin's family life just as much as his moments of eloquence.

To embrace the whole of Tuzenbach's personality is something that Irina, however, is incapable of doing. She cannot reconcile herself to his unimpressive appearance, which is made even worse when he relinquishes military uniform. Irina is romantic and idealistic. She was only nine when the family left Moscow, and for her it has acquired a fairy-tale quality, being linked in her mind with romantic dreams of love and marriage; it is always Irina who expresses the most passionate yearning for Moscow. Her idealism takes the form of a deep commitment to the ideal of 'work', and it is here that she and Tuzenbach are able to find common ground. Irina's enthusiastic speech in Act I—' . . .

Man must toil, must work by the sweat of his brow, whoever he may be, and that alone constitutes the meaning and purpose of his life, his happiness and his joy...'—evokes an immediate response from Tuzenbach:

> ... The time has come, an avalanche is bearing down on us, there's a healthy powerful storm gathering which is already quite close and will soon sweep away from our society all idleness and indifference, all prejudice against work and rotten apathy. I'm going to work, and in twenty-five or thirty years' time everyone will be working. Everyone!

Divorced from context and character, as it sometimes is, this passage can be read as a forecast of impending revolution; within the play it suggests little more than an emotional protest by Tuzenbach against the prejudices of his class. Work is still a completely unknown quantity for both Tuzenbach and Irina, and they talk about it in improbably romantic and poetic terms. They are not concerned with work as purposeful action, they do not talk in terms of earning a living, or making a useful contribution to society; they are much more concerned with the emotional satisfaction which they believe work can provide. 'You know how sometimes you long for a drink on a hot day?', says Irina. 'Well, that's how I long to work.' Tuzenbach offers Irina selfless love and devotion, but so far as attitudes to work are concerned, Irina is the prime mover who always seems to be at least one jump ahead. It is she who first plunges boldly into work, while Tuzenbach is still making up his mind to resign his commission, and she who learns from bitter experience that it has none of the poetry she had dreamed of.

On the night of the fire in Act III all the play's emotional involvements pass through a critical phase; and what is particularly striking is the way in which each of the Prozorovs involved (Masha in her attitude towards Vershinin, Andrei towards Natasha, and Irina towards Tuzenbach) attempts to relate what is happening to them now in the present with their common Prozorov past.

Writing to Olga Knipper, Chekhov had this to say about the scene in which Masha tells her sisters that she wants to 'make confession':

> Darling, Masha's confession in Act III isn't a confession at all, it's just a frank conversation. You're on edge but you're not desperate, so don't shout, put in at least an occasional smile, and in general

let the audience feel the exhaustion of the night. And let them feel you're cleverer than your sisters, or at least think you are.[16]

It is not a question then of Masha being overwhelmed by an attack of conscience and feeling compelled to lay bare the guilty secret that she loves Vershinin (and in any case it is unlikely that Olga and Irina would have had no previous inkling of this). Chekhov has invested the love of Masha and Vershinin with a mood of sad inevitability rather than of dramatic passion, and whether they should be censured for their behaviour is not a question that he seeks to provoke in the minds of his audience. Masha is not afraid of her sisters' moral condemnation (impatiently brushing aside Olga's hesitations), but neither is she especially seeking their approval. It is just that she feels an urge to bring them in officially, as it were, on what is happening in her life, to make a bridge between her present individual experience and the shared experience of the past. That she feels a need to do this is an indication of the importance that Vershinin has now acquired in her life.

Olga's reaction to the confession is indicated only briefly, yet it is very subtle. The warm-hearted, reliable and even-tempered Olga is a person with a strong sense of duty, who sets high standards for herself and for others. When Masha says that she is in love with Vershinin, Olga turns away from her sister and disappears behind the screen round her bed, saying: 'That's quite enough. I'm not going to listen to you'; and when Masha continues to speak about Vershinin, Olga again says from behind the screen: 'I'm not listening to you, you know. I don't care what nonsense you're talking, I'm not going to listen. Now Olga knows full well that Masha's confession is not a real confession at all, and that her sister is seeking, if not approval, then a sympathetic understanding of her position. Behind Olga's refusal to listen one is aware of a conflict: between immediate sympathy, making it impossible for her to condemn her sister's behaviour (and unconsciously, of course, Masha knew that she could count on this), and her high moral standards, which refuse to let her be made a party to what Masha is doing.

Andrei now comes in, and when he asks Olga for a key to the cupboard, one senses that this is no more than a pretext for starting up a conversation. But Olga hands him the key in silence and Andrei, piqued because his peaceful overtures have met with no response, decides that it is time to 'have it out once and for all' with the sisters. What is remarkable about his self-justification is the way in which its emotional undercurrents contradict the actual words spoken. When he is speaking about Natasha, for example, he uses certain phrases, italicized below, which tell us more about his deeper feelings than he himself is prepared to admit:

> Natasha is a fine, honest person, she's decent and straightforward —*that's my opinion.* I love my wife and I respect her—*yes, I respect her*—and I expect other people to respect her too. *I repeat,* she's an honest, decent person, and all your grievances against her, *if you don't mind me saying so,* are nothing but childishness.

He then goes on to review other aspects of his present life—his work for the town council, how he has mortgaged the house to pay off debts—and the manner of his exposition suggests that he has gone over all this in his own mind many times before. The turning-point comes quite unexpectedly—for Andrei, one feels, no less than for the audience:

> They're not listening. Yes, Natasha's a fine, honest woman. (*Walks silently up and down the stage, then stops.*) When I got married, I thought we'd be happy . . . I thought we'd all be happy. But oh my God! (*Cries.*) Sisters, my dear sweet sisters, don't believe what I've been saying, don't believe it . . .

'I thought we'd all be happy': how clearly this reveals that Andrei has failed in his attempt to have the best of both worlds! He has tried desperately to convince himself that it is the sisters who must adjust to the present, not *vice versa.* But when the flash-point is reached, Andrei finds that the past is too strong, and that his present life with Natasha and his Prozorov past are irreconcilable.

It is Irina, however, who is most acutely and consciously aware of the gulf between her present experience and the built-in expectations of the past:

> . . . I'm twenty-three, I've been working a long time, my brain's dried up, I've become old and ugly and thin, and for nothing, nothing, I've had no satisfaction, and time's going by, and I keep feeling that I'm leaving behind the real life, the beautiful life, and being swallowed up in some kind of abyss.

Tuzenbach's devotion is powerless to change this situation; but in agreeing to Olga's suggestion that she should marry the Baron, albeit on condition that they still go to Moscow, Irina is prepared to strike a compromise between past and present.

Just as in *Uncle Vanya* the psychological action is concluded some time before the end of the play, so in *Three Sisters* the psychological action is substantially concluded in Act III, although the stories themselves have yet to run their full course. The story of Andrei and Natasha has no surprises in store. Their incompatibility is merely further accentuated in the final act. Right from the beginning of Act II Natasha has been treating her husband as just another object on her horizon to be manipulated; and now Andrei too remarks that whatever else Natasha may be, 'she's not a human being'. Outwardly he continues to be entirely dominated by his wife, but inwardly his resistance to Natasha and her standards has become much stronger. Chekhov himself insisted that in Andrei's final speech, when he is deploring the squalid life of the provincial town, 'he must be just about ready to threaten the audience with his fists'.[17]

By the time of the last act, Masha is scarcely bothering to conceal her feelings for Vershinin from anyone. Kulygin is certainly well aware of them. Chekhov's Masha has been likened to Tolstoy's Anna Karenina, and the lines from Pushkin ('A green oak by a curving shore, And on that oak a golden chain') are used by Chekhov to frame Masha's story in the same way that the train motif frames the story of Anna. Like Anna, Masha has been married at an early age to a considerably older man for whom she soon ceases to have more than a slight affection. When Kulygin says that the most important thing about everyday life is that it should be lived in accordance with certain prescribed forms, one is reminded of Karenin and how, when he decides to speak to Anna after her over-animated conversation with Vronsky at Princess Betsy's, 'the form and sequence of the speech he had to make took shape in his mind as clearly and distinctly as an official report'. Like Anna, Masha is a person of great natural warmth and vivacity, whose sufferings would have been less had she not possessed these qualities in such full measure.

Yet the nature of the two portraits is clearly very different. Tolstoy brings the full glare of his powerful psychological spotlight to bear upon the different transformations that overtake the emotional life of his heroine. What Tolstoy spells out psychologically, Chekhov suggests. We know far more about Anna than we do about Masha, and yet of the two women Masha would perhaps be the easier to recognize. This is because Masha is seen in the way in which we do normally see people in life—that is to say, we see her from outside, or more precisely, we see her from the vantage-point of an unseen extra member of the family (as with the Rostovs when they are growing up). Because the Tolstoyan psychological spotlight is so powerful and picks out each detail with such life-like conviction, everything about Anna becomes very public; and on looking back at the novel one may feel as if one had been present at a totally absorbing ritual demonstration (and ultimately it may seem a strangely cruel demonstration) of what will happen to a woman like that. Chekhov does not make us live through every stage of Masha's feelings, yet on looking back at the play one is more persuaded than with Tolstoy that 'this is the way such things do happen'. In Tolstoy, when Anna and Vronsky have been making love for the first time, the scene is described in highly coloured terms: 'And as with fury and a kind of passion the murderer throws himself on the body, drags it and slashes it—so he covered her face and shoulders with kisses'. When Vershinin kisses Masha's hand and tells her what a wonderful woman she is, how he dreams of her eyes and the way she moves, Masha feels scared and yet she is also to be heard *laughing quietly*! Tolstoy's extended judgement on Anna leads to the final degradation of a bloody suicide. Masha and Vershinin are attracted to one another—not very dramatically or even very passionately, but inevitably, with little awareness of moral transgression—they enjoy a certain happiness, though there is always a sense of living on borrowed time and Masha talks of having to take one's happiness in snatches, and then at the end of their story, they have to part, without jealousy, without self-destruction, but sadly and for good.

The story of Irina and Tuzenbach is the last to be concluded, coming to a dramatic if not altogether unexpected end. Although they are to be married on the following day, Irina and Tuzenbach's feelings for one another are basically unchanged, and it is still Irina who leads the way in relation to work, since in becoming a schoolteacher she will be putting her abilities to good use. The scene between the two of them, just before Tuzenbach leaves for the duel, is emotionally beautifully sustained. It is a variation on the 'snack' scene in *Uncle Vanya*. In *Uncle Vanya* Sonya loves Astrov but her love is not returned—indeed he knows nothing about it. Tuzenbach's love for Irina in *Three Sisters* is not returned either; but Irina is extremely well aware of what Tuzenbach feels for her. Here are two people who would both *like* to be in love, but one of them can't be—as Irina explains, 'it's not within my power'.

To that extent it is not necessary for the audience to participate as the third party, since both characters are only too conscious of their predicament. But what the audience knows, and Irina does not know (or at most half-suspects), is that Tuzenbach may shortly be killed, and this gives added emotional poignancy to his inability to find the 'lost key' to Irina's soul. Turning back to look at Irina for what may be the last time, Tuzenbach falters, and ends up by asking her lamely to have some coffee prepared for him. Here the audience does step in to supply the contrast between the everyday simplicity of his words and the complexity of what we know he must be feeling. Tuzenbach would dearly love to take Irina in his arms, knowing that he may never have another chance, but he cannot bring himself to do so: partly because he must give no hint of the impending duel, but rather more because he is held back by the knowledge that Irina does not feel as strongly for him as he does for her.

The announcement that Tuzenbach has been shot by Solyony concludes the action of *Three Sisters*. Since his death hammers the final nail into the coffin of the sisters' hopes, why does the play not come to an end at this point, but considerably overrun it? To find an explanation it is necessary to go back and to consider in greater depth the most important of the play's outsiders.

viii. VERSHININ

To devote a whole section to one character would seem to run counter to the spirit of this book, which has been concerned to stress the primacy in the Chekhov play of emotional *relations*; and indeed I do believe that what finally matters about Vershinin is not so much his 'personality' as the way in which he and his philosophy of life interact with the people round him. But of all the characters in Chekhov Vershinin is probably the one who has aroused most controversy; and how a person understands Vershinin is a quick guide to how he is likely to understand the Chekhov play as a whole. Hence the present discussion.

Vershinin is the successor to Astrov in *Uncle Vanya*. If Astrov's name suggests the stars, then that of Vershinin suggests *vershina*, meaning 'peak' or 'summit'. Like Astrov Vershinin appears to be concerned not so much with his own personal life as with life in general. But whereas Astrov's philosophy of life is revealed only once in *Uncle Vanya*, under exceptional circumstances and near the end of the play, Vershinin has no such inhibitions. On the contrary, as he knows him-

self, he is rather apt to talk too much and is always eager to philosophize, which means that in *Three Sisters* the philosophy of life element
is present from early on in the play.

Let us look at the scene in Act I where Vershinin makes his first
philosophizing speech:

OLGA. Oh, now I've remembered who you are. Yes, I remember
you.
VERSHININ. I knew your mother.
CHEBUTYKIN. She was a good woman, God rest her soul.
IRINA. Mama's buried in Moscow.
OLGA. At the Novo-Devichy convent . . .
MASHA. Do you know, I'm already beginning to forget what
she looked like? And no one will remember us either. We shall
be forgotten.
VERSHININ. Yes, we'll be forgotten. That's our fate, and we
can't do anything about it. What seems to us so serious and
meaningful, so full of importance, in time will be forgotten or
will seem trivial.

(*Pause.*)

And it's curious that we have no means at all of telling what
will be considered great and important, and what will seem
pitiful or absurd. Didn't the discoveries of Copernicus, or
Columbus, say, at first seem pointless and absurd, whereas some
rubbish written by a crank was regarded as a great truth? And
it may well be that our present life, to which we are so reconciled, will in time appear odd, awkward, unintelligent, not very
moral, even perhaps sinful . . .

It is striking, of course, that this almost complete stranger should
launch into this kind of speech within about ten minutes of his arrival.
But what is particularly striking here is the way in which Vershinin
changes the *level* of the conversation. The talk has been of a fairly
trivial, personal kind. Masha's remark is more of a general reflection.
Vershinin seizes this opportunity of opening the conversation out and
revealing much wider vistas: individual considerations are left behind
as he tries to see our present life in relation to life in the past and
life in the future. (Later, in Act III, the frightened faces of his daughters
during the fire lead him in a similar way to see the sufferings of
the present in relation to the far worse horrors of past ages, and

the wonderful life which lies ahead.) It is Masha again who in Act I prompts what is probably Vershinin's best philosophizing speech. She is complaining, in personal terms, that in a town like theirs knowing three languages is 'a useless luxury'; and Vershinin once more changes the whole tenor of the conversation, not only seeing the sisters' lives within the context of how their town as a whole may develop, but using them, we feel, as examples of a process that may happen throughout the world:

> Well now! (*Laughs.*) You say you know too much! I don't think there exists, or ever could exist, a town so dull and dreary that a clever, educated person would be superfluous in it. Suppose that among the hundred thousand people living in this town— which admittedly is a coarse and backward place—there is no one else like you three. It stands to reason that you will not prevail against the mass of ignorance surrounding you; during your life-time you'll gradually have to give way to the hundred thousand, you'll be lost in the crowd and swallowed up by life. But that doesn't mean that you'll disappear completely and have no influence. After you've gone, perhaps half-a-dozen people will turn up like you, then a dozen and so on, until eventually the people like you will become the majority. In two or three hundred years life on earth will be inconceivably beautiful, it will be wonderful. Man needs a life like that, and if it doesn't exist yet, he must feel that it is coming, he must look forward to it, dream about it, prepare for it, and to do that he must see and know more than his father and his grandfather did. (*Laughs.*) And you complain that you know too much.

The reactions of the Prozorovs to this speech are of interest. Masha is sufficiently intrigued to decide to stay to lunch. Irina is spell-bound, as much perhaps by Vershinin's eloquence as by the content of what he has said. Andrei in the course of the speech has dis-appeared: his thoughts are no doubt on Natasha. Olga is silent; but later, when Vershinin is preparing to leave, she eagerly persuades him to stay.

Not everything that Vershinin says is on this same generalizing level. His description to Masha early in Act II of the row he has had with his wife shows that he is no stranger to personal suffering and diffi-culties. But he is back in generalizing mood again not long after, when he and Tuzenbach philosophize about happiness. Vershinin argues that everything is changing gradually for the better, and that we

must work and suffer now for the sake of a distant happy future. He
continues:

> ... My hair's turning grey, I'm practically an old man, and I
> know so little, so very little! All the same I feel that the most
> genuine and important thing I *do* know, and know quite firmly.
> And how I wish I could prove to you that for us there can be no
> happiness, there ought not to be and there will not be. We must
> just go on working and working, and happiness will be for our
> distant descendants.

It is significant that Vershinin says that there *ought* not to be
any happiness for us now. To seek for personal happiness in a world
that is full of suffering can only be regarded as immoral. This is the
same conclusion that the narrator comes to in the short story *Gooseberries* (1898). For him there is no worse sight than that of a 'happy
family sitting round the table drinking tea'. This happiness is only
possible because those who are unhappy remain silent:

> It's a universal hypnosis. Behind the door of every happy, satis-
> fied person there ought to stand a man with a hammer whose
> constant knocking would be a reminder that there *are* unhappy
> people in the world, and that however happy he may be, life
> sooner or later will show him its claws and disaster will strike—
> illness, poverty, bereavements—and then no one will take any
> notice or listen to him, just as now he does not take any notice or
> listen to others. But there is no man with a hammer, the happy
> person goes on his way, and the petty cares of life disturb him
> faintly, like the wind in the aspen trees—and everything is exactly
> as it should be.[18]

Tuzenbach takes the opposite view to Vershinin, arguing that life
obeys its own inscrutable laws and will never change:

> ... Think of migrating birds—cranes, for example—which go
> on flying and flying, and it doesn't matter what kind of thoughts
> come into their heads, great thoughts or little thoughts, they'll
> still fly on and on without knowing why or where they're going.
> They'll go on flying, quite oblivious of any philosophers they
> may manage to produce; let the philosophers say what they
> choose, so long as they go on flying.
> MASHA. Yes, but where's the point?

TUZENBACH. The point? Look out there, it's snowing. Where's the point in that?

The discussion between the three of them eventually breaks down, not because they cannot understand one another's points of view, but because they cannot understand one another's emotions. The argument as such is quite inconclusive, though Tuzenbach's remarks are sometimes quoted as if they were distinctively 'Chekhovian' and expressed the whole spirit of *Three Sisters*.[19] That Chekhov's sympathies would have lain more with Vershinin can be inferred from the play in general.[20] It seems odd at first that Tuzenbach should take such a gloomy view, when he himself has so much to live for; but the reason why he can talk as he does is that he himself feels happy and is therefore quite content for life to go on just as it always has done. His experience of life is, however, superficial. What he says about work immediately afterwards—'If only I could spend one day in my life working so hard that I'd come home in the evening, tumble into bed with exhaustion and go straight to sleep . . . I should think labourers must sleep very soundly!'—is reminiscent of the naive Irina in Act I, before she began to discover the realities of work at first hand; and he is unacquainted with suffering. Vershinin, however, has taken some hard knocks in his life, and when he talks of working and suffering, we feel that he knows what he is talking about. As in the case of Astrov, Chekhov seems to suggest that an experience of suffering is necessary before a person begins to take the broad view of life. At this stage in the play, none of the other characters has experienced suffering in the same depth as Vershinin, though in time they will do. Only Tuzenbach continues to soar high through the first three acts, while those around him are becoming more and more depressed and disillusioned; but it is Tuzenbach who is finally shot down, almost as if he were paying the price for continuing to be happy in an unhappy world.

It may be objected here, following the more orthodox approach, that Vershinin's faith in the future is no more than a comfortable illusion with which he consoles himself for the miseries of his life in the present, and that the distinction we have been making betweeen the 'personal' and the 'general' is not valid. Too weak to extricate himself from a life of misery with an impossible wife, he tries to conceal his inertia behind a smokescreen of grandiloquent phrases. How can his inspiring belief in a better future for mankind be reconciled with his nondescript showing in the present world of human affairs?

The Soviet critic would argue that it cannot be reconciled, and that it was indeed Chekhov's intention to show up the ineffectuality of Vershinin and those like him. To the objection that it seems strange that Chekhov should have taken such obvious care to make Vershinin's speeches eloquent, if his aim were to produce no more than a sceptical smile, the answer would be that this eloquence only makes the contrast in Vershinin more poignant.

The Western producer may not be so concerned with Vershinin as a social representative but he is not inclined to take him very much more seriously My recollection of the recent National Theatre production is that Vershinin's opening entrance was handled in such a way as to leave the impression that this man was obviously a bit of an ass—a likeable ass, but an ass just the same—who has this comically endearing habit of philosophizing all the time. Here it is necessary for Vershinin's eloquence to be ignored, and the words he uses obscured. Instead, his speeches have to be delivered in a rather hurried and apologetic manner (perhaps even cut), so as to make it clear that no serious attention need be paid to the content of what he is saying.

Now I think that this whole vexed question of how to interpret Vershinin is resolved if one sees in him a character who is quite unequivocally emotion-centred. Of all the characters in the play he is the one who possesses to the highest degree that emotional awareness, so lacking in Natasha, of the extent of human suffering and of human potentialities. As with the sisters, we are sympathetic to him not for what he might do in life, but for what he *is* emotionally; like them, he is not adaptable. There is little doubt in my mind that when Vershinin is expressing such a deep faith in man's future, Chekhov was writing 'from the heart', intended his character's enthusiasm to be genuine and infectious, and hoped that his faith would evoke a warm emotional response from the audience. Emotional, certainly, and not intellectual; for Vershinin has no 'programme'. Intellectually, there is nothing to choose between saying that life will be wonderful in two hundred years' time, and that life will never change. It is unlikely that Vershinin—or, for that matter, his creator—had ever given serious thought to the future in the manner of the political or social reformer for whom this is a very real *intellectual* issue. But Chekhov did want us to feel the full emotional force of Vershinin's yearning for a better world—one of the few emotions that can be made to stand up against the feeling of letdown and disappointment that otherwise pervades the play. To prepare

the ground for change was a sufficient aim—both in Vershinin's mind
and in Chekhov's.

ix. THE FINALE

In dashing Irina's last hopes, Chebutykin's announcement of Tuzenbach's death has the effect of bringing the sisters on to the same level
of suffering as Vershinin. Let us now look at the speeches that follow
Chebutykin's announcement:

> IRINA (*cries quietly*). I knew it, I knew it.
> CHEBUTYKIN (*sits down on a bench at the back of the stage*). I'm
> exhausted . . . (*Takes a newspaper out of his pocket.*) Let them
> have a little cry . . . (*Sings softly.*) Tarara-boom-di-ay, there will
> be rain today . . . Anyway, what does it all matter?
>
> (*The three sisters stand pressing close to one another.*)
>
> MASHA. Oh, just listen to the band! They're all going away,
> one of them has gone for good, gone away for ever, and we shall
> be left alone to start our lives all over again. We must go on
> living . . . We must go on living . . .
> IRINA (*puts her head on Olga's breast*). There'll come a time
> when everyone will understand why these things happen, what
> all this suffering is for, and there'll be no more riddles . . . but
> now we must go on living . . . we must go on working, just go
> on working. Tomorrow I'll set off on my own, I'll teach in the
> school and devote all my life to those who may perhaps have
> need of it. It's autumn now, it'll soon be winter, everything will
> be covered in snow, and I shall be working, working . . .
> OLGA (*puts her arms round her sisters*). The band's playing so
> bravely and cheerfully—and I feel that we want to go on living.
> Dear God! Time will go by, we shall go away for ever and be
> forgotten, they'll forget our voices and our faces, and how many
> of us there were, but our sufferings will turn into joy for those
> who live after us, peace and happiness will reign on earth, and
> we who are alive now will be remembered with affection and
> gratitude. My dear sisters, our lives are not yet over. We shall
> go on living! The band's playing so cheerfully, so joyfully, it
> feels as if in no time at all we shall understand why we are living
> and suffering . . . Oh, if only we could know, if only we could know!
>
> (*The music grows fainter and fainter; Kulygin, cheerful and
> smiling, brings Masha's hat and coat, while Andrei pushes the
> pram in which Bobik is sitting.*)

CHEBUTYKIN (*sings quietly*). Tarara-boom-di-ay, there will
be rain today . . . (*Reads the newspaper.*) What does it matter?
Nothing matters!
OLGA. If only we could know, if only we could know!

CURTAIN

It is worth observing at the outset that there is nothing very
naturalistic about this scene, especially when compared with the opening of the play, where the sisters are also seen together as a group.
Their statuesque immobility (whereas at the start Olga had been
pacing to and fro correcting exercise books), the degree of artistic
licence that allows Irina to recover her spirits so quickly after the bad
news, the way that Olga in her final speech is presumably intended to
face the audience rather than her sisters: details such as these suggest
that Chekhov was not making trueness to life his highest priority.

When Stanislavsky pointed out that the ending of *Three Sisters*
recalled *Uncle Vanya*, Chekhov replied that this was 'no great disaster. After all, *Uncle Vanya* is my play and not someone else's, and
they do say that it's a good thing to remind people of oneself in one's
work.'[21] Certainly, there are similarities between the two finales: the
general raising of the emotional pitch (or 'coda' effect), the theme of
reapplying oneself to the business of living in the face of present
distress, and the tableau scene in the background which suggests that
life will go on just the same as usual. Yet Chekhov need not have
defended himself on the grounds that this was not a bad thing anyway,
for the contrasts between the finales are of considerably greater interest
than the similarities.

In their distress the sisters are not crushed and abject, as one might
have expected, but dignified and even curiously cheerful. Whereas
Sonya in her final speech speaks 'in a tired voice' and 'through tears',
in the sisters' final speeches there are no such directions. The sisters
seem able to draw on reserves of emotional strength which were not
available to the characters of *Uncle Vanya*. That strength derives from
their sense of emotional harmony, which had been so clearly suggested
in the opening act, and which now, in adversity, again comes into its
own. The sisters feel perhaps closer to one another now than they have
ever done before; and although their lives are about to diverge, they
are able to derive from this harmony a considerable degree of emotional
courage.

Chekhov conveys their emotional harmony partly on a physical level—the sisters 'stand pressing close to one another'—but more especially through the harmonious composition of the speeches themselves. The end of *Uncle Vanya* can also be called musical, for Sonya's words are beautiful and moving, and an actual musical accompaniment is provided by Telyegin, softly playing his guitar. But there is only the one human voice. In *Three Sisters*, against the background of the military band playing in the distance, a number of human voices blend and contrast with one another. The contrasting notes are provided by Chebutykin, sitting apart from the sisters, quite alone, and totally oblivious to what is going on around him. He really does seem almost literally to have become a disembodied voice. But in the sisters one is aware, not only of the simple beauty of their words, very rhythmical and assonant, but also of how they pick up and complement one another's remarks. Neither Masha's speech nor Irina's is concluded, but is broken off by dots as the next sister takes over. The speeches appear dovetailed; and the impression is created that the sisters are thinking and feeling as one person. Masha talks of what has just happened, Irina thinks of what she will do in the immediate future, while Olga concentrates on a more distant future still. Masha begins very quietly and sadly, thinking of both Vershinin and Tuzenbach, but she finds enough courage to say that 'we must go on living'. Irina's voice comes in softly too, but she looks ahead a little more hopefully to the time when the meaning of their suffering will become clear. She picks up Masha's phrase 'we must go on living', and then develops the special 'work' motif that we have associated with her throughout the play. The note of courage that is sounded by Irina's decision to go off alone to work is taken up by Olga, who 'embraces her sisters' both literally and in what she says. Their phrase 'we must go on living' (*nado zhit'*) is replaced by the stronger 'we *want* to go on living' (*i khochetsya zhit'*). Irina's question about the meaning of their suffering is picked up and answered as Olga expresses her faith in a happier future. The eloquence of her long sentence 'Time will go by . . .', and her confident prediction that 'peace and happiness will reign on earth', are an unmistakable echo of Vershinin. Though he is not physically present, Vershinin's voice is thus clearly heard in the finale, and one is aware of how his philosophy of life has affected the other characters. The musicality of the sisters' speeches merges once more with the music in the background as Olga refers to the cheerful sound of the band. But the music is beginning to die away, and Olga's speech likewise ends on a note of quieter reflection, as heady thoughts of a glorious future are checked by the memory of their present lives and sufferings.

So that the immediate impact of the end of *Three Sisters* is to communicate a sense of emotional harmony, and to suggest how such harmony can mitigate personal distress. But the long-term impact of the finale is of a different nature. In *Uncle Vanya* one feels that Sonya's final speech is peculiar to her, that however much we may sympathize with the intensity of her feeling, this is *her* vision, her emotional emergency measure. In the finale of *Three Sisters*, however, the personal current of the play becomes absorbed by the general current. By this I mean that Chekhov is no longer just drawing our attention to his characters as particular individuals, who have passed through certain unpleasant experiences, but is using their fates as a means of commenting on human life as a whole. Just as Vershinin changes the level of a conversation, so here Chekhov changes the level of the play, giving it a remarkably centrifugal, or emotionally open-ended quality. What is now important is that the characters express and illustrate certain very critical responses to life: the responses of indifference (Chebutykin), of work to relieve human suffering (Irina), and of faith in the future (Olga). These responses all take it for granted that the present world is a place full of suffering. This indeed seems to be a basic assumption of *Three Sisters* (and, no doubt, of Chekhov himself at this time). Only people like Natasha, because of limitations in their natures, can remain unaware of suffering. Tuzenbach was a much more sensitive person, but in resisting the idea of suffering so obstinately, even he was courting disaster.

Chebutykin's indifference now sounds with more finality than ever before. There is a remarkable transition from the comic doctor of Act I, copying down in his notebook a newspaper formula to prevent hair falling out, or proving to Tuzenbach that human life cannot be lofty by standing up and demonstrating how short he is, to the drunken figure of Act III, who, like the Prozorovs, comes to an emotional turning-point when he tries to relate past and present. So meaningless does his past appear to him that he wonders whether he even exists. He picks up the china clock that belonged to the sisters' mother. His love for her, he thinks, maybe that was real? But it all happened so long ago, now only Irina still reminds him . . . At that moment, out of the blur of conversation there comes Irina's cheerful voice: 'And we'll be leaving too!' This final realization, that what happens to him is of course totally unimportant to Irina, that she

L

cannot remain for ever the affectionate young girl with a soft spot in her heart for uncle Ivan Romanych, is the last straw. He drops the clock; and we feel that in so doing he is destroying his own most cherished memories as well. From now on elements of cynicism and indifference become predominant:

> . . . Perhaps I didn't smash the clock and it only seems as if I did. Perhaps it only seems to us that we exist and really we're not here at all. I don't know anything, and neither does anyone else.

The idea that 'we don't exist, we only think we do' appeals to him greatly, and he repeats it in Act IV. The 'placid mood which does not leave him throughout the act' is that of a man to whom everything seems equally nonsensical. Chebutykin, like Vershinin, has been through an experience of suffering, but this does not lead him to adopt Vershinin's broad view of life, his involvement with our present plight and future possibilities. It leads him instead to an exactly opposite position—to a position of total indifference concerning what happens to human beings, whether now or in the future. He does nothing to stop the duel (though a single word, to Vershinin for example, would have been enough), indeed he helps it to take place; he looks on while a disaster overtakes the lives of the little circle of which he forms part. Everything in his mind has become so fragmented that he refuses to see the connection between Irina, for whom he still feels a residual affection, and the duel, in which her future husband may be hurt or killed. Indifference, in other words, offers no easy escape from a suffering world. To adopt the laissez-faire attitude of a Chebutykin is not *merely* to let human events take their course, for in so doing we cannot avoid contributing to human suffering and evil.[22]

It is only at the end of *Three Sisters* that the 'work' theme assumes a general significance. Previously it had been very much tied up with the individual lives of Irina and Tuzenbach. And Irina's decision to go off alone does still leave us thinking about her personal fate. Will the vulnerable Irina have enough stamina to persist in a job that is almost certain to be hard and unrewarding? In his short story *A Journey by Cart* (1897), about a rural schoolmistress, Chekhov had written that 'the lively, highly-strung, impressionable girls, who talked of their vocation and their ideological involvement, were the ones who soon became tired and gave up'.[23] But the question-mark against Irina's future is not the main reaction that we feel to her final speech. It is the general idea, the general response to life, that is important here. The sisters, unlike Chebutykin, cannot close their minds to the sufferings of the present. The present is much too vivid and painful; they suffer, and know they will continue to suffer. But this makes them more aware of the suffering in the world as a whole, more conscious of the feeling that 'we're all in this together'. Irina's decision to devote her life to those 'who may perhaps have need of it' ought not to be thought of in a heroic light. If the extent of human suffering is seen sufficiently clearly, then the *only* course of action should be to work to relieve that suffering. In a suffering world, as Vershinin had implied, no one has the right to seek personal happiness. This rationale of work, with its general significance, is on an altogether different level from that enthusiasm for the working life which Irina and Tuzenbach had expressed earlier. Then Irina was reacting emotionally against the idleness and prejudices of her class. Her enthusiasm for work did not form part of a wider view of the world, and we would have had little hesitation about classifying her as one of the highly-strung, impressionable girls mentioned above. Now that her attitude to work forms part of a more consistent scheme, there is a much better chance that she will be able to carry out her resolve: so that the personal and the general currents might be said to merge together at this point in the play.

In contrast to the 'work' theme, Olga's theme of the future is already familiar to us from Vershinin's speeches. The sisters have lost everything that gave hope and promise to their lives at the beginning of the play—yet here is Olga cheerfully proclaiming her faith in a glorious future for the human race. No reasons are given as to why or how this might come about; it is something that she feels very deeply, and she recognizes that the cheerful music in the background is helping to reinforce the feeling inside her. How are we to react to Olga's faith? Is she the victim of a delusion merely? No, since none of us is able to predict the future. In two or three hundred years (whether from now or 1900—'the length of time', as Vershinin would say, 'is not important'), human life *may* be incomparably better. This is a possibility, just as it is possible that we shall never achieve any insight into 'why we are living and suffering'. Or is Chekhov's intention to evoke in us feelings of pity? Surrounded by the debris of their hopes, the sisters cling pathetically to their poetic vision of a happy future for generations ahead. This might indeed provide a very moving finale to the play; but it is hard to make such a view consistent with the decidedly unpathetic tone of the sisters' speeches. Natasha, we might guess, would be very likely to *pity* the sisters. We can imagine her making another tour of inspection of her newly-acquired domain, and at the sight of the three sisters, sighing to herself and exclaiming with mock intensity: 'Oh, the poor dears!' But is not the 'happy' Natasha ultimately more to be pitied than the 'unhappy' sisters?

Here again, it is not so much the personal fates and feelings of the sisters, as the general idea expressed by Olga, that deserves our attention. Olga now rounds off the picture that Irina has begun. In a suffering world, we should work to relieve suffering, and at the same time we should keep faith with the idea that a better future might come about, which gives to our lives a more positive sense of purpose, complementing the 'repair work' of the relief of suffering. There is one further implication of what is said by Olga and Vershinin. When they express their faith in a happy future for mankind, they are by implication expressing their faith in *human nature*. Man *needs* a life like that, said Vershinin, 'and if it doesn't exist yet, he must feel that it is coming, he must look forward to it, dream about it, prepare for it . . .' Such a life, in other words, is *natural* to man, and he needs it just as much as he needs food or drink; it is his natural state.

*   *   *

The closing stage directions, and the last remarks by Chebutykin and Olga, are additions made by Chekhov when he came to revise *Three Sisters* in 1902 for his collected works.[24] His only other important change was the insertion at various points in the play of Chebutykin's phrase 'What does it matter?' (*Vsyo ravno!*) Does Chekhov's decision to reintroduce Chebutykin's pessimistic motif at the very end of the play, and to strengthen it elsewhere, perhaps point to a mood of increasing cynicism in Chekhov himself? It is more likely, I think, that Chekhov became increasingly conscious of the profound but implicit contradiction in his previous finale between Olga's faith and Chebutykin's indifference. In the new version this contrast is made explicit, and the audience presented with the two clear alternatives. The increased prominence given to Chebutykin's pessimism required Chekhov to prepare the ground more carefully by strengthening the pessimistic motif elsewhere. Musically we might say that the new ending provides a striking final 'counterpoint' to a play that can well be described as a complex emotional symphony. On a deeper level the changes seem to reflect Chekhov's desire to 'give a full picture': to give full expression to one's worst fears and doubts about human life—for life may be just as hollow and absurd as the little tune that Chebutykin keeps monotonously singing to himself—no less than to one's deepest hopes. It is right too that Olga should repeat her equivocal phrase 'If only we could know', rather than a simple statement of optimism (though the latter might have provided a more immediately striking contrast). If only we could know *now* what meaning our lives have, if only we could be *sure* that they do have some meaning: these are the kind of unresolved doubts that are introduced by Olga's final remark, and which qualify but do not undermine the basic feeling of optimism.

To believe in Vershinin's 'wonderful life' and his 'natural state of man', as conceived of in *Three Sisters*, clearly involves an act of faith. Vershinin's convictions are emotionally rather than intellectually persuasive. They stimulate us to bring our most sensitive emotional faculties to bear on the problems round us. Chekhov was using the fates of his fictional characters as a means of illustrating his own emotional appreciation of the world he lived in, its problems and its possibilities. If we look at our world today, we find that very much the same problems and possibilities are reflected. There is the threat of a disaster that may envelop all our lives, and the attendant problem of whether, like Chebutykin, we can remain indifferent to it on the grounds that everything in the world is nonsensical anyway. There is our increased awareness of the vast extent of human suffering, and the problem that is presented to the individual conscience, as it was to Irina, of what can be done to relieve that suffering. Above all, perhaps, there is the question of how we interpret our own natures and whether or not we believe, along with Vershinin, that it would be *natural* for men to live in peace and harmony on the earth; since the answer to that question is bound to influence, if not to determine, what life will be like in two or three hundred years' time. The main difference between our world and Chekhov's is that these problems have acquired a far more agonizing relevance today than they had at the time when he was writing *Three Sisters*.

The Emotional Network
An Appreciation of 'The Cherry Orchard'

I. THE SOCIAL LANDSCAPE

THE scene is southern Ireland, in the year 1888. After an interval oɪ sixteen years, the Martin family has recently returned to its ancestral home of Ross House. Violet Martin, better known as Martin Ross, co-author with Edith Somerville of *Some Experiences of an Irish Resident Magistrate* (1899), describes in a letter to Edith an incident that occurred on the day after her arrival. Paddy Griffy was a tenant who had held some position of authority, such as bailiff, on the estate:

> I wish you had seen Paddy Griffy on Sunday night when he came down to welcome Selina and me. After the usual hand-kissings on the steps, he put his hands over his head and stood in the doorway, I suppose invoking his saint. He then rushed into the hall. 'Dance Paddy' screamed Nurse Barrett, our maid-of-all-work. And he did dance, and awfully well too, to his own singing. Mama, who was attired in a flowing pink dressing gown and a black hat trimmed with lilac, became suddenly emulous, and with her spade under her arm joined in the jig. This lasted for about a minute, and was a never-to-be-forgotten sight. They skipped round the hall, they changed sides, they swept up to each other and back again, and finished with the deepest curtseys. Mama is indeed a wonderful woman.[1]

This description strikes an immediate chord with *The Cherry Orchard*; for surely Ranyevskaya in those circumstances would have reacted in just the same kind of way? To find a parallel in English life to the situation in *The Cherry Orchard* is not difficult—one thinks of a stately English home with its historical avenue of trees, mentioned in all the guide-books, which are to be chopped down to make way for a caravan site or a holiday camp; but it is late nineteenth-century Ireland which provides something comparable to the particular social relations that are to be found in Chekhov's play.

Of course, as the biographer of Somerville and Ross points out, 'things were not quite what they had been sixteen years before. The

Home Rule movement had gained considerable momentum; agrarian unrest had been fomented by the Land League. The landed gentry stood for a regime that was passing away . . . the Martins were still paid the respect due to The Family, a respect belonging to a past order, but it could not be hidden that times had changed.'[2] And seen in the light of the events that convulsed Ireland in the early part of the twentieth century, the world that is glimpsed in Violet Martin's letter begins to seem very distant.

Strong echoes of Chekhov here too; for the world of *The Cherry Orchard* was likewise to be overtaken by history and to become distanced from us by the revolutionary events of 1905 and 1917. Chekhov's earlier plays all seem to be firmly enclosed within the nineteenth century, and within nineteenth-century Russia at that; but in *The Cherry Orchard* there is for the first time an awareness of a world outside Russia, and the twentieth century has begun to creep in. People now travel by train as a matter of course; telegraph wires can be seen from the grounds of the estate; English prospectors discover 'some kind of white clay' in Simeonov-Pishchik's soil; while Ranyevskaya at the beginning of *The Cherry Orchard* has just returned from Paris and is on her way back there again when the play ends.

In social content and implication Chekhov's final play is much richer than its predecessors. There is little social content in *The Seagull*, concerned as it is with the acting and writing community, while *Uncle Vanya*, though it does provide some insight into how the landed gentry live and the difficulties which they have in making their estates pay, is one-dimensional from the class point of view. This is not so, of course, with *Three Sisters*, where Chekhov points a sharp contrast between the classes represented by the Prozorovs and by Natasha. In *The Cherry Orchard*, however, Chekhov not only expands the theme of the landowners' financial plight, but also draws his characters from much wider social backgrounds. The most striking contrast is between the representatives of the landed gentry (Ranyevskaya and Gayev) and Lopakhin, the son of a serf on Ranyevskaya's estate and now a successful merchant. But a further element of contrast is provided by Trofimov, a representative of the student intelligentsia; and he too is contrasted most obviously with Lopakhin—the one tending to be idealistic and revolutionary, the other materialistic and conservative.

The minor characters in *The Cherry Orchard* also have a much more important part to play on the social level. Characters like Marina in

Uncle Vanya and Anfisa in *Three Sisters* had been faithful old family retainers, whose contribution to the play, though important, was on an emotional level only. But in *The Cherry Orchard* the retainers form a distinct group, a separate servant world. Each has a particular social background, each a distinctive attitude towards the masters and his or her fellow-servants. There is nothing in the earlier plays to compare with the opening of Act II, when the servants hold the stage alone for a while and are seen together in their normal relations. Very often the servants' world seems to be parodying that of their masters (it is an obvious comment on the bankruptcy of the masters' world that the only people still left around them should be such an odd bunch of individuals); and within the servant world there is a contrast between generations—the older generation being represented by Firs—just as in the masters' world there is a contrast between the middle-aged generation of Ranyevskaya, Gayev and Lopakhin, and the younger generation of Anya and Trofimov. If one wants to measure the kind of social change that was overtaking Russia around the turn of the century, it is enough to compare an 'old' master-servant relationship with a 'new' one. Gayev's attitude towards Firs, as towards the peasants generally, is the old nineteenth-century paternalistic attitude; while Firs for his part is absurdly devoted to the masters—'The mistress is home again! And I've lived to see it! I don't mind if I die now . . .' (*Weeps with joy.*)—and even proprietorial in his attitude to 'young' Gayev: 'You went off this morning and you never said a word.' It is Firs who feels more keenly than anyone the social degradation that is involved when the family has to invite the local postmaster to a ball. Yasha, on the other hand, is a former peasant who has acquired a thin veneer of town sophistication, irresistible to Dunyasha, as a result of living abroad as Ranyevskaya's personal servant. In addressing him she uses the more formal second person plural, rather than the condescendingly familiar second person singular used to Firs. The self-seeking Yasha is servile to Ranyevskaya, knowing that she may take him back to Paris. Gayev resents his brash behaviour, but when he tries to put Yasha in his place, the young upstart just laughs at him quite openly. And there is nothing Gayev can do about it. He has no authority left. More and more the younger servants are infiltrating the masters' world. Dunyasha is asked to make up the numbers at the ball because there are not enough ladies to go round. Yepikhodov is playing billiards, and breaking a cue, in the masters' billiard-room.

At the very centre of this social landscape there stands the orchard itself. It is not the first time that trees have figured prominently in the Chekhov play. In *Uncle Vanya* considerable symbolic importance had been attached to the destruction and replanting of the forests, while in *Three Sisters* Natasha unwittingly anticipated the theme of *The Cherry Orchard* when she announced that her first task, once the sisters had left, would be to cut down all the old trees in the Prozorovs' garden.

The image of the orchard may be associated with the past, the present and the future. Firs can look back to a distant time when the cherry orchard meant real affluence, when cartloads of dried cherries were sent off to the cities and money flowed into the estate. For Ranyevskaya and Gayev, the orchard is associated with memories of the past. 'Look, there's Mama walking through the orchard,' Ranyevskaya exclaims joyfully in Act I, 'wearing a white dress'; and Gayev does not disbelieve her. Looked at through their eyes, the orchard conjures up the whole way of life of a leisured, cultured class, it evokes the poetic, Turgenevan atmosphere of white dresses, cherry trees in blossom, and dew on the spring grass. By rights this poetry of the past should now be handed down to Anya. But Trofimov makes Anya think of the orchard's past in quite a different way: don't you see the faces of human serfs looking out at you from every branch, he asks her, can't you hear their voices?

By the time of the play itself, the orchard still retains its outward beauty, but it has become absurdly unproductive. The recipe for drying the cherries has been lost. And Ranyevskaya and Gayev have likewise lost the recipe for the gracious way of life of earlier generations. The work-shy Gayev spends all his time talking or playing billiards, while his sister has frittered away her life on men who were unworthy of her, and who either died from drinking too much champagne like her husband, or else robbed her like her present lover in Paris. The orchard has become identified in her mind with the innocence and happiness of youth. At the end of the play, when the cherry trees are cut down, the door back to that earlier period is symbolically closed to her once and for all, and the orchard's destruction also symbolizes that the way of life of a certain class has come to an end, hinting perhaps that the class itself will soon become extinct. The characters react to the fate of the orchard in different ways. Trofimov and Anya have no regrets. Lopakhin looks upon it as just another commercial venture on which he has already wasted far too much time. Even Ranyevskaya and Gayev will muddle on somehow. Their lives are not yet over, though the world in which they were central and 'belonged' has gone for good. Weighed down by the attachment to her lover, Ranyevskaya returns to Paris; while her weightless brother will bob about for a few more years on the surface of life like some comic impoverished nobleman out of Dostoyevsky. Only for Firs there is no longer a place anywhere. He was part of the old feudal Russia, the Russia that was undermined by the peasant Emancipation —'the disaster', as he calls it—of 1861. His only place is in the old feudal home. It is right that he should remain there.

But the orchard is also used by Chekhov as a poetic symbol of a better life ahead. 'The whole of Russia is our orchard,' Trofimov tells Anya in Act II; and at the end of Act III, Anya consoles her mother by saying that 'we'll plant a new orchard, even more splendid than this one'.

ii. A CRITICAL IMPASSE

What does Chekhov himself feel about the passing of the old order?

Stanislavsky had no doubts about the answer to this question. After reading through the manuscript, he at once reported to Chekhov: 'This is not a comedy or a farce, as you wrote; it is a tragedy, no matter what solution you may have found in the second act for a better life.'[3] The passing of the old order, he felt, was presented by Chekhov in the most deeply moving terms, and any production of the play must bring out the extreme pathos of the situation. But Chekhov had described *The Cherry Orchard* as 'a comedy' and was insistent about this. Painful disagreements took place between author and director that were never properly reconciled. After watching the original production, Lunacharsky, the future Minister of Education in the Soviet government, wrote in a newspaper review:

> But what makes the play so unbearably sad is the general idea of man's helplessness before life, before the blindly elemental nature of the process being worked out. It is we who are controlled by life. . . .[4]

The roles of Trofimov and Anya, and the theme of the future, must clearly have been very much played down by Stanislavsky; and indeed Chekhov himself was criticized for making Trofimov and Anya too shadowy.

More recently, Stanislavsky's emphasis has been exactly reversed by the Soviet critic, Yermilov.[5] He argues that far from bidding the past a fond farewell, Chekhov in *The Cherry Orchard* was quite clearly satirizing the old regime—laughing it out of existence—and that the play looks forward optimistically to a brighter future. 'A parody of tragedy': this is how Yermilov describes *The Cherry Orchard*. Everything about Ranyevskaya and Gayev is absurd, their sufferings are trivial: 'we expect a tragedy but what happens is that the central characters are not merely perfectly reconciled to the appalling catastrophe, but are actually pleased with the misfortune that has overtaken them'. He is unequivocal in his verdict on Lopakhin, who brings with him into life 'vulgar bourgeois prose which destroys every kind of beauty', and who is necessary only 'for the execution of a brief social function'. Yermilov admits that Trofimov cannot be taken seriously as a fighter in the social struggle, but he places special emphasis on Anya, who is 'an image of spring, an image of the future'. Anya is to be associated with Nadya, the heroine of Chekhov's last short story, *The Fiancée* (1903): 'readers and spectators could see perfectly clearly what Chekhov, for censorship reasons, was unable to make explicit: that both Anya and Nadya had entered the revolutionary struggle for the freedom and happiness of their country'.

Now this view of Anya is not only important to Yermilov's interpretation of *The Cherry Orchard*, but also provides a climax to his general thesis on Chekhov, which presents him as someone who sympathized intuitively with the forces of revolution but did not have the good fortune to come into contact with those who were actively engaged in the revolutionary struggle. Chekhov's own comments on Anya, however, give little support to such a view. Reacting strongly to the suggestion that Anya was like Irina in *Three Sisters*, Chekhov wrote that 'first and foremost Anya is a child, cheerful all the way through, with no experience of life',[6] and that 'Anya can be played by anyone you like, even by a completely unknown actress so long as she's young ... This is not one of the important parts.'[7] Anya's shoulders seem altogether too frail to bear the weight of interpretation that Yermilov wishes to place on them. As for Lopakhin, Chekhov had gone out of his way to prevent this character from being squeezed into a narrow pattern of class representativeness, so much so that early critics were confused because Lopakhin did not bear more resemblance to the stage merchant they were used to.[8] What finally of the claim that Ranyevskaya and Gayev 'are actually pleased with the misfortune that has overtaken them'? It is based on Gayev's speech in Act IV when he remarks 'cheerfully' (*vyeselo*) that 'everything's all right now', and on Ranyevskaya's reply that her nerves are better and that she is sleeping well. But it is true as a simple matter of psychological observation that people are always less distraught after a disaster than while waiting for it to occur; and it is also obvious that during the last act the older couple are putting a brave face on things, so that their mood will not jar with the unmistakable happiness being radiated by Anya. Left on their own just before the play ends, they throw themselves into one another's arms and sob quietly. The stage direction for Gayev now is 'in despair' (*v otchayanii*): not the kind of direction that Chekhov was in the habit of using lightly.

But if Yermilov's approach has not found much favour outside the Soviet Union, that of Stanislavsky has also come in for its fair share of criticism. By origin Stanislavsky belonged to Lopakhin's class rather than to the landed gentry. He was still, at the time of *The Cherry Orchard*, one of the directors of the factory of Alekseyev & Co., founded by his father;[9] and no doubt it was for this reason that Chekhov felt that he had been writing the part of Lopakhin specially for him.[10] Stanislavsky declined to take Lopakhin, however, playing Gayev instead. It almost looks as if Stanislavsky regarded his production of *The Cherry Orchard* as a kind of personal expiation for the wrong that had been done by his class to the landed gentry. This would account for its extreme pathos. But one can readily understand Chekhov's exasperation at the high-handedness of a director who prolonged the agony of the final act, which is unusually short, to a full forty minutes[11]—when the playwright himself had so deliberately abstained from all emotional indulgence.

In time other counsels came to prevail at the Moscow Art Theatre, in particular that of Nemirovich, whose judgement in such matters always seems more reliable than that of Stanislavsky. The pall of gloom that had descended on *The Cherry Orchard* was lifted. Nonetheless, opinion on *The Cherry Orchard* in the West has always been closer to the extreme represented by Stanislavsky than to that of Yermilov, placing the emphasis on the poignant departure of the old life rather than on the hopefulness of the new. The Western position may be summed up by saying that although the destruction of the orchard and the disappearance of the way of life it symbolizes may be inevitable as part of the grim process of social evolution, yet the disappearance of anything fine and beautiful is bound to cause us sadness.

To challenge such an apparently unexceptionable view may seem strange, and indeed it would be a hard-hearted critic who tried to

claim that Gayev and Ranyevskaya's final leave-taking, and the sound
of the distant axe on the trees, were not moments of great poignancy.
But is it possible to say more than that Chekhov sympathizes with the
two of them as individuals? Is it fair to go on to say that Chekhov
is taking a nostalgic last look at the old regime? On the contrary, it
seems to me that as Chekhov has arranged his play, there could be no
reason for us to feel grief at the particular course being taken by social
evolution. The poetry of the past, as Trofimov points out, could only
flourish in a system of gross social injustice; and there is every reason
to think that Chekhov, with his first-hand experience of the workings
of the social system in Russia, shared Trofimov's view that the aristocracy had been living 'on credit', and that it was impossible for any
sensitive thinking person to ignore the sinister implications behind the
orchard's beauty. And in any case where is all that poetry now? Is it
to be found in the life of Ranyevskaya? Here there is only the vulgar
prose of the stuffy Paris apartment filled with cigarette smoke. In the
life of Gayev, reduced to discussing literature with the waiters in the
local restaurant? Or in that of Simeonov-Pishchik, who can 'only
think of money'? There is nothing to grieve over here. But it may be
objected that this is to overlook the orchard itself. Surely Chekhov
would have been profoundly saddened by the destruction of a beautiful
orchard, when he himself devoted so much time to planting trees
at Melikhovo and Yalta? Quite true. But Chekhov was never a
writer who exalted nature above man. For him the beauty of nature
was not impersonal. The aesthetic pleasure that the orchard gives
is not more important than what the orchard reflects about relations
between men. At the end of the play Trofimov's speech has not been
forgotten.

It may well be felt that at this point we have reached an impasse!
To suppose that Chekhov was bidding the old regime a fond farewell
seems no more straightforward than to argue that he wanted to laugh
it on its way to oblivion. Can anything unequivocal be said about
Chekhov's own feelings towards the old regime? I think not. The
reason, I suspect, is very simple. It is that, notwithstanding the vivid
economy of its social landscape, the social content of the play was
never in the forefront of Chekhov's mind. What has happened is not
just that *The Cherry Orchard* has been overtaken by history, but that
its whole character has been obscured by subsequent events. How a
person decides between the two extremes discussed above is not so
much a judgement on *The Cherry Orchard* as a judgement on the

relative merits of the Tsarist and Soviet regimes. To take a fresh look at Chekhov's play, one must start by trying to free one's mind of the knowledge of what happened in 1905 and 1917, and by recognizing that Chekhov's approach was not in any sense partisan.

iii. 'IN PLACES EVEN A FARCE'

Back in 1901, not long after the first performance of *Three Sisters*, Chekhov had written to Olga Knipper that his next play 'would definitely be funny, very funny' and that there were times when he felt 'an overwhelming desire to write a four-act vaudeville or comedy for the Art Theatre'.[12]

It seems that he never entirely lost sight of this earlier intention; for what most clearly distinguishes the style of *The Cherry Orchard* from its predecessors is the extent to which Chekhov makes use of elements derived from farce and broad comedy. 'What I've got isn't a drama, but a comedy, in places even a farce,' he wrote in September, 1903, when the play was already well advanced.[13]

There are two characters in *The Cherry Orchard* who seem to have stepped straight out of farce: Simeonov-Pishchik and Yepikhodov. Pishchik's father used to claim that the ancient stock of the Simeonov-Pishchiks was descended from the horse that Caligula made into a senator. 'Yes, there *is* something horse-like about your appearance', observes Trofimov. Pishchik is perpetually being astonished by the extraordinariness of life, and his invariable response—'Just fancy that!' (*Vy podumaitye!*)—becomes a comic catch-phrase. Fortunes are farcically reversed in Act IV when Pishchik, that indefatigable borrower of money and firm believer in lottery tickets, suddenly finds himself the possessor of quite undeserved wealth.

In contrast to Pishchik, Yepikhodov has a predecessor—the semi-educated Medvyedyenko in *The Seagull*—but the character in *The Cherry Orchard* is presented in much broader comic terms. Yepikhodov, otherwise referred to in the servants' world as 'twenty-two misfortunes', is an accident-prone incompetent who, like the sad-faced clown, always comes up for more—'not that I'm complaining,' he says, 'I'm used to it. I can even raise a smile.' Chekhov makes fun of his actions and of the would-be intellectual way in which he talks—'forgive my frankness, but you've reduced me to an absolute state of mind'; and in the following remarks Chekhov seems to be sending up all introspective literary heroes, his own included (Kostya from *The Seagull* and Uncle Vanya both cross one's mind):

I'm a man of culture, I read all kinds of remarkable books, but I simply can't make out what direction I want my life to go in. What I mean is, am I to go on living or am I to shoot myself? Anyway, I always carry a revolver round with me to be on the safe side.

There is a third character who appears to be a suitable candidate for farcical treatment. This is Charlotte Ivanovna, the governess, who goes out shooting in an old peaked cap, and whose chief function in the household is to perform conjuring tricks. Stanislavsky has left a description of the prototype for this character, which is sufficiently amusing to be worth quoting in full:

> In the summer of 1902, when Anton Pavlovich was preparing to write *The Cherry Orchard*, he and his wife . . . were living in our cottage on my mother's estate of Lyubimovka. Nearby, in our neighbours' family, there lived an Englishwoman, a governess, a small, thin creature with two long girl's pigtails and wearing a man's suit. Because of this combination it was difficult at first to be sure of her sex, where she came from and how old she was. She was on hail-fellow-well-met terms with Anton Pavlovich, much to the writer's delight. They would meet every day and tell one another the most outrageous nonsense. For example, Chekhov would assure the Englishwoman that in his youth he had been a Turk, that he had his own harem, that he would be returning shortly to his native country to become a pasha, and would then summon her to join him. As if to show her gratitude, the agile English gymnast would then jump on to his shoulders, and settling herself there would greet all the passers-by on Anton Pavlovich's behalf, i.e. she would take his hat off his head and doff it, adding in clownishly comical broken Russian:
> 'Gut mornink! Gut mornink!' (*zdlas'te! zdlas'te! zdlas'te!*)
> Then she would give Chekhov's head a jerk as a sign of greeting.
> Anyone who has seen *The Cherry Orchard* will recognize in this original figure the prototype of Charlotte.
> When I read the play through, I realized this straight away and wrote a highly enthusiastic letter to Chekhov. How worked up he became! With what energy he assured me that Charlotte must definitely be German, and definitely not small—someone like the actress Muratova, who bore no resemblance at all to the English-woman from whom Charlotte had been copied.[14]

Stanislavsky had no doubt guessed correctly, for Chekhov, like Tolstoy, preferred to rely on observation rather than on invention;

but it is significant that Chekhov only made use of the superficially memorable qualities of the English governess. His finished product bears no real similarity to its prototype, for there is nothing in Stanislavsky's description to suggest that the Englishwoman felt emotionally alienated from her surroundings in the way that Charlotte Ivanovna does. Charlotte is one of Chekhov's eccentrics, and though she may seem comic and even farcical at first, the lasting impression is more serious than that created by Yepikhodov or Pishchik. Chekhov was fond of Charlotte. 'If only you could play the part of the governess,' he wrote to his wife. 'It's the best part. I don't like any of the rest of them.'[15]

There are farcical elements to be found in other characters too—in Gayev, for example, and in Firs (*Lopakhin.* They're saying you've aged a great deal! *Firs.* I've been alive a long time . . .)—to say nothing of the comic love triangle formed by Yasha, Dunyasha and Yepikhodov; but the element of farce is also apparent in the large amount of comic stage business to be found in *The Cherry Orchard.* Predictably, Pishchik and Yepikhodov make a substantial contribution here. On his first entrance, Yepikhodov's new shoes are squeaking uncontrollably, and during the play he seems unable to move without dropping something, knocking something over or squashing something flat. Pishchik contributes to the play two passages of near-slapstick. The first comes in Act I:

YASHA (*handing some medicine to Lyubov' Andreyevna*). Would you care to take your pills now?
PISHCHIK. Don't ever bother with medicine, my dear. It does you no good and it does you no harm. Hand them over to me, dearest lady. (*Takes the pills, pours them out on to the palm of his hand, blows on them, puts them in his mouth and washes them down with kvass.*) There!
LYUBOV' ANDREYEVNA (*in alarm*). You must be mad!
PISHCHIK. I've taken the lot.
LOPAKHIN. What an appetite!

(*Everyone laughs.*)

FIRS. His Honour was here during Holy Week. Finished off half-a-bucketful of salt cucumbers. (*Mutters.*)
LYUBOV' ANDREYEVNA. What's that he's saying?
VARYA. He's been muttering like this for the last three years. We're used to it.

Here the audience sees the appositeness of what Firs is saying much more quickly than the other characters. It is a rare example in the Chekhov play of the technique which Gogol' relies upon so heavily in *The Inspector General*: the technique of referring to detail *outside* the play, which sets the audience's imagination racing and which gives the playwright room for considerable comic exaggeration—not that Firs is necessarily exaggerating on this occasion! Later Yasha reports that Yepikhodov has broken a billiard cue; again we imagine the scene, just as we imagine the history teacher in *The Inspector General* who was always breaking chair legs when he began to talk about Alexander the Great. Pishchik's unseen daughter, Dashenka, who never fails to send her regards, is another such character who has to be imaginatively inferred by the audience.

The second moment of obvious farce which Pishchik contributes comes from Act III:

PISHCHIK. Nietzsche, the philosopher, that great and famous man—and what an intellect!—says in his works that it's all right to forge bank-notes.
TROFIMOV. You've read Nietzsche then?
PISHCHIK. Well . . . actually Dashenka told me. The way things are just now, I might as well forge some bank-notes. Three hundred and ten roubles due the day after tomorrow. I've got a hundred and thirty so far. (*Feels his pockets with alarm.*) It's gone! The money's gone! (*Through tears.*) Where's it gone to? (*Joyfully.*) Oh, there it is, inside the lining. I'm sweating all over.

It is worth observing that these two farcical moments, apart from being memorable, have also been carefully chosen by Chekhov to be appropriate to this particular character. After all, Pishchik's horse-like appetite and his preoccupation with money, both visibly demonstrated on these occasions, are the two things that we remember best about him. In *The Inspector General* Gogol' likewise makes the gossip-monger Bobchinsky fall through a door while eavesdropping, and the rank-conscious Mayor pick up a hat-box instead of his official Mayor's hat. When Trofimov falls downstairs or loses his galoshes, these are also fitting moments, while all the comic stage business that is involved in Charlotte's conjuring and her ventriloquism are appropriate to her, because it is only in these artificially created worlds that Charlotte seems to be a real person.

M

Finally, the farcical element also rubs off on the dialogue of *The Cherry Orchard*. Chekhov deformalizes Charlotte's monologue at the start of Act II by making her pull a cucumber out of her pocket and start to munch it. But it is in the opening act that comic deformalization is most apparent. This little scene takes place early in Act I:

ANYA. Well, how's everything? Has the interest been paid?
VARYA. That's a hope.
ANYA. Oh, heavens!
VARYA. The estate'll be up for sale in August.
ANYA. Oh, no!
LOPAKHIN (*puts his head round the door and bleats*). Me-e-e. (*Disappears.*)
VARYA. Ooh, I'd like to give him what for! (*Shakes her fist.*)

Magarshack finds this exchange significant for the plot of *The Cherry Orchard*, commenting on Lopakhin that he is so full of his plan for saving the estate 'that he walks about restlessly all over the house and, happening to hear the young girls' conversation, is unable to control his excitement and, thrusting his head in at the door, bleats to show his contempt for their search for a solution of the problem that he believes he has solved already'.[16] The audience however knows nothing as yet of this plan, and Lopakhin's bleating seems to me to have other and simpler functions. It deformalizes the dialogue; it varies the emotional key, in that a serious, worried conversation is followed by this absurd interruption; and it also tells us something about the relations between Lopakhin and Varya. Lopakhin knows from experience how easy it is to tease the quick-tempered Varya; humour is not her strong point, and she will always rise to the bait. The scene suggests that they are on terms of a certain bantering intimacy, and indeed, as the play progresses, it becomes clear that their relations can never quite pass beyond that point.

As with Ferapont in *Three Sisters*, the use of a deaf character, especially one who mutters incoherently to himself and makes up words of his own, like the untranslatable *nyedotyopa*, is a certain way of upsetting rational communication:

LYUBOV' ANDREYEVNA. But I really must drink up my coffee. Thank you, Firs. Thank you, dear old friend. I'm so glad you're still alive.

FIRS. The day before yesterday.

GAYEV. He doesn't hear too well.

Gayev himself punctures formal speech in a more suitably civilized manner. Every so often he breaks off what he is saying to take a box of sweets out of his pocket and to pop one in his mouth. In moments of heightened emotion, particularly of emotional stress, we find him making imaginary billiard strokes in the air, to which he provides his own commentary. On such occasions his tone of voice is always very revealing. As for Simeonov-Pishchik, he has a disconcerting habit, equally fatal to rational utterance, of dropping off to sleep in the middle of talking, giving a loud snore and promptly waking himself up again: it must be something to do with his horse-like constitution. He is also liable to forget what he was going to say:

... And Dashenka says ... she also says that ... well, she says various things actually.

iv. MORE EVOLUTION

What most clearly distinguishes the content of *The Cherry Orchard* from its predecessors is that it has by far the simplest of Chekhov's plots. The play's 'shape' is no more than a straight line, which passes through the threat to the estate, ineffectual attempts to save it, the sale, and the dispersal of the family. It is the simplest and also the least dramatic of Chekhov's plots, in which for the first time, as he himself noted, 'there isn't a single pistol shot'.[17] A certain amount of suspense is generated in Act III, but whether or not the estate has been sold seems trivial when compared, for example, with the outcome of the duel in *Three Sisters*. The final act may be very poignant, but again it has none of that deep anguish which one associates with the finales of *Uncle Vanya* and *Three Sisters*.

Moreover, the complex interlocking love intrigues of *The Seagull* and *Uncle Vanya* are not repeated in *The Cherry Orchard*, except in the comic love triangle of the minor characters; nor can it be described as a 'polyphonic' play in the manner of *Three Sisters*, where four distinct stories are developed in parallel. What happens to individuals in *The Cherry Orchard* is seen largely within the context of what happens to the estate, and the 'individual fates hanging in the balance' quality of *Three Sisters* is never so keenly felt. In contrast to the young characters of the earlier play, Ranyevskaya and Gayev are both well into middle age; they are not standing at the crossroads, they have already made or marred their lives, whatever happens to them now. Ranyevskaya's inability to break finally with her lover in Paris is an emotional under-current that runs beneath the surface throughout the play, but the outcome of this story is obviously dependent on whether or not the estate is sold. Trofimov claims that he and Anya are 'above love', but even if one overrules him and sees their relationship as a 'love story', it is neither very dramatic nor of great interest in its own right: Anya changes, she grows up perceptibly during the few months of the play, but this is because Trofimov makes her see the orchard and the whole of her past in an entirely different light. Only the story of Varya and Lopakhin does have some dramatic interest of its own—will Lopakhin propose or won't he? Their story recalls Irina and Tuzenbach, and Sonya and Astrov. Varya, like Sonya, is twenty-four, at the crossroads; yet even here the parallel is not quite exact, for what Varya would really like to do with her life is not to marry Lopakhin, but to become a pilgrim and to wander from one holy place to another.

So what then is *The Cherry Orchard?* What has made it the best known of Chekhov's plays, and why does it exert such a continuing fascination?

When Stanislavsky recalls that by the autumn of 1903 Chekhov had still not decided on a title,[18] his memory must certainly have been at fault, for Chekhov had referred to his new play as *The Cherry Orchard* as far back as December 1902, not only long before the time recalled by Stanislavsky, but before he himself had even put pen to paper.[19] And indeed it does seem to me of considerable importance for the evolution of the Chekhov play that this particular title had been chosen at such an early stage of composition. In contrast to *The Seagull* (a symbol to be identified with one or more characters), *Uncle Vanya* (one individual) and *Three Sisters* (a group of individuals), the new title is both inanimate and 'supra-individual'. It immediately conjures up the whole *situation* of the play (the inevitable sale of the estate of which the orchard forms part), a situation that is bound to cause disruption in the lives of all the characters. The play's disruptive element, in other words, is contained within the situation itself and not, as before, within particular individuals. Previously Chekhov had used the technique of making his outsiders cause disruption in the lives of the residents. Emotional tension had been generated by making these characters bring with them into the play elements of friction and antagonism, so causing the emotional network to vibrate in painful and urgent ways.

Now it would not have been at all difficult for Chekhov to follow a similar procedure in *The Cherry Orchard*, since at first sight the merchant Lopakhin appears to be an obvious successor to Natasha in *Three Sisters*—if not more than a successor, for he wields much greater power. Strikingly, however, Lopakhin is not treated as an unsympathetic figure by Chekhov. Soviet critics may regard him as the villain of the play, but one need only quote Chekhov's remark that Lopakhin is 'a very decent man in every sense'[20] to refute such a view. Moreover, with the possible exception of the minor character, Yasha, *The Cherry Orchard* alone of the four major plays has no unsympathetic characters whatsoever. At the end of the play, *all* the characters depart with the exception of Firs; and this avoids that sense of contrast and unresolved opposition between outsiders and residents, between sympathetic and unsympathetic characters, which is implicit in the endings of *Uncle Vanya* and *Three Sisters*.

Thus in *The Cherry Orchard* Chekhov is no longer relying on the contrast between sympathetic and unsympathetic characters as a means of activating the play's emotional network. This change would have come about because he was attracted in the first place to a situation rather than to particular characters (the sisters, for example).[21] That situation—the plight of the aristocratic family forced to sell its beautiful estate—would have seemed to him rich in emotional and social implication, though, as in *Three Sisters*, I have suggested that the social landscape interested Chekhov not so much for its own sake, but more as a backcloth for the emotional processes. In itself the situation was neither especially dramatic nor momentous: it would not be possible to activate the emotional network by introducing intense drama into the characters' personal lives—exposing them to extreme emotional situations so as to evoke an extreme response; nor would it have seemed appropriate to activate the network by making the characters fall in love with one another. On the other hand, many people might be involved in this situation, for a variety of reasons, and their lives would all pass through the situation as through an emotional focal point, each life being more or less deeply affected by the orchard's fate. Their common relationship to this situation would create the emotional network between them.

The new and final evolutionary departure in *The Cherry Orchard* is therefore to bring out the emotional interrelatedness of a group of people who are not 'linked' by emotional hostility, and who at the same time are not linked by special ties of family or background. It was by making the situation central that Chekhov found himself able to do this. In *Three Sisters* emotional responsiveness is largely associated with the harmonious family relations among the Prozorovs. In *The Cherry Orchard*, though family relations play a part, there is less harmony but more general responsiveness. It is not necessary for characters to be all that close to one another for emotional responsiveness to start to operate. Lopakhin and Ranyevskaya, for example, are divided by their background, yet Chekhov brings out the emotional interrelatedness between these two very different characters.

We have come a long way from *The Seagull*, where emotional interaction only occurred within the suffocatingly close relationship of mother and son.

V. THE EMOTIONAL LANDSCAPE: ITS CENTRAL FIGURE

If the orchard itself is at the centre of the play's social landscape, then the character who stands at the centre of the emotional landscape in *The Cherry Orchard* is Ranyevskaya. It is true that Chekhov referred more than once to Lopakhin's role as the central one, but he was then still hoping to flatter Stanislavsky into taking the part.[22] To regard Lopakhin as the central character is only possible in the limited sense that such action as there is in *The Cherry Orchard* revolves around him. But I would have no hesitation in saying that if she is not the central character—for our argument has been that after *Ivanov*, there are no 'central characters' in the Chekhov play—Ranyevskaya is the character who is placed at the centre of the play's emotional network. She takes over the role that might have been played by the absent General Prozorov in *Three Sisters*. She is central not only because she appears to be most closely associated with, and to feel most deeply about the orchard, but also in the sense that what other people feel about the orchard is seen in relation to what she feels.

Yermilov argues that Ranyevskaya only gives the appearance of being deeply affected by the fate of the orchard, whereas in reality she is incapable of feeling deeply about anything. She and her brother, he writes, are 'children who have not grown up . . . they are spoilt children, spoilt by their upper-class upbringing'. It is no coincidence, he suggests, that they are both so often recalling childhood, and that the room in which we first meet them is their former nursery; and he draws attention to the revealing nature of Gayev's remark: 'Now I'm fifty-one, strange as it may seem.'[23]

This description of Gayev as a spoilt overgrown child does strike one as very close to the mark. Memories of childhood are still unusually vivid and meaningful to him. Near the end of the play, he recalls how 'on Trinity Sunday, when I was six years old, I sat on this window-sill and watched Father going off to church'. It seems that he is scarcely able to dress and undress himself without the assistance of Firs, and even when he is expressing impatience with the way Firs fusses round him, he still does what he is told:

(*Firs comes in, carrying an overcoat.*)

FIRS (*to Gayev*). Please put this on, sir, it's damp out here.
GAYEV (*putting on the overcoat*). What a trial you are.

Gayev's self-indulgence over sweets ('They say I've eaten away my whole fortune on sweets,' he says with a laugh in Act II, as he pops another one into his mouth) could not be more characteristic of the spoilt child; and there is something very adolescent about his passion for playing billiards, and his love of his own voice as he delivers high-flown speeches at all the wrong moments. One may not agree with Yermilov's verdict that Chekhov showed 'a plebeian severity'[24] towards characters like Gayev (Chekhov himself saw 'gentleness and elegance' as the main ingredients of the part),[25] but it may aptly be said of him, in the words used by a small boy, that 'some grown-ups aren't really grown up at all, they're just old'. Never having needed to fend for himself, Gayev has not become a full member of the adult world, and in times of difficulty is liable to withdraw into the escapist worlds of childhood. The 'parody of tragedy' view of *The Cherry Orchard* seems especially apposite in the scene where Gayev returns from the auction, wiping the tears away from his eyes—but not having omitted to purchase in town some anchovies and some special herrings which he now carefully hands over to Firs—and when the expression of resigned suffering on his face is transformed by the sound of billiards being played in the next room. Gayev's grief is genuine though, as Chekhov's closing stage direction, 'in despair', indicates; it is just that he is childishly unable to face up for long to the demands and realities of life.

But what of Ranyevskaya? Are she and her brother just two of a kind?

That they are not is suggested by the way in which the other characters' attitudes to Ranyevskaya are so very different from their attitudes to Gayev. Lopakhin knows the Gayev type through and through. 'He'll never stick it, he's far too lazy,' Lopakhin comments on Gayev's proposed job in the bank; and earlier on he has had no hesitation in telling Gayev that he's nothing but 'an old woman'. Lopakhin's first assessment of Ranyevskaya, however—and as always in the Chekhov play, the first assessment carries special weight—is very complimentary: he describes her in his opening speech as 'a good person, an easy, straightforward kind of person'. It is remarkable that both Lopakhin and Trofimov should have absented themselves from their very contrasting worlds—Lopakhin from the staid world of commerce and Trofimov from the hectic world of student political agitation—in order to be present on the estate when Ranyevskaya returns from Paris. But what is there about this middle-aged woman from an entirely different class that so fascinates them?

When Ranyevskaya first appears, she immediately establishes herself at the centre of the emotional network (as indeed the emotional tone of each subsequent act will be closely related to the mood that she happens to be in). It is quite true that the theme of childhood soon figures prominently in her conversation, but it is not so much that she has failed to grow out of the state of childhood, as that she has grown too far away from it. Now she looks back to childhood across a great divide of adult misery, the innocence of childhood, symbolized by the white cherry trees in blossom, being contrasted with the complicated mess that she has made of her adult life. In the first act she is evoking that childhood and rediscovering what was most meaningful about her past life in Russia, joyfully recognizing familiar faces, and familiar rooms and furniture.

But when, in the excitement of recognition, she crosses the room and plants a kiss on her 'own little cupboard', a shadow of doubt may begin to cross one's mind, or the mind at least of the phlegmatic Anglo-Saxon. Isn't there something over-demonstrative, not entirely convincing, about her display of emotion? When she relates how the sight of her native land moved her so much that she was unable to look through the carriage window for tears, isn't this perhaps histrionic and not very deeply felt?

The question becomes more pressing later, for it may be argued that the tears which she sheds over the fate of her orchard are also superficial. Her behaviour in the third act seems to confirm this view. She says to Trofimov: 'I feel so depressed today, you just can't imagine. It's too noisy here, every sound sends a shiver through me, I'm trembling all over, but I can't go up to my room, I feel so scared alone in the silence.' And yet in the course of this act, when, as she herself puts it, her fate is being decided, Ranyevskaya can be seen enthusiastically applauding one of Charlotte's conjuring tricks, humming to herself a cheerful dance tune, the *lyezginka*, and dancing in the ballroom with Trofimov. Varya is dancing too; but she by contrast is constantly dabbing at her eyes with a handkerchief. Should not Ranyevskaya be doing the same?

I think that the explanation of her behaviour is this: that in Ranyevskaya Chekhov is presenting us with a character who has a quite unusual capacity for giving herself up wholeheartedly to the emotion of the moment. She is perfectly sincere in what she says to Trofimov—and equally genuine in her reaction to the *lyezginka*. Such behaviour undoubtedly *is* child-like, but it is not the behaviour of a spoilt overgrown child. It is much closer to the way in which a small child's attention can be diverted by something which makes him laugh with pleasure even before the tears of frustration have begun to dry. To an outsider, Ranyevskaya seems one of the most 'Russian' of Chekhov's characters, and it may well be that she incorporates in extreme form a quality that is common among Russians as a whole.

By comparison with the three sisters, Ranyevskaya is very much lacking in emotional reticence. One recalls Chekhov's comment, *à propos* of Masha, that 'people who have long borne grief inside them and have grown used to it, merely whistle from time to time and often become lost in thought'.[26] This is a comment that could never be applied to Ranyevskaya. She is not the kind of person who can bottle things up inside her. It would be unfair to say that she lives her emotional life in public—she is too well-bred for that—but it is noticeable that when she is trying to explain to Lopakhin what she feels about the estate, she does not refrain from going into all the details of how her lover in Paris robbed her, and how she tried to poison herself. The effect of such disclosures is to make Ranyevskaya a much less dignified character than the sisters.

This capacity for giving herself up to the emotion of the moment seems to me to have very clearly defined positive and negative aspects. On the positive side, she is a person who is capable of generating great emotional warmth among those around her; all the satisfaction that she derives from life is to be gained from her emotional contacts with other people. It is this underlying warmth which has drawn Lopakhin and Trofimov to the estate. Her warmth derives partly from the spontaneous way in which she gives expression to what she herself is feeling.

If a person looks older, Ranyevskaya—like Masha when she recalls Vershinin as a young man—comes straight out with it and tells him so, whether it be Firs, or her brother, or Trofimov: 'Well, Petya? Why are you looking so much uglier? Why have you aged so?' But her warmth also derives from her responsiveness to emotion in others. She has the capacity to enter into someone else's emotional world—her brother's, for example:

RANYEVSKAYA. Now how does it go? Let's see if I can remember . . . Pot the red into the corner! Double into the middle!
GAYEV. And a screw shot into the corner!

She is unusually quick to perceive any emotional changes in other people, noticing in Act II that Anya has tears in her eyes, or that Trofimov's face has begun to assume a stern expression (Act III). And contrary to Yermilov's verdict, she is not a selfish person. The unhappiness of people close to her, like that of Varya at the end of the play, causes her genuine concern and she does what she can to put matters right.

The negative aspects of Ranyevskaya's emotional orientation are evidenced all too clearly in the course that her life has taken. She is completely vulnerable to every passing emotional stimulus, and her affections are so comprehensive that they embrace unworthy objects as readily as worthy ones. Gayev says of her: '. . . whatever allowances you make, you still have to admit that she's an immoral woman. You can sense it in her slightest movement.' The remark of a prudish schoolboy, perhaps, but not entirely without foundation: as the play shows, Ranyevskaya will never be able to resist for long the pull of 'being in love', however disastrous the consequences. Chekhov rejected the suggestion that by the time of the play Ranyevskaya was a woman who had 'calmed down'. 'Only death', he wrote, in a memorable phrase, 'can subdue a woman like that.'[27]

vi. WIDENING THE EMOTIONAL HORIZONS: ACT II

'Writing the second act was difficult, very difficult, but I think it's turned out all right'; 'the third act is the least boring, but the second act is as boring and monotonous as a spider's web'.[28] There are no incidents in this second act, no obvious landmarks, yet taken as a whole, it is perhaps the most intriguing individual act that Chekhov ever wrote. In evolutionary terms, it might well have provided the links between *The Cherry Orchard* and the plays which Chekhov's early death prevented him from writing.

By the normal standards of the Chekhov play, the stage directions for Act II of *The Cherry Orchard* are unusually elaborate:

> Open country. An old chapel, leaning to one side and long since abandoned. Beside it a well, some large stones which were evidently once tombstones, and an old bench. A road leading to Gayev's estate can be seen. On one side loom dark poplar trees: it is there that the cherry orchard begins. In the distance a row of telegraph poles, and far, far away on the horizon the faint outlines of a large town, which is visible only in very fine, clear weather. It will soon be sunset. Charlotte, Yasha and Dunyasha are sitting on the bench; Yepikhodov is standing beside them playing his guitar, while the others sit lost in thought. Charlotte is wearing a man's old peaked cap; she has taken a shot-gun from her shoulder and is adjusting the buckle on the strap.

To these stage directions should be added Chekhov's comments in a letter to Nemirovich-Danchenko: 'in the second act you must give me proper green fields and a road, and a sense of distance unusual for the stage'.[29]

It is this 'sense of distance', I believe, that gives the second act its distinctive character, for what Chekhov is doing is to widen the play's emotional horizons. Act II of *Three Sisters* is also a very fluid act, largely free of incident and relying heavily on group scenes; but in *The Cherry Orchard* Chekhov was able to explore new possibilities that were not open to him with the single indoor setting of *Three Sisters*. He was able to show how the natural scene—the fine summer evening drawing to a close—might interact with the feelings of his characters; and to do this more directly than in *Three Sisters*, where the evocation of a winter atmosphere has to be achieved verbally. His use of sound for emotional purposes could also be more ambitious.[30] There are sound effects in *Three Sisters* too, of course; but the playing of a piano indoors is somehow less emotive than a guitar being played in the open air, and the sound of the wind whistling in the stove less mysterious than a sound from a far distance, which seems to come from the sky itself. And in *Three Sisters* the outside world (the mummers down below in the street) never passes beyond the front door; whereas in *The Cherry Orchard*, the tipsy traveller who has lost his way blunders right into the closed circle of Chekhov's group.

When the act opens, Chekhov is careful not to play his cards too soon. The sun about to set, the guitar, the rustic figures seen against the timeless background of a deserted chapel, Charlotte's pensive monologue . . . all this seems very idyllic. But the young heroine, Dunyasha, instead of picking up the strains of Yepikhodov's plaintive melody, takes out a hand-mirror and starts to powder her nose; and her two swains sing so atrociously that Charlotte calls them jackals.

After this comic, trivial opening scene Chekhov immediately varies the emotional key by introducing a serious, worried conversation among the main characters about the future of the estate. From the outset Ranyevskaya is irritable, and this affects the general mood: there is friction and bad feeling. Only the arrival of the young people from the house is able to break this mood in Ranyevskaya. At first the atmosphere of ill-feeling seems to continue. Lopakhin and Trofimov make what sound like quite wounding remarks to one another, Lopakhin twitting Trofimov for being 'an eternal student', and Trofimov comparing Lopakhin to 'a predator that devours everything in its path'. But just as animals may have automatic signals to indicate to one another that what they are doing is 'in play', so here there is inserted into the conversation a kind of human 'play' signal. This is the use of the familiar second person singular in the exchange:

LOPAKHIN. But why are you (*ty*) getting so worked up, you funny chap?
TROFIMOV. Well, don't you (*ty*) keep pestering me.

Varya nonetheless does not like to hear Lopakhin described in these terms, suggesting that they change the subject, and it is Ranyevskaya who returns to the previous day's discussion about 'the proud man'. This hackneyed topic from nineteenth-century Russian culture has no relevance to the play. It is just a means of starting the characters off philosophizing. And as always, the effect of this philosophizing is to widen the context, from the personal (the earlier discussion about the estate, Ranyevskaya's account of her past life) to the general (the state of Russia). The mood is now quite different: more relaxed and reflective. Of course, it is not really a *discussion*. The mood is such that each participant is enabled to express something of what he feels about life. Lopakhin's comment that human beings should be more worthy of their magnificent natural surroundings follows on very indirectly from Trofimov's speech about the Russian intelligentsia, but it does follow on emotionally in the sense that he too is expressing something that he feels deeply.

Music (Yepikhodov playing his guitar in the distance) is now used as a signal that this discussion sequence is at an end, and to introduce a more purely emotional passage. The absent-minded way in which Ranyevskaya and her daughter repeat the same phrase—'There goes Yepikhodov'—suggests how thoughtful and dreamy their mood has now become. At this moment, Gayev notices that the sun has gone down, and before anyone can stop him, he has begun to address himself to Nature:

> GAYEV (*softly, as if declaiming*). Nature, glorious Nature, shining with an everlasting radiance, so beautiful and so indifferent, you whom we call Mother Nature, uniting in yourself both Life and Death, you create and you destroy . . .
> VARYA (*imploringly*). Uncle, dear!
> ANYA. Uncle, you're doing it again.

Anya and Varya had tried to persuade their uncle in Act I—playing the wise older relatives to his incorrigible small child—that he really would feel better in himself if he didn't talk quite so much and make such tactless remarks. Now they seem to be saying to him: 'Uncle, we know that deep down you feel just the same way about the sun setting as we do, so why spoil this shared experience by putting it into words? It's like someone talking at a recital—even if they are praising the music.'

Suddenly, in the silence that follows, 'a distant sound is heard, as if from the sky, the sound of a breaking string, dying away, mournful'.

Interpreters of Chekhov have often attached to this sound, to be repeated right at the end of the play, very precise meanings. Thus, Magarshack writes:

> The dying, melancholy sound of a broken string . . . is all Chekhov needed to convey his own attitude to the 'dreary' lives of his characters . . . It is a sort of requiem for the 'unhappy and disjointed' lives of his characters.[31]

A different view of the sound in the second act was expressed by Francis Fergusson, who said that '(though distant) it is sharp, almost a warning signal';[32] while Valency associates the sound with the speech that Gayev has just made:

> In his apostrophe to nature is said all that can be said of the mystery of life, and in this moment Gayev gives voice to what all

those present must feel in their hearts. It is the essential theme of the play. But the young people find his words unbearable, and they force him to be silent. It is at this point that we hear the sound of the breaking string in the sky.[33]

An unlikely interpretation, I feel; for Gayev's theme of Nature, 'so beautiful and so indifferent', is trite and alien to Chekhov.[34]

The very diversity of these views, however—and one could go on multiplying them indefinitely—suggests that Chekhov did not intend that one specific meaning should be attached here to the sound of the breaking string. The trouble perhaps is the adjective, 'dying away', which suggests an obvious symbolic parallel to the 'dying away' of the estate and the old regime. But Chekhov himself was not anxious that the sound should be a long drawn-out one: 'tell Nemirovich', he wrote to his wife in March, 1904, 'that the sound in Acts II and IV of *The Cherry Orchard* must be shorter, much shorter, and must be felt to come from very, very far off.'[35] Moreover, one has to bear in mind that this sound was not *invented* by Chekhov for the purposes of his play. It was familiar to him from time spent in his youth in the Donets Basin, the mining area of Russia, where a bucket falling in a distant mine-shaft would produce this strangely evocative sound.[36] The sound is mournful (Chekhov's own word) and mysterious ('as if from the sky'), but it would be wrong to attach to it here a more precise emotional meaning.

Why then did Chekhov choose this particular moment in the play to introduce his evocative sound? The characters are all in a very quiet, dreamy kind of mood. Their attention, like ours, has just been drawn to the sounds of music: Yepikhodov 'softly and sadly' playing his guitar. Then the emotional context changes. The characters are seen in relation to the world of nature, to the sun that has just set. There follows a pause, a moment of emotional rest, but one in which characters and audience are particularly responsive to sounds and to their natural surroundings. Suddenly this mysterious sound is heard—a musical sound in its way but contrasting so strangely with the thoroughly familiar sounds of Yepikhodov's guitar—and emanating from somewhere in the world of nature, from some distant point, so it seems, in the sky itself. For a brief moment the characters, and perhaps the audience too, seem very close together, linked by a common emotional awareness. Then the emotional network, drawn so fine and taut for that brief moment, slackens again as each of the characters interprets the sound in accordance with his or her own nature. The practical Lopakhin gives the correct explanation, about the bucket falling in the mine-shaft; Gayev, still preoccupied with nature, thinks that it might be some kind of bird; the emotional Ranyevskaya, who feels that something dreadful is going to happen, finds the sound disturbing and gives a shudder; while the reaction of Firs is typically oblique and drawn from the past. It reminds him of how the owl hooted ominously and the samovar kept on singing, 'before the disaster'.

In this short passage with the sunset and the breaking string, Chekhov is widening the emotional horizons by presenting on the stage the mysterious emotional relationship that exists between men and the world of nature, and between men and the realm of sound. Here the Chekhov play seems to me to be moving closer to the world of Chekhov's short stories. The stage directions themselves for the second act have a markedly literary quality. In the stories Chekhov's descriptions are seldom objective, but are presented more in terms of the emotional interaction between the observer and what is being observed. In the following paragraph from the opening of *The House with a Mezzanine* (1896), the same time of day is evoked as in Act II of *The Cherry Orchard*, and Chekhov shows how the impact of the natural scene on the observer's senses—of sight, hearing, and even smell—all combine to produce in him a very distinctive emotional reaction:

One day, as I was returning home, I wandered by chance on to an unfamiliar estate. The sun was already disappearing, and evening shadows stretched across the flowering rye. Two rows of very tall, closely planted old fir trees stood like two solid walls, forming a dark and beautiful avenue. I climbed easily over the hedge and walked along this avenue, slipping on the fir needles, which were an inch deep underfoot. It was quiet and dark, and only a bright golden light trembled here and there in the treetops, producing rainbow reflections in the spiders' webs. The smell of the fir needles was strong, overpowering. Then I turned into a long avenue of lime trees. And here too there was neglect and old age; last year's leaves rustled sadly beneath my feet and in the twilight between the trees shadows lurked. On the right, in an old orchard, an oriole was singing, reluctantly and in a weak voice; a veteran, too, no doubt. But now the lime trees also came to an end; I walked past a white house with a terrace and a mezzanine, and suddenly there opened up before me a view of a courtyard and a wide pond with a bathing hut, and on the far side a collection of green willow trees and a village, with a tall narrow church steeple on which a cross burned, reflecting the sunset. For a moment I was entranced by the peculiar sensation that this scene was part of me and very familiar, as if I had already seen it all at some time in my childhood.[37]

The richness and subtlety of the sensual details in this description cannot of course be reproduced in *The Cherry Orchard*, but the play does have one very strong compensating advantage. It is able to suggest the *shared* experience of being present when the sun sets. Although the individual observer may find the sunset beautiful and moving, he may also feel that the experience is in some way emotionally incomplete unless it is shared with other human beings.

The intrusion of the drunken traveller now provides the sharpest variation in emotional key during the course of this second act. When the older characters decide to go back to the house, Trofimov and Anya are left on their own, and once more the emotional context changes. Now we are invited to respond to the feelings of two young people whose thoughts are all of the future, and here too human feelings and the natural scene are interwoven. The audience may have its doubts about the tone of Trofimov's first speech, but not Anya. 'How well you speak!' she says, throwing up her arms in delight, and after a pause she adds: 'It's so wonderful here today!' A way of changing the subject? I think not. It is one of those remarks in the Chekhov play that are emotionally complementary: in response to the obvious emotion behind Trofimov's words, Anya speaks of what she at that moment finds emotionally most moving. Trofimov himself is not indifferent to the world of nature. He and Anya watch the moon begin to edge its way up above the horizon, and this makes Trofimov think of how in his vision happiness is also just on the point of edging its way into the human world. The act ends with a final evocation of the natural scene: to escape from Varya's constant surveillance, Anya and Trofimov run off down to the river.

Chekhov had originally intended to conclude the second act with quite a long and very quiet scene between Charlotte and Firs.[38] Stanislavsky felt that this would lower the tempo too much, and at his request the scene was omitted, though most of Charlotte's remarks were transferred to her opening monologue. Had the scene been retained, it would have provided Act II with yet another emotional context, contrasting with that of the previous scene: the context of the past. Here we become involved in the feelings of two characters who are recalling their past lives: the governess, who does not know how old she is or who her parents were, and the very old man who is remembering an incident that happened at least sixty years ago. They strike us as a totally dissimilar pair, but at the end of the scene Chekhov builds an emotional bridge between them. Firs now appears to have moved on to some totally different episode, involving a cart and a sack, and something inside the sack which made a noise. Firs imitates the noise, and Charlotte picks it up, laughing to herself with quiet pleasure.

Stanislavsky seems to have had pangs of conscience about the omission of this scene, which he describes at length in his memoirs.[39]

vii. RANYEVSKAYA AND LOPAKHIN

In *The Cherry Orchard* the most subtle vibrations of the emotional network occur because the main characters (Ranyevskaya, Lopakhin and Trofimov), though fundamentally well disposed towards one another, yet cannot help viewing the orchard in quite different ways.

Lopakhin is the kind of man who would be miserable if he were forced to watch a Chekhov play. He would want to stand up, move around, wave his arms about. He needs to be active: 'I can't manage without work, I don't know what to do with these arms of mine; look at the funny way they hang down, as if they don't really belong to me.' Lopakhin is not one of those Russians who have no notion of time, and who appear to take a perverse delight in not consulting clocks or watches: in Act IV he announces that there are forty-six minutes to go (not forty-five, but forty-six) before the train's departure. But Lopakhin, the successful business man who has raised himself up from the humblest origins, is more than a conventional self-made man of action (and much less one-dimensional than Natasha in *Three Sisters*). There is also an emotional side to him, even an artistic side. Surprisingly it is Trofimov who comments: 'Your fingers are fine and sensitive, like an artist's, you've a fine, sensitive soul . . .' This duality of artist and business man is well illustrated by his remark to Trofimov shortly after:

> In the spring I put almost three thousand acres down to poppy, and now I've made a clear profit of forty thousand. And when my poppies were all in flower, what a splendid sight that was!

It is the emotional side of Lopakhin that makes him value Ranyevskaya as a person, and that has drawn him to the estate for her homecoming. He feels moreover that he has his own special contribution to

N

make to the joy of the occasion. By putting his financial expertise at
their disposal, he can help Ranyevskaya and Gayev to salvage the
family fortunes. He is quite sincere when he says that he has something
'very pleasant and cheerful' to tell them, going on to elaborate his
scheme for converting the estate into a dacha colony (a dacha being a
Russian summer residence, in this case presumably a small wooden
chalet). Quite apart from the satisfaction of arranging a good business
deal on behalf of Ranyevskaya, Lopakhin believes in his scheme, for
as an enlightened capitalist he deplores the sight of all this valuable land
being wasted on an unproductive cherry orchard ('the only remarkable
thing about the orchard', he says, 'is that it's very big') when it could
be put to so much better use.

The scheme is received with scorn or incomprehension. Lopakhin is
not to be regarded as the hero of the hour. He is not to feel that he has
repaid his debt of gratitude to Ranyevskaya, who must have made his
whole business career possible in the first place. On the contrary, it is
Lopakhin who finds himself in the position of the supplicant. 'Do please
think about my scheme,' is the tone of his parting remark to Ranyevskaya, before an angry Varya shoos him out of the door.

To say that this breakdown in communication comes about because
the two sides view the orchard from the standpoint of different social
classes is true, but the breakdown is also more fundamental. Gayev and
Ranyevskaya value the orchard for its emotional associations, and to
them it is inconceivable that others fail to see it in the same light.
Lopakhin regards the orchard as part of a problem, the problem of
what action will be most appropriate to save the estate-owners from
financial ruin. 'Don't you realize that there's a practical problem here?'
he seems to be imploring them. 'And can't *you* see how much the
orchard means to us emotionally?' they seem to be asking in return;
though neither side is able to make its question explicit.

Lopakhin may be disappointed by his rebuff, but he must feel that
it is only a matter of time before the two of them come round to his
point of view. But when he puts a straight question in Act II, he finds
them infuriatingly evasive. In Gayev this does not surprise him. But
surely Ranyevskaya will not be so unrealistic? She too however is
irritable and evasive from the beginning of the scene:

LOPAKHIN. You must come to a definite decision, time's
running out. After all, the question couldn't be simpler. Are you
willing to lease your land for dachas or aren't you? You need only
say one word: yes or no? Just one word!

LYUBOV' ANDREYEVNA. Who's been smoking such abomin-
able cigars round here. . . .

When, at long last, Lopakhin does receive his answer, it comes from
Ranyevskaya:

LYUBOV' ANDREYEVNA. Summer chalets, holiday visitors—
you must forgive me, but it's so vulgar.
GAYEV. I couldn't agree with you more.

One feels that she does not *want* to have to say this, since to her it
seems so obvious that it ought not to need saying; and that her previous evasiveness, unlike Gayev's escapism, has been more of an
attempt to head Lopakhin off, so that it will not be necessary for her to
say something that may offend him. Lopakhin finds it preposterous: to
think that considerations of vulgarity are to be allowed to settle a
problem of such grave consequence for those concerned! He explodes
with frustration. Ranyevskaya is alarmed. She knows that Lopakhin
means well, that he would not react in such an extreme way unless
there were good cause; and though her long autobiographical speech is
not addressed to Lopakhin in particular, indirectly she is trying to
explain to him, and to herself, why she feels about the estate in the
way that she does.

This speech reveals in her a new depth and capacity for introspection. She is contrasted with her brother, who can summarize his sinful
life in just one sentence: 'They say I've eaten away my whole fortune
on sweets.' Ranyevskaya sees her life as a repeated cycle of sin and
punishment. Now she is uneasily aware that the whole cycle, briefly
interrupted by her return to Russia, may be going to start up all over
again. In the first act she had thrown away the telegrams from Paris
without opening them. By this time she is tearing them up only as an
afterthought, having obviously read them and kept them by her. There
is an ominous ambiguity of attitude about the way in which she takes
out the telegram and says: 'This came today from Paris . . . he begs
my forgiveness, implores me to return'—as if inviting her listeners to
agree with her, before she destroys the telegram, that to return to Paris
would not after all be so unjustifiable.

What she feels about the estate and what she feels about her past life
are obviously inextricable. If the estate is to be sold, this will be a
punishment to her for having lived her life so badly. When she speaks

of living in a state of apprehension, 'as if the house were about to collapse around our ears', she seems almost to desire to take this punishment upon herself, to be punished in advance for feeling this urge to return to Paris. As for Lopakhin's scheme, there has already been far too much vulgarity in her life to add to it the further vulgarity—involving not just herself, but her family, her ancestors—of converting the estate into a dacha colony. 'Oh Lord, Lord, be merciful, forgive me my sins! Don't punish me any more!' If only God would save the estate in some miraculous way, and save her from herself and the telegrams! If only she could be given one last chance!

But to Lopakhin the details of Ranyevskaya's private life must seem to have curiously little relevance to the problem in hand, and the dialogue between them is not resumed.

Whether Lopakhin goes to the auction with the express purpose of bidding for the estate is not made clear by Chekhov. I am inclined to think that he acts upon impulse, that the wild idea of becoming the owner of the cherry orchard suddenly attracts and takes possession of him. For what emerges most immediately from the big scene in which Lopakhin returns with Gayev from the auction and announces his triumph, is that purchasing the estate has released in him a whole flood of deep feelings: feelings that had been submerged previously when the estate's plight had presented itself as little more than an abstract problem, to be approached and solved disinterestedly. These feelings now released are feelings of resentment. They are deep and they are bitter; and they are bound up, in just the same way as Ranyevskaya's feelings towards the estate are, with childhood and with ancestors. But it is not the happy associations of childhood that Lopakhin looks back to:

> ... Don't anyone laugh at me! If only my father and grandfather could rise from their graves and see everything that's happened, could see how their Yermolai—who was flogged, and never taught to read or write properly, and who ran about barefoot in winter—if only they could see how this same Yermolai has bought the estate which is the most beautiful place on God's earth. I've bought the estate where my father and grandfather were serfs, where *they* weren't even allowed into the kitchen.

The very beauty of the orchard intensifies the resentment, and it is with a sense of paying off old scores that Lopakhin invites everyone to come and see him take an axe to the cherry trees. Previously Chekhov has suggested that Lopakhin is still very sensitive about his peasant origins.

Now, in becoming the owner of the estate, it must seem to him that he is symbolically erasing those earlier painful childhood memories and at the same time redeeming his ancestors' past. Ranyevskaya's childhood memories have also been symbolically wiped out; but what she must feel, as she listens to Lopakhin recalling the past, is that through her sinful life she has betrayed her ancestors and is now merely walking out on them. Perhaps this bitterness of betrayal might have been sweetened if the estate had been bought by a member of her own class, who would have been aware of the orchard's emotional associations and not destroyed it, but that it should have been purchased by Lopakhin, Yermolai Lopakhin, one of her own former serfs, is a crushingly ironical blow.

In the headiness of his triumph Lopakhin has quite forgotten about Ranyevskaya herself. At the end of his speech he orders the musicians, who will now do as *he* commands, to strike up a tune, and he himself is presumably about to go through to the ballroom. Had he done so, and had Chekhov concluded the scene at this point, the effect would have been striking: the emotional network between these two characters would have been cut completely, and the audience would have been left reflecting on the anguish and mutual incomprehension that are involved in the processes of social change. A striking effect, perhaps, but not characteristic of the Chekhov play. In the Chekhov play the scene continues:

(*The musicians are playing. Lyubov' Andreyevna has sunk into a chair and is weeping bitterly.*)

LOPAKHIN (*reproachfully*). But why didn't you listen to me, why? My poor good friend, it's too late now. (*With tears.*) Oh, if only this could all be over quickly, if only these unhappy, disjointed lives of ours could somehow be transformed.
PISHCHIK (*taking him by the arm, in an undertone*). She's crying. Come along into the ballroom, let her be by herself. . . . Come along. . . . (*Takes him by the arm and leads him into the ballroom.*)
LOPAKHIN. What's going on? Musicians, let's hear you playing properly. Everything must be as I want it now. (*Ironically.*) Here comes the new squire, the owner of the cherry orchard! (*Bumps into a small table and almost knocks over the candelabra.*) Never mind, I can pay for it all!

Lopakhin is brought up sharply by the sight of Ranyevskaya's bitter tears. The sense of triumph and achievement had left no room for other feelings. His immediate reaction to the sight of her distress is defensive, self-justifying: I kept on telling you, but you just wouldn't listen. But he is conscious of some inadequacy in this response, and his next remark is on an altogether different emotional level. It is delivered *with tears*, Chekhov's way of indicating the expression of an unusually deep emotion: 'Oh, if only this could all be over quickly, if only these unhappy, disjointed lives of ours could somehow be transformed.' The remark is unexpected and very moving. On a personal level, Lopakhin is trying to reach out to Ranyevskaya emotionally, trying very belatedly to bridge the gap between them by looking ahead to a future where this kind of situation could never arise. But the remark is also striking because it is the only occasion in *The Cherry Orchard* where one of the characters manages very briefly to place himself outside the situation in which they all find themselves. Lopakhin's choice of phrase to describe their situation—'these unhappy, disjointed lives of ours'— is peculiarly accurate. The adjective, *nyeskladnyi*, which I have translated here as 'disjointed', gives the idea of not fitting together properly, or in musical terms, of failing to harmonize. Unlike *Three Sisters*, where friction and disharmony are often sharp and obvious, *The Cherry Orchard* presents a set of characters whose lives, while seeming to tend towards agreement and harmony, yet refuse to be quite fitted together, refuse to blend harmoniously.

The moment passes quickly. When he shouts at the musicians to start playing properly, Lopakhin seems to have returned to the mood of swaggering defiance of his earlier speech. But not really. Lopakhin has undermined his own triumph. Now he can only refer to himself as the owner of the cherry orchard in a tone of irony; and in his exit line—'Never mind, I can pay for it all!'—there is a strong suggestion of self-mockery.

viii. RANYEVSKAYA AND TROFIMOV

If Gayev and Ranyevskaya value the orchard for its emotional associations, and if Lopakhin looks upon it, initially at least, as a practical problem, then it is the *idea* of the cherry orchard that matters to Trofimov: the orchard as a symbol of an unjust and outdated social system.

Chekhov presents Trofimov as an idealist, an optimistic believer in the cause of a better Russia. He is ready to serve these lofty ideals with complete singlemindedness, refusing to let his life be influenced by private emotional considerations; as he says of himself and Anya: 'We are above love.' This singlemindedness is both comic and endearing. He can do without money. He does not mind where he lives: when the play opens we learn that rather than make a nuisance of himself indoors, he has decided to camp out in the estate bath-house! His personal appearance does not bother him, but there is more than a touch of self-consciousness about the way in which he tells Ranyevskaya that he has 'no desire to be good-looking'. He does not mind labelling himself 'an eternal student', nor does he hesitate to describe how the peasant woman in the train (Trofimov must have been travelling third class) referred to him as 'a moth-eaten gent'; though here too Chekhov brings out an element of self-consciousness. In the second act he claims that he is scared of 'earnest conversations', yet he gives every impression of being a great talker himself. On the practical level he is a bungler: not quite in the Yepikhodov class, perhaps, but not so very far off. He falls down the stairs. He loses his galoshes. This would not be so bad, but he makes a great song and dance about losing his galoshes and seems to expect everyone else to start searching for them. And when Varya finds the galoshes, and they turn out not to be *his* galoshes . . . !

If Vershinin in *Three Sisters* is the middle-aged character who becomes involved with a group of people much younger than himself, then it is Trofimov who injects a mood of essentially youthful optimism and idealism into the predominantly middle-aged atmosphere of *The Cherry Orchard*. In outlook Trofimov has more in common with Tuzenbach. 'You solve all the most serious problems with such confidence,' Ranyevskaya says to him, 'but tell me, my dear, isn't that because you're young, because you haven't had time yet to experience any one of these problems for yourself?' (literally, 'to have *suffered through* any one of these problems'). This is the same kind of question mark that stands against Tuzenbach's philosophy of life. Vershinin, on the other hand, has 'suffered through' his problems, and in his philosophizing speeches it is hard to detect any suggestion that Chekhov was not taking him seriously. Can this be said of Trofimov also? 'Forward!' he cries in Act II. 'We're marching on towards that bright star burning in the distance, and there's no stopping us! Forward! No falling back, my friends!' A brave youthful sentiment on a fine summer's night; but, bearing in mind that Trofimov is addressing a captive audience of one, not to be taken too seriously.[40] Or consider his remarks to Lopakhin from Act IV:

> ... I'm a free man. And all the things that the rest of you praise
> and value so highly—rich men and poor—all those things have no
> more hold over me than a speck of dust floating in the air. I can
> pass you by. I'm strong and I'm proud. Mankind is marching
> towards the highest truth, the highest degree of happiness that is
> possible on earth, and I'm one of the vanguard.

Here he goes against what he had said during the discussion on 'the
proud man', for his argument then was that human beings have
precious little to be proud about anyway! It is also hard not to feel that
these remarks confirm the suspicion that there is in Trofimov an element of self-conscious striking of attitudes. But what is perhaps most
damaging here is his insistence on the first person, the arrogance of the
first person. How different this arrogant tone is from that of Vershinin:

> ... My hair's turning grey, I'm practically an old man, and I
> know so little, so very little! All the same I feel that the most
> genuine and important thing I *do* know, and know quite firmly.
> And how I wish I could prove to you that for us there can be no
> happiness. ...

Trofimov emerges from *The Cherry Orchard* as the type of the youthful
Russian social idealist, more of this world than Vershinin (he talks of
the need for crèches and reading-rooms, which in Vershinin would
seem unlikely), more individualized as a character but without Vershinin's generalizing dimension, and therefore, to my mind, making
considerably less impact.

In the first two acts the divergence between Ranyevskaya and
Trofimov is brought out only indirectly, through Anya. At the
beginning of the play, Anya is still a very young girl, seeing the world
through the same eyes as her mother and uncle, who represent the safe
old world of childhood. But by the end of Act II she has swung round
completely and can no longer feel the same way about the orchard. One
guesses that through Petya she has been brought into contact for the
first time in her life with ideas, and has been quite swept away by them—
just as her mother is naively impressed by his speculation that when we
die, 'only the five senses known to us perish, whereas the other ninety-
five go on living' (the practical Lopakhin refuses to be in the least
awed by such brilliance!) But in spite of her change of heart towards
the orchard, Anya remains her mother's daughter in the sense that it is
not really the ideas in themselves that interest her, but only ideas as a

means of replacing one emotional world by a new one—the emotional world that is suggested to her by Petya's more poetic flights of rhetoric. This is why, as he is expounding his ideas, Anya will come in with a little remark that the weather is wonderful, or that Petya speaks so beautifully, or that the moon is rising.

It is in Act III, in their famous duologue, that the divergence in attitude between Ranyevskaya and Trofimov is thrown into sharpest relief, and that the most subtle vibrations of the emotional network take place between them. And here it is important to bear in mind that just as Lopakhin is rather more than the conventional man of action, so too Trofimov is more than a conventional man of ideas or ideals. There is in him too an emotional element which makes him value Ranyevskaya as a person and which has drawn him to the estate for her homecoming. Without this element the scene in Act III obviously would not work.

This scene from *The Cherry Orchard* recalls the 'bandage' scene between Arkadina and Kostya in *The Seagull*. There is the same confrontation between an experienced middle-aged woman whose morals are open to criticism, and an inexperienced, rather pure-minded young man; and in both scenes tension builds up until finally hurtful things are said. Ranyevskaya's attitude to Trofimov has in it much of a mother's attitude towards a son, or certainly a future son-in-law. But what distinguishes the 'bandage' scene is that mother and son are really very much alike and behave very similarly, each taunting the other, for instance, with rude epithets; whereas in *The Cherry Orchard*, because there is not the same long-standing intimacy between them, Trofimov would never dream of calling Ranyevskaya names, and sees the world in a genuinely quite different way from her.

In appealing to Trofimov to sympathize with her in her anguish over the estate, to help her, to say something to her, Ranyevskaya is appealing to the person whose sympathy she would most like to have. Petya may be odd, he may seem comic at times, but she feels that he belongs to a different world—a purer, more moral, more elevated world than the world in which her life has been lived. He has an honesty, a strength and conviction that she wishes she could share. His reply, when she pleads with him to say something helpful to her, is sensible enough, if a little patronizing:

TROFIMOV. Whether the estate's sold today or not—does it really make any odds? It was finished and done with long ago.

There's no going back, the path's overgrown. You must calm down, my dear. Don't deceive yourself, for once in your life look the truth straight in the eye.

But this was not the kind of answer that Ranyevskaya had been hoping for, and in her next speech she makes an all-out attempt to win his sympathy:

> What truth? You can see what is true and untrue, but I seem to have lost my sight, I can see nothing. You solve all the most serious problems with such confidence, but tell me, my dear, isn't that because you're young, because you haven't had time yet to experience any one of these problems for yourself? You look so confidently towards the future, and isn't that because life is still hidden from your young eyes and you can't see or imagine anything terrible? You've more courage and honesty, more depth, than the rest of us, but stop for a moment, see if you can't find a tiny spark of generosity inside you and be merciful. Just think, Petya, I was born here, my mother and father lived here and my grandfather, I love this house, I can't conceive of life without the cherry orchard, and if it really has to be sold, you'd better sell me with it . . . (*Embraces Trofimov and kisses him on the forehead.*) My son was drowned here, Petya . . . (*Weeps.*) Have pity on me, my good, kind friend.

Ranyevskaya here speaks movingly and very well. It is a speech that should dispel once and for all any suggestion that she is a lightweight, frivolous character. She is using all her powers of persuasion. When she talks of being born on the estate, and of her son being drowned there, she begins each sentence with the particle *ved'*, which is used in Russian when one is trying to be particularly persuasive—'surely you must agree that . . .' (I have translated it very freely here by making Ranyevskaya introduce Petya's name). She embraces him, she kisses him, and her last emotional appeal is to remind him of the drowning of her son, an event which Trofimov will remember especially vividly. Behind this persuasiveness of Ranyevskaya's there is a complexity of feeling which Trofimov can know nothing about. It concerns her feelings of guilt. If the estate is sold, this will be a punishment to her for having lived her life so wickedly, and for weakening now in the face of the bombardment of telegrams from Paris. If only 'good, kind' Petya would give her some support, if only he would tell her that she is right to feel that the orchard is the most important thing in the

world, then possibly she might still manage to stop short on the brink
of that abyss which the thought of life in Paris conjures up before her.
This is why she is so eloquently—so desperately, almost—persuasive.

Trofimov replies: 'You know that I feel for you with all my heart';
and one is to imagine that these words are spoken in a wooden, unemotional tone of voice.

He is not being callous or perfunctory, nor is he incapable of showing emotion. No, he is making a rather exact, thought-out statement:
he does feel sorry for her, but only up to a certain emotional point.
Ranyevskaya, on the other hand, is asking much more of him than
this. She is asking that he should abandon himself completely to an
emotional state, should let his emotions take full possession of him,
just as they always take full possession of her; and here he must draw
the line. He cannot allow this to happen, any more than he can pretend
to an emotion that he does not truly feel, as a less singleminded person
might have done. 'I'm sorry, but I cannot really be like you,' is the
emotional message behind his wooden comment. The perceptive
Ranyevskaya realizes that his profession of sympathy carries little
emotional weight—'But you should have said that differently, quite
differently'—and she realizes also that it is futile to pursue the matter:
her persuasions will never be effective.

At this point Chekhov allows the emotional temperature of the
scene to drop considerably. Ranyevskaya describes her overwrought
state, offering this as a kind of explanation, almost an excuse, for her
impassioned plea a moment earlier. It is her turn to be a little patronizing—but affectionately so—as she tells Petya that it really is about
time he took his degree, and tried to make his beard grow properly.
And there the scene might have ended, had not Ranyevskaya dropped
the telegram from Paris, which Petya now hands back to her. The
conversation enters its final phase.

At first Ranyevskaya talks of her lover in Paris in much the same
terms that she had used in Act II—'he begs my forgiveness, implores
me to return'—but now she goes on: 'and really I do feel I ought to
go to Paris and be with him for a while'. Petya frowns; like her, he is
incapable of concealment. Ranyevskaya ignores this warning signal. It
is not in her to hold back, to leave well alone, to bottle things up inside
her:

> . . . You're looking very stern, Petya, but what's to be done,
> dear boy, what am I to do? He's ill, he's lonely and unhappy, and

who's going to look after him in Paris, who'll stop him making a fool of himself and give him his medicine at the right time? And why should I hide it or keep quiet about it—I'm in love with him, that's obvious. Yes, yes, in love with him . . . He's a millstone round my neck and he'll drag me down to the bottom, but I love that millstone and I can't live without it. (*Presses Trofimov's hand.*) Don't think badly of me, Petya, don't say anything to me, don't say anything . . .

Persuasion again, but of a very different kind: not 'say something to help me', but 'don't say anything'. Ranyevskaya now sees Trofimov as her own conscience and better judgement. Conscience and better judgement tell her that she is heading for disaster; but she feels powerless to stop herself. 'You mustn't try to stop me' is the emotional message that she is trying to communicate to Trofimov.

Petya understands this message, but his affection for her is such that he feels that it is his duty to try to stop her. And in contrast to the tactlessness of his earlier remark about being 'above love', he realizes that what he is going to say will be emotionally painful:

> TROFIMOV (*through tears*). Do please forgive me for being so blunt, but don't you see that this man has *robbed* you?

Here it is Trofimov's turn to introduce his question with the persuasive particle *ved'*. Just as Lopakhin cannot begin to understand how anyone might not be aware that the fate of the cherry orchard has to be regarded as a practical problem, so too it is incomprehensible to Trofimov that emotional considerations could blind anyone to the most glaringly obvious facts of a situation. 'Don't you see that this man has *robbed* you?' To him it seems incontrovertible; and after all, he is saying no more than Ranyevskaya herself has admitted publicly in Act II:

> . . . And then last year, when the villa had to be sold to pay off the debts, I left for Paris, and it was there that he robbed me. . . .

But now she no longer wants to hear this and covers her ears, begging him to say no more. Petya continues however; and again he starts off with the persuasive *ved'*:

> But don't you see, he's no good—and you're the only one who doesn't realize it! Just a petty good-for-nothing, a nobody . . .

A strange coincidence that it should be this same word, *nichtozhestvo* ('nobody' or 'nonentity')—not, one would have thought, an exceptionally venomous word—which occupies such a prominent position both in this scene and in the 'bandage' scene. But in *The Seagull* it is the word itself that is damaging, for the fear of being a nonentity haunts Kostya above all other fears; whereas in *The Cherry Orchard* it just happens to coincide with the moment when Ranyevskaya finds that she can take no more.

She does not try to answer Trofimov's criticisms of her lover (in contrast to Arkadina, who defends Trigorin to Kostya). Clearly, there is no answer. Trofimov has inadvertently driven her into a corner. He has refused to endorse the difficult option for her, which would have been to try and continue living in Russia; and here he is refusing to endorse the easy option, which is to rush back to Paris. It is this feeling of being trapped, of having no way out, which in a person of Ranyevskaya's temperament was bound to cause a sudden upsurge of emotion:

LYUBOV' ANDREYEVNA (*angrily, but restraining herself*). You're twenty-six or twenty-seven, but you're no more grown up than a second-year schoolboy.

Driven into a corner, she responds by being angry and defiant. The emotional import of this remark seems to parallel that of Trofimov's 'You know that I feel for you with all my heart.' He is asking of her more than that she should just renounce her lover in Paris. He is asking that she should allow judgement and reason to dictate how she behaves; and here *she* must draw the line. 'I cannot be like you, Petya, and it's no use pretending that I could ever become like you.' But her tone, of course, is very different to Trofimov's: instead of his unemotional wooden statement, putting a damper on all further discussion, there is that in her voice which suggests that her anger may need to run its full course. And this is how the scene develops, with Ranyevskaya being seized by her new emotion of angry defiance, letting herself be swept away by it, just as she will always abandon herself to whatever emotion is uppermost in her at any given moment:

LYUBOV' ANDREYEVNA. You ought to be a man, at your age you ought to understand people who are in love. And you ought to be in love yourself . . . Yes, that's it. And you're not 'pure', you're just a prude, a laughing-stock, a freak . . .
TROFIMOV (*horrified*). What is she saying?

LYUBOV' ANDREYEVNA. 'I'm above love!' You're not above love, you're just what old Firs would call a wash-out (*nyedotyopa*). Fancy not having a mistress at your age! . . .

TROFIMOV (*horrified*). This is awful! What *is* she saying? (*Walks quickly into the ballroom clutching his head.*) This is awful . . . I can't stand it, I'm going . . . (*Goes out, but comes back again immediately.*) It's all over between us! (*Goes out into the hall.*)

'What is she saying?'—it is noticeable that Trofimov puts the question in this form, and does not exclaim, as one might have expected: 'What are you saying?' Certainly, he is horrified, but not so much by the words that she has used—this kind of attack, one feels, is unlikely to touch him very deeply—as by the fact that she, Ranyevskaya, should have wanted to say them. Coming from her they seem so totally beyond his comprehension. To defend himself, or to answer her back, never enters his head. Ranyevskaya has exposed him to a purely emotional situation, and he is at a loss to know how to behave. When Chekhov brings him back on to the stage to deliver the comically melodramatic line—'It's all over between us!'—it is as if he has had a sudden after-thought and decided that this kind of remark is 'the done thing' in such circumstances!

The electric flashings of the scene cease abruptly. Ranyevskaya's emotion has expended itself. Characteristically, she recovers her composure again straight away. The heavy thump of Petya falling down the stairs, and the screams and laughter of the two girls, break the highly-charged atmosphere completely. Within a few moments, Trofimov and Ranyevskaya are dancing together in the ballroom. She tacitly withdraws her earlier words when she calls him a *chistaya dusha* (literally, 'a pure soul'). The emotional network, which had briefly seemed in danger of being broken, remains intact. The reconciliation is effected so quickly because she understands that he was only trying to help, just as he understands that her words were only an overflowing of emotion inside her and were not directed at him personally.

ix. DISMANTLING THE EMOTIONAL NETWORK

In contrast to the finales of *Uncle Vanya* and *Three Sisters*, there is no coda effect in the last act of *The Cherry Orchard*. Chekhov had used the effect already for the finale of Act III, in the speech where Anya consoles her mother with the vision of planting 'a new and even more splendid orchard'. At the end of the final act there is no such coda speech, no brave resolve to apply oneself again to the business of living in the face of present distress, but just the mumblings of a very old man who finds that there is not an ounce of strength left in his body. And this is consistent with the general character of the final act, where the atmosphere seems to be one of decompression, of prolonged anti-climax (reaching its nadir in Firs's mumblings), as if the situation were being resolved by its own momentum and did not require the active intervention of the playwright.

The last act of *The Cherry Orchard* is also distinguished from previous final acts in the Chekhov play by a greater sense not so much of antagonism, as of divergence among the characters: a sense of the characters all going their own separate ways. In *Uncle Vanya* Sonya and her uncle are at least still together when the play ends, while the sisters, though their lives are diverging, convey a strong impression of spiritual unity. But in *The Cherry Orchard*, Ranyevskaya is returning once more to Paris, Lopakhin is off to Kharkov, Gayev, that unlikely recruit to the world of high finance, is going to live in the local town, Varya has taken the job of housekeeper on a nearby estate, and heaven knows what will happen to Charlotte Ivanovna. Of all the characters, only Trofimov and Anya remain close to one another.

This sense of anti-climax appears so hopeless, and the sense of divergence so inevitable, that one might well see in them profound implications for the play's interpretation as a whole: implications of a pessimistic, if not tragic nature.

The Marxist critic observes how in *The Cherry Orchard* the class struggle has followed a predictable pattern. No matter that Lopakhin is said to have the soul of an artist and would like to help Ranyevskaya if he can. What *happens* in the play is that he, the *nouveau riche* bourgeois merchant, purchases the old feudal estate and displaces the decadent members of the aristocracy. That Lopakhin longs for a better world only deepens this tragic inevitability. But one does not have to be a Marxist to feel that the characters in *The Cherry Orchard* are trapped by forces of social evolution that they can do nothing about. No one actually wants to evict Ranyevskaya and Gayev, and yet, almost from the very beginning, it seems inevitable that this is going to take place. As Lunacharsky wrote: 'It is we who are controlled by life.' Alternatively, one might see in *The Cherry Orchard* an illustration of the idea that the most fundamental divisions between men are not so much the divisions of social class, as divisions of a more abstract, conceptual

nature. Because the three main characters approach life so differently
—'interpreting' it primarily in terms of emotion, or action, or thought
—they each see in the orchard something quite different. To each of
them the significance of *my* orchard is perfectly clear. But it remains
my orchard: they make no progress in persuading one another to
see the orchard through different eyes. Indeed the problem was bound
to remain unresolved because its fundamental nature was never consciously recognized.

The theme of irreconcilability, whether between different class
interests or different interpretations of life, is potentially tragic. True,
Chekhov presents it on a miniature scale, so that nothing more vital is
at stake than the future of a cherry orchard; but this does not lessen the
theme's tragic implications. If one pursues this line of thought, *The
Cherry Orchard* begins to seem an even more sombre play than its predecessors, for it has no compensating factor of hope or consolation.
But then one remembers that Chekhov described *The Cherry Orchard* as
'a comedy', refused to budge from this position and even told his wife
that the mood of the last act would be 'merry';[41] and further, that
Yepikhodov does indeed manage to flatten a hat-box, and that to the
equal astonishment of audience and other characters, something does
turn up at last for Micawber-Pishchik.

What is one to make of this contradiction? The tragic implications,
in my opinion, *are* there and can be quite reasonably deduced from
Chekhov's text. But at the same time I have never felt, whether watching
or reading the final act of *The Cherry Orchard*, any very profound
awareness of tragedy or even pessimism. It seems that reason has to
come along and detect these implications some time after the event. And
since an underlying assumption of this book has been that Chekhov in
his plays was appealing to the emotional responses of his audience
rather than to their reasoning faculties, I am inclined to suspect that he
himself was never very aware of tragic implications in *The Cherry
Orchard*. It was the emotional content of the final act that concerned
him, and will concern us here.

Do you recall the little tableau scenes inserted by Chekhov at the
very end of *Uncle Vanya* and *Three Sisters?* Telyegin was playing his
guitar, Mariya Vasil'yevna making notes in the margin of a pamphlet
and Marina knitting stockings . . . while Andrei pushed Bobik along in
his pram, and a smiling Kulygin fetched Masha's hat and coat from the
house. There was a sense of timelessness, of a continuing present, about
these images. In *The Cherry Orchard* I feel that Chekhov creates this

same effect of timelessness, but much more powerfully, by making the whole of the final act into a kind of extended tableau scene: a tableau scene, however, in which words are spoken and where the relations between the individual figures are not so much dramatic or representational as emotional. It is a tableau of how they stand in relation to one another emotionally. The sense that the situation is resolving itself by its own momentum appears at first to result from the way in which the terminal stages of the cherry orchard story are being allowed to run their course. But this is only a superficial impression. On a deeper level it is the logic of this particular emotional network (a logic which has been thrown into relief by the play's sequence of events) that is being worked out, quietly and inevitably. Reassemble this particular set of characters and you feel that they would always stand in precisely the same emotional relationship to one another. This is the special achievement of the final act of *The Cherry Orchard*. And it is that awareness which makes it so hard to feel that the divergence at the end of *The Cherry Orchard* is the divergence of rupture, with pessimistic or tragic implications. It is rather that each of the characters is stepping down from the emotional network in turn—in a simple succession of poignant leave-takings, first from one another, and then from the estate—and stepping down in ways that are particularly characteristic and memorable, in the manner of a tableau. Chekhov is quietly dismantling the emotional network.

*   *   *

When the last act opens, the state of the room, the piled-up luggage, and the sound of the peasants in the background saying goodbye to Gayev and Ranyevskaya establish immediately the atmosphere of leave-taking. Trofimov is also ready to leave, but first there will be a long talk between him and Lopakhin, for these two important characters have not previously been seen on their own together. In response to Trofimov's claim that he is in the vanguard of those who are advancing 'towards the highest truth and the highest happiness', Lopakhin asks, with the man of action's mixture of scepticism and tolerant amusement: 'And will you get there?' One is reminded of his ironical reaction to Trofimov's 'brilliant' idea that perhaps only the five senses known to us perish when we die. But it is typical of the Chekhov play that although Lopakhin is unaffected by Trofimov's youthful vision, he is encouraged by his tone of voice, his general mood, to express a deep if

o

intangible feeling of his own: 'When I work for a long stretch without getting tired, my mind becomes easier and I feel as if I too understand the purpose of my existence. But what a lot of people there are in Russia, my friend, who have no idea what they are living for.' This excursion into Trofimov's area of philosophizing and speculation is short-lived however. Lopakhin's train of thought passes on quickly to the prosaic subject of Gayev's new job; and when Anya comes in to ask Lopakhin to stop the felling of the cherry trees, at least until the family has departed, the image of the man of action is re-created for us once more.

After the light relief of Yasha's leave-taking from Dunyasha, Ranyevskaya says farewell to her daughter. What makes this scene moving is the extreme unlikelihood that Ranyevskaya will ever return from Paris, even when her money does run out. Inwardly they are both aware of this, but they cannot face up to such a devastating realization. Anya would have liked to draw her mother into the new emotional world that Trofimov has inspired in her imagination. She talks dreamily of books and autumn evenings (can one imagine Ranyevskaya ever calming down sufficiently for that kind of life?), but she must know that this is wishful thinking, and her voice is full of uncertainty. Ranyevskaya, quick as ever to respond to the moods of other people, is immediately reassuring: of *course* I'll be back soon, my treasure. But these two emotion-centred characters are playing out a charade together. So strong is the desire to persuade themselves that they are in a state of emotional harmony that they are willing to settle for a good imitation.

Perspiring, breathless, but saved at the eleventh hour by the English prospectors—those 'men of extraordinary intellect'—Simeonov-Pishchik now irrupts boisterously into the quiet atmosphere of the final act. He does not at first notice the preparations for departure, nor that his cheerful voice sounds hollow in the empty room, and when he does, his mood of elation vanishes abruptly. Pishchik bows out of *The Cherry Orchard* in a beautifully characteristic way, as he makes his adieus to Ranyevskaya:

> If you should hear that my time has come, just remember this old ... horse, and say: 'There used to be such-and-such a fellow ... Simeonov-Pishchik his name was ... God rest his soul' ... Most remarkable weather we're having ... Yes ...
>
> (*Goes out in considerable confusion, but comes back immediately*

and speaks from the doorway.) Dashenka sends her regards!
(*Goes out.*)

His request is reminiscent of Bobchinsky in *The Inspector General*.
Bobchinsky had only one favour to ask, and this was that on his return to St. Petersburg, the Inspector General should say to any important people whom he met that in a certain town there lived a certain
Pyotr Ivanovich Bobchinsky. That was all.

It is time for Chekhov to take up the one part of his plot where there
is still unfinished business to attend to. This is the story of Lopakhin
and Varya. In the short scene between them, the emotional network,
which has been vibrating very quietly so far in the act, begins to
vibrate again with painful intensity. But nothing is explicit. In contrast to the emotional flashings of Act III nothing more can be immediately detected than an exchange of commonplace remarks. Even
Varya's tears at the end of the scene are quiet and quickly restrained,
so that the overall atmosphere of decompression is not affected.

At first sight, Lopakhin and Varya, like Andrei and Natasha in
Three Sisters, seem an ill-assorted couple. What can they possibly
have in common? A love of hard work is one obvious answer. Without any occupation, Varya is 'like a fish out of water', just as Lopakhin does not know what to do with his arms when he is idle. But
can there be much in common between a girl who dreams of walking
round on foot and visiting all the holy places in Russia, and a successful
business man who dreams of building more and more summer dachas?

The answer may well be that Varya sees in Lopakhin something that
other people do not see. This is the spiritual side of Lopakhin, the side
of him that responds to the beauty of his poppy fields.[42] But the period
when they were most attracted to one another has become somewhat
remote, and now they seem to be growing apart rather than together.
Varya appreciates that 'he's making money, he has business matters to
attend to and he's no time for me'. She could never begin to share those
business interests. As for Lopakhin, he is no longer able to speak to
Varya except in a bantering tone. To suggest that he is inhibited from
proposing to Varya by feelings of guilt or social inferiority seems
unnecessary. Though he may not yet realize it consciously, surely
Lopakhin just does not *want* to marry Varya (or anyone else for that
matter)? Varya too does not regard marriage to Lopakhin as her highest
ambition in life, but like Olga in *Three Sisters*, she has a very strong
sense that it is her *duty* to marry.

The scene between the two of them has often been singled out as one of the most remarkable in Chekhov's plays: 'Chekhovian' not in any wistful sense, but in the sense of being perfectly tuned emotionally. In 1889, at the very start of his career as a dramatist, Chekhov is reported as saying: 'Let everything on the stage be just as complicated and at the same time just as simple as it is in life. People eat their dinner, just eat their dinner, and all the time their happiness is being established or their lives are being broken up.'[43] Easier said than done, this combination of the very simple and the very complicated; but at the end of his dramatic career Chekhov shows that it is not impossible.

What is remarkable about the scene is the complete lack of importance of the words themselves. They are being used not to convey meaning, but as emotional messengers, and the pauses and dots in the text are of much greater significance. The tense feeling in Lopakhin of knowing that something is required of him, is matched by the tension of anticipation in Varya. Her immediate impulse, when she realizes what Ranyevskaya has arranged for her, is to run; and when she finds herself trapped inside the room, she tries desperately to relieve the tension by pretending to search for some mislaid object.

Lopakhin, equally tense, is quite happy to play along with this: 'What are you looking for?' he asks her.

But Varya is in no state to think up a suitable lie on the spur of the moment. She feigns preoccupation. 'I packed it myself and I still can't remember.' (*But I must stop saying things. He must speak, he must be the one to speak.*)

Lopakhin shifts uneasily. (*Well, I suppose I'll have to say something, that's why I'm here after all.*) 'And where are you off to now, Varvara Mikhailovna?': the occasion seems to demand this formal mode of address.

Varya tries to conceal her excitement. 'I? (*Oh, you mean where am I off to?*) To the Ragulins ... I've agreed to go and look after their place ... as a kind of housekeeper, I suppose.' (*And not a very attractive prospect, is it?*) This exchange is the closest that either of them will come to the subject that is throbbing away in the forefront of both their minds. Lopakhin has been given his cue for a speech beginning: 'I wondered whether, instead of going to the Ragulins—after all, they can find someone else easily enough—you might instead be willing to consider ...' But the cue is ignored.

'At Yashnevo, isn't it? That'll be about fifty miles from here ...

(Don't you see, I can't do it, I can't bring myself to do it.) . . . So life has come to an end in this house . . .'

There is a feeling of panic in Varya at these words—Lopakhin is just making conversation!—and she falls back on her displacement activity of pretending to search among the luggage. 'Where can it be . . . or maybe I put it in the trunk . . . *(but I must keep the conversation going, I must do that at least)* . . . yes, life has come to an end in this house . . . there'll be no more life here . . .' *(Oh, how absurd! I'm just repeating myself!)*

'And I'm off straight away to Kharkov . . . on the same train. I've a lot to attend to. *(So don't judge me too harshly. I've my own life to lead. And it probably wouldn't have worked out between us.)* And I'm leaving Yepikhodov behind here . . . *(she won't like that!)* . . . I've taken him on.'

'Really!'

Varya is quick to let Lopakhin see what she thinks of the idea that Yepikhodov of all people should be left in charge of the estate. Her characteristic response helps to ease the tension for Lopakhin. He is now quite unashamedly making conversation. 'If you recall, by this time last year it was already snowing, but now it's calm and sunny. A bit cold though . . . About three degrees of frost.'

'I've not looked. *(Is it all over?)* And anyway our thermometer's broken . . .' *(Yes, all over.)*

Outside someone is shouting for Lopakhin. 'Just coming!' he shouts back, full of relief, and goes out quickly, closing the door on Varya for the last time.

This scene concludes the series of leave-takings among the characters of *The Cherry Orchard*. Now the moment has come when the characters must take leave of the estate itself. They leave in the order that one might expect. Those who are least attached to the estate—Anya and Trofimov—go first. They are followed by Varya, Yasha and Charlotte with her dog (reminding us immediately of the arrival scenes at the beginning of the play). Before she leaves, Varya takes a good look round the room. Is she carrying out her last household duty and making sure that nothing has been left behind? Or is she anticipating that in the years ahead she will find herself returning to this memory time and again? Then she is described as going out 'unhurriedly'. Anya and Trofimov may be full of eagerness to start the new life, but there is no reason for Varya to hurry. Lopakhin follows shortly after. He might well have been leaving with Varya, but as it is, he leaves alone, associated neither with the younger nor the older generation. Gayev and Ranyevskaya are now left together, but theirs was not the deepest involvement in the life of the estate; that honour belongs to Firs.

What is striking about these scenes of departure is that Chekhov does not dwell for any length of time on the feelings of particular individuals. He must have been very tempted to isolate the feelings of Gayev and Ranyevskaya, and to concentrate the audience's attention on those feelings alone. (Since Chekhov had failed to do this, Stanislavsky decided that he would have to do it for him!) But Chekhov's technique of emotional shorthand is so highly developed that it is only necessary for him to touch the right emotional nerve in the audience very briefly to trigger off a deep response. Nor does he confine himself to evoking a simple reaction to the anguish of Gayev and Ranyevskaya. Throughout the final act the feelings of the older couple are always juxtaposed with those of the younger pair: the two sets of feelings are harnessed together. Gayev and Ranyevskaya's feelings are anguished and complex. It is not just that they are leaving the ancestral home where they were born and grew up. Ranyevskaya has failed in her attempt to pick up the threads of her old life in Russia and is being thrust back into the terrible world of Paris, just as Gayev is being thrust out for the first time into the (for him) equally terrible world of having to stand on his own feet. For the younger couple the outside world has no such fears. When Gayev and Ranyevskaya see how joyfully Anya is looking forward to the new life, they manage to forget their own worries for a moment. 'I'm a bank employee, I'm a financier now,' Gayev says cheerfully, but then, as if doubting his own words, he pauses and plays an imaginary billiard shot in the air. When at last the older couple are left alone together, they throw themselves into one another's arms and sob quietly, but Chekhov allows them only the briefest of moments in which to express their feelings before they are interrupted:

GAYEV (*in despair*). Sister, dear sister . . .
LYUBOV' ANDREYENVA. Oh my orchard, my darling, precious, beautiful orchard! . . . My life, my youth, my happiness, goodbye! . . . Goodbye!
ANYA (*off-stage, cheerfully and appealingly*). Mamma! . . .
TROFIMOV (*off-stage, cheerfully and excitedly*). Hallo-o!
LYUBOV' ANDREYEVNA. One last look at these walls, these windows . . . Mother used to love walking about this room . . .

GAYEV. Sister, dear sister! . . .
ANYA (*off-stage*). Mamma! . . .
TROFIMOV (*off-stage*). Hallo-o! . . .
LYUBOV' ANDREYEVNA. We're coming! . . . (*They go out.*)

Here we are Gayev and Ranyevskaya inside the house, but are we not also Anya and Trofimov calling from outside?

In the play's final sequence the audience does not look but listen, and listen very hard. There is nothing to focus the attention of the eye, nothing comparable to the image of Sonya kneeling in front of her uncle, or of Olga embracing her two sisters. Only Firs moves; but after a while he lies down, silent and motionless, and there is no reason for the spotlight to remain on him. The clear youthful voices of Anya and Trofimov calling in the background have accustomed us to the idea of paying attention to sounds from off-stage. We listen: recognizing immediately the sound of doors being locked and of carriages slowly moving off; interpreting the dull thud, heard briefly once before in the act, of an axe upon trees; spellbound and mystified, pricking up our ears to catch the thin shuffle of slippers as Firs approaches the empty room; straining our attention to hear his weak voice and to try to understand his incoherent mumblings; and in the final silence, experiencing a thrill of recognition as the sound of the breaking string is heard, while the now familiar axe continues to spell out its same message. When the curtain falls, further silence may ensue, for the audience cannot immediately switch off its concentrated attention.

A gruesome element has sometimes been detected in this last appearance of Firs. Yermilov, for example, writes that his masters 'leave him alone, ill, in the boarded-up house, like some unwanted object'.[44] This kind of melodramatic interpretation is however not consistent either with the situation—for Chekhov would not have left Yepikhodov behind on the estate if he had wanted to suggest that Firs had been 'locked in to die'—or with the generally decompressed, undramatic nature of the final act. The scene is gentle, not gruesome. That Firs will die soon is very probable, but his closing words suggest that his death will be quiet and natural:

FIRS (*goes up to the door and tries the handle*). Locked. They've gone. (*Sits down on the sofa.*) Forgot all about me. Never mind . . . I'll sit here for a bit . . . And I bet Leonid Andreyevich hasn't put his fur coat on, he'll have gone off in his light one . . . (*Gives a worried sigh.*) I should have seen to it . . . They've no sense, these young people! (*Mutters something which cannot be made out.*) Life's gone by as if I'd never lived . . . (*Lies down.*) I'll lie down for a bit . . . There's not an ounce of strength in you, there's nothing left, nothing at all . . . You, you're an absolute wash-out! (*Lies motionless.*)

This speech on the threshold of death is just what we would have expected from the Firs that we have known in his lifetime. At the end of his eighty-seven years he has nothing profound to say, no wise revelations to pass on to future generations. There is nothing to be learned here about the secret of life. Like all the other characters he is bowing out of *The Cherry Orchard* in an entirely characteristic way. What concerns him most is his dereliction of duty. Though he is the last character to depart, he is still seen in emotional relationship to Gayev, worrying about which coat Gayev has put on and repeating his catch-phrase: 'They've no sense, these young people!'; and this is the final link in the play's emotional network to be dismantled. At the last Firs turns on himself the favourite criticism that all his life he has used about other people: 'You, you're an absolute wash-out!'

The silence that follows these words is exceptionally taut. Why does the curtain not fall? What else is there to happen? I suspect that the idea of introducing the sound of the breaking string at this very last moment, when the stage is completely still and silent and the effect would be most striking, was one that Chekhov had nurtured from an early stage. This would explain why the sound has to be heard *twice*. Had it been heard for the first time at the end of the play, it would have been meaningless; as it is, the sound is already quite familiar from Act II, when it was heard by a number of characters and discussed at some length.

To say on this second occasion that the sound of the breaking string is sad and mysterious in its own right, and to leave it at that, no longer seems tenable. There must be some link between the sound, introduced at such an important moment, and the play as a whole. But a link of what nature? Ranyevskaya had shuddered when she first heard the sound, as if it were an evil omen; now the disaster has happened, and the omen has come true. Firs had also had a premonition of disaster, and one might just be tempted to make the sound coincide with the moment of his death. But both these links seem too partial, too closely identified with one particular character; the sound needs rather to be seen in relation to everything that has gone before it in the play. Valency, for example, writes that 'whatever of sadness remains unexpressed in *The Cherry Orchard*, this sound expresses', and he goes on to say, thinking of the sad but inevitable destruction of the orchard, that 'if the world is an organism, a living thing, perhaps it too has its moments of heartbreak'.[45] This is more convincing; but have not implications of that nature already been adequately suggested by the sound of the axe on the trees? Chekhov did not describe this sound in neutral terms. On the contrary, his stage direction reads: 'The silence is broken by the dull thuds of an axe striking a tree. The sounds are sad and forlorn.' That 'sad and forlorn' is very open-ended in implication; and it seems unlikely that the later sound was meant to do no more than duplicate this effect.

'Tell Nemirovich', Chekhov had written, 'that the sound in Acts II and IV of *The Cherry Orchard* must be shorter, much shorter, and must be felt to come from very, very far off.'[46] His tone is uncharacteristically sharp. Chekhov's stage direction had referred only to 'a distant sound, as if from the sky'. Why was he now so emphatic that it should come 'from very, very far off'?

The answer, I believe, is that by this means Chekhov creates the effect of emotional 'distancing'. Our own affairs of the moment are always in the forefront of our minds, and occupy our whole attention; but if we are able to stand outside them, or to see them in retrospect, they no longer seem to have the same importance. Prince Andrei in *War and Peace*, when he was lying wounded on the battlefield at Austerlitz, realized that Napoleon must be looking down at him, but that same Napoleon, whom he had once idolized and whose activities had seemed to him so important, now appeared totally insignificant by comparison with the vast sky that Andrei saw overhead; and this sky was to introduce a new dimension, a new emotional perspective, into Andrei's life. In Chekhov's play the fate of the orchard has preoccupied the characters and given rise to all the vibrations in the emotional network that we have witnessed. But now Chekhov allows the network to be dismantled, and he uses the character of Firs as a means of distancing all the previous events in the play. Firs is approaching death, and as we watch him and listen to him, all the emotion that had until so recently been expended on the estate no longer seems to matter very much. But Firs in his turn is distanced by the sound of the breaking string. His single life coming to an end is seen against the background

P

of something very, very far way—of infinite time, perhaps, as opposed to our finite lives—so that it too seems to dwindle into insignificance.

In contrast to what Stanislavsky and Nemirovich thought, the sadness contained in the sound of the breaking string is not one of anguish or despair. This was why Chekhov wanted the sound to be 'shorter, much shorter'. It is a lighter, more elusive kind of sadness, evoked by the fleeting awareness of discrepancy: between, on the one hand, the importance that we attach to our affairs of the moment, the emotional capital that we invest in them; and on the other, the feeling of emotional bankruptcy that comes over us when we look back at those affairs and find them no longer of importance. Firs is aware of that discrepancy when he looks back at the past and comments: 'Life's gone by as if I'd never lived.'

It is as though, in these closing moments of *The Cherry Orchard*, one had been looking intently at a painting, in which a house, an orchard and human figures were depicted with beautiful and intricate detail; and had then realized that this was not the whole of the picture but only the foreground; and that beyond it there was a much wider landscape and beyond that the sky itself.

X. RETROSPECT

In her book on Chekhov, written between the wars, Princess Toumanova considers at one point what is likely to have happened to the characters of *The Cherry Orchard* and their real-life counterparts:

> The rich Lopakhins, the *kulaks*, are most certainly ruined. The Gayevs have lost everything. Varya works somewhere and dreams, in great secrecy, about travel to holy places; Trofimov tries to adapt himself to the new conditions in the hope of a future happiness for humanity. And the Ranevskys, what do the Ranevskys do? They sell dresses in the shops of the Champs-Elysées or Fifth Avenue, or teach foreign languages if they are educated.[47]

The speculation is attractive, especially the picture of Ranyevskaya selling dresses in some fashionable shop in the Champs-Elysées, which recalls how Chekhov told his wife that to play Ranyevskaya 'you must think up a smile and a way of laughing, you must know how to dress';[48] but though such speculation is intriguing, I also find that it jars somewhat. For of all Chekhov's major plays, *The Cherry Orchard*, it seems to me, least invites speculation about 'what happened to the characters afterwards'. It is not like *Uncle Vanya*, where one imagines Sonya growing old, or *Three Sisters*, where one wonders how Irina is going to cope in her village school. In both the earlier plays the tableau scenes in the background, suggesting a continuous present, had involved minor figures only, while in the foreground the main figures were wondering what life would be like in the future. But in *The Cherry Orchard* the tableau, the continuing present, becomes central, and the audience's thoughts are not projected into the future in the same way; on the contrary, the characters of *The Cherry Orchard* definitely seem to stop at the end of Act IV. This, I believe, comes about because the play's emotional network has been so complete in itself that there is no desire to speculate on the individual fates of the characters outside that context.

Instead, when one thinks of the characters in *The Cherry Orchard*, one remembers them as they appear in that final tableau act. Particular images and particular phrases come to mind. Yepikhodov has just flattened a hat-box, while in an obscure part of the room Yasha is stealthily draining the last glass of champagne and hiccupping politely. A worried-looking Trofimov peers shortsightedly at the dirty pair of galoshes that Varya has flung towards him from the next room. 'But those aren't *my* galoshes!' he exclaims, with sudden realization. Now everyone is turning round to look at the doorway where Simeonov-Pishchik has unexpectedly reappeared: 'Dashenka sends her regards!' The falling cadence is clearly to be heard in Varya's voice as she says to Lopakhin: 'And anyway our thermometer's broken . . .' while he gratefully answers the summons to some practical task that awaits him. Gayev is speaking now, bidding farewell to the old house. His voice gathers strength as he launches into one of his elaborate sentences, but Anya and Varya cut him off in mid-flight: 'Uncle, please!' Rummaging tenaciously among the suitcases, Varya has managed to unearth an umbrella. Does it still work, she wonders? She moves to open it up, and as she does so, Lopakhin backs away from her in mock fright. Next an imaginary scene, outside the house. Ranyevskaya and Gayev have turned round to take a last look at the estate. They seem much older and their expression is anxious. Anya and Trofimov are standing a little distance away, looking in the opposite direction, laughing and talking together animatedly. Meanwhile, inside the boarded-up room, Firs still mutters on: 'They've no sense, these young people! . . . You, you're an absolute wash-out!' These are the things, Chekhov seems to suggest, that we shall remember about people; we shall always remember them in that way.

The theme of time passing and sweeping aside the frail defences that are placed in its path, is very fully brought out in *The Cherry Orchard*. There might seem to be more continuity in the life of a family than in the life of an individual: a family with its traditions and memories (of an occasion forty-five years ago, for example, when you sat on a window-sill and watched your father walk across the fields to church on Trinity Sunday), a family with its historic home, spanning the generations, and an orchard that is 'even mentioned in the encyclopaedia'; but no, all this can be swept into oblivion in the brief moment of an auction sale. And indeed, no perception of human life would be complete unless it conveyed an awareness that time passes and that death lies ahead; for such an awareness is an essential emotional ingredient of life itself. Only an insecure person like Arkadina in *The Seagull* would try to suppress that awareness; only a selfish person like the Professor in *Uncle Vanya* would start complaining about the personal injustice of it all. 'We look down our noses at one another,' Lopakhin says to Trofimov, 'but life keeps going by just the same'; while Simeonov-Pishchik also recognizes that 'everything in this world comes to an end'.

Yet the very strength of the theme also serves to point up the timeless quality of *The Cherry Orchard*, for it seems to act as a constant reminder that this life is all we have. When the play's immediate poignancy has worn off, it is the feeling of timelessness that remains with one. In the clear light of an October day—calm, sunny and just right for building—the emotional network of *The Cherry Orchard* seems to detach itself from its particular context in place and period and to stand out in sharp relief, as fresh and enduring as when Chekhov first created it. Individual human lives may come to an end, but the emotional interrelatedness of human beings remains constant. To leave this lasting impression of emotional interrelatedness is perhaps the finest achievement of the Chekhov play.

In Place of a Conclusion

In the view of life that it implies, *The Cherry Orchard* differs from *Uncle Vanya* and *Three Sisters*. Behind *Uncle Vanya* there still seems to be a feeling that if only more people had the 'right' emotions, if only there were more givers and fewer takers in life, what a much better place the world would be! For all its sombre qualities, the note of quiet indignation that may be detected in the play suggests an underlying hope on Chekhov's part that it may yet be possible to put matters right, given sufficient goodwill. In *Three Sisters* this hope is made to look over-optimistic. 'Nothing ever happens as we'd like it to' in that play, and it is further implied that to seek happiness for oneself (as the givers in *Uncle Vanya* do, however modestly) represents in these circumstances a 'wrong' emotion. Given that the world is full of suffering, Chekhov casts round for those emotions that can still sustain us: what emotions are still valid, he asks, how can we adapt ourselves emotionally to the given situation? This play I take to be the fullest statement of Chekhov's own 'philosophy of life'.

In *The Cherry Orchard* his emotional position has become narrower, less speculative; and here it seems reasonable to admit the knowledge of his impending death as an important and perhaps decisive cause. If there is less philosophizing about the future in Chekhov's final play, this is because he is concentrating more on the near things in life, on the emotional relations that we have with other people here and now. No one's 'wrong' emotions are exposed in *The Cherry Orchard*, for whether people have the 'right' or the 'wrong' emotions no longer appears so critical. The emotional network *itself*, Chekhov seems to imply—the to-and-fro of emotion between people, the complex emotional interconnections that we form with those round us, whether comic or serious, painful or tender—that alone is meaningful and constitutes the sum total of our lives.

It was a performance of *The Cherry Orchard* in English that first brought me into contact with Chekhov's plays some fifteen or more years ago; and I remember feeling surprised and even cheated because this 'masterpiece' did not seem as tragic or profound as I had been led to believe, but was really quite funny in places. My most vivid memory of that occasion is of the governess, sitting on a bench with a rifle slung over her shoulder and munching a very long green cucumber.

Yet there was something about the play that fascinated; and later, when I became able to read Chekhov's stories and watch his plays in their original language, this elusive fascination increased, and with it the desire to find out just what made these plays so intriguing.

This is not the place to give a formal summary of my answer to that question, since, as I explained in the foreword, it seemed more helpful to do so before and not after discussing the plays individually. But I would like to hark back to the general conclusion that I drew in the opening chapter—that more than any other dramatist before or since, Chekhov is the dramatist of the emotional side of man's nature—and to insist again that the time has come to bury alike both Chekhov, the social partisan, and Chekhov, the ironist who smiled wryly at the tragi-comedy of life. The Chekhov presented above has been, I hope, both simpler and more convincing. If he has also seemed to the reader a more attractive figure, so much the better, for I should like to think that in the long run he will have greater powers of survival.

Notes and References

The *Works* referred to below are the *Polnoye sobraniye sochinenii i pisem A. P. Chekhova* ('Complete Collection of the Works and Letters of A. P. Chekhov'), published in twenty volumes (Moscow, 1944–51). The abbreviation *Chekhov v vospom.* refers to *A. P. Chekhov v vospominaniyakh sovremennikov* ('A. P. Chekhov Recalled by his Contemporaries'), published in Moscow (1960). In the Appendixes to his translations of Chekhov's plays contained in Vols. I–III of *The Oxford Chekhov* (London, 1964–68), Ronald Hingley provides a very helpful selection of material translated from Russian into English, covering the composition of the plays, variant readings, comments on the plays by Chekhov himself, and the reception given to the plays when first produced in Russia. Unless otherwise indicated below, all translations from the Russian are my own.

CHAPTER ONE

1 Recalled by Bunin, *Chekhov v vospom.*, p. 520.
2 Recalled by P. P. Gnedich. See N. N. Gusev, *Letopis' zhizni i tvorchestva L'va Nikolaevicha Tolstogo, 1891–1910* (Moscow, 1960), p. 340.
3 Recalled by Bunin, *Chekhov v vospom.*, pp. 518–19.
4 Recalled by Gnedich, *op. cit.*, p. 422.
5 *Works* 11, 584.
6 A. B. Goldenveizer, *Vblizi Tolstogo*, p. 113. Quoted by R. F. Christian in *Tolstoy: A Critical Introduction* (Cambridge, 1969).
7 *Works* 14, 268–74.
8 V. I. Nemirovich-Danchenko, *My Life in the Russian Theatre*, translated by John Cournos (London, 1937), p. 62. First published in 1936 (Boston).
9 *Chekhov v vospom.*, p. 394.
10 *Works* 20, 172–73.
11 *Chekhov v vospom.*, p. 379.
12 *Two Plays by Tchekhof*, translated, with an introduction and notes, by George Calderon (London, 1912), pp. 8–9.
13 *Ibid.*, p. 8.
14 *Works* 18, 292.
15 *Works* 16, 413.
16 A. Roskin, *A. P. Chekhov. Stat'i i ocherki* (Moscow, 1959), p. 238.
17 Chekhov's views on Bernhardt all taken from his article, *Opyat' o Sare Bernar* (*Works* 1, 483–88).
18 Calderon, *op. cit.*, p. 10.
19 Nemirovich-Danchenko, *op. cit.*, p. 17.
20 Letter to Chekhov from A. F. Koni, quoted by P. Henry in his introduction to *The Seagull* (Letchworth, 1965), p. 38.
21 *Chekhov v vospom.*, p. 397.
22 *Works* 20, 163.
23 See his article, 'Intonation and Rhythm in Chekhov's Plays', in *Chekhov. A Collection of Critical Essays*, ed. Jackson (Englewood Cliffs, New Jersey, 1967), p. 166. First published in *Anton Čechov: 1860–1960. Some Essays*, ed. T. Eekman (Leiden, 1960), pp. 168–80.
24 D. S. Mirsky, *A History of Russian Literature*, edited and abridged by Francis J. Whitfield (New York, 1960), p. 365. First published in 1925 and 1926 (London).
25 David Magarshack, *Chekhov the Dramatist* (Dramabook edition, New York, 1960), pp. 196–97. First published in 1952 (London).
26 Nilsson, *loc. cit.*, p. 167.
27 Maurice Valency, *The Breaking String. The Plays of Anton Chekhov* (New York, 1966), p. 285.
28 Nilsson, *loc. cit.*, p. 169.

[29] *Ibid.*, p. 170.
[30] Mirsky, *op. cit.*, p. 366.

[31] Calderon, *op. cit.*, p. 10.

CHAPTER TWO

[1] See Valency, *op. cit.*, pp. 104–05.
[2] Letter from Chekhov to his brother Alexander (*Works* 13, 372).
[3] *Ibid.*, p. 373.
[4] *Works* 14, 268–74.
[5] Nemirovich-Danchenko, *op. cit.*, pp. 57 and 58. I. Gurlyand, however, recalls that in the summer of 1889 Chekhov said to him: 'If you hang a pistol on the wall in Act I, then it must be fired in Act IV' (*Chekhov v vospom.*, p. 754).
[6] *Works* 15, 388.
[7] *Works* 11, 573.
[8] *Works* 16, 271.
[9] Cf. the article by Robert Louis Jackson, 'Chekhov's *Seagull*: The Empty Well, the Dry Lake, and the Cold Cave', in *Chekhov. A Collection of Critical Essays*, ed. Jackson, pp. 99–111.
[10] The figure of the stage-struck young girl occurs twice in Chekhov's stories: in *A Tragic Actor* (1883) and, more importantly, in *A Boring Story* (1889).
[11] Quoted by Ernest J. Simmons in *Chekhov: A Biography* (London, 1963), p. 424. First published in 1962 (Boston and Toronto).
[12] See *Chekhov v vospom.*, p. 754.

CHAPTER THREE

[1] *Works* 16, 366.
[2] *Works* 16, 409.
[3] See N. I. Gitovich, *Letopis' zhizni i tvorchestva A. P. Chekhova* (Moscow, 1955), pp. 282–83; Hingley, *The Oxford Chekhov*, Vol. III (London, 1964), p. 300.
[4] *Works* 15, 7.
[5] V. Yermilov, *A. P. Chekhov*, expanded edition (Moscow, 1959), p. 435.
[6] Magarshack, *op. cit.*, p. 206.
[7] Yermilov, *op. cit.*, p. 434.
[8] *Ibid.*, p. 435.
[9] See the article by Sophie Laffitte, 'Čechov et Tolstoj', in *Anton Čechov: 1860–1960. Some Essays*, ed. T. Eekman (Leiden, 1960), p. 129.
[10] *Ibid.*, p. 130.
[11] *Works* 9, 87.
[12] This theme of the impoverishment of the countryside is anticipated in Chekhov's short story, *The Pipe* (1887). See *Works* 6, 250–57.
[13] *Chekhov v vospom.*, p. 386.
[14] *Works* 19, 10.
[15] *Works* 18, 235.

CHAPTER FOUR

[1] 'Nothing is more painful than failure,' Chekhov had written to Suvorin in October 1895, referring to the hostile critical reception given to a performance by the actress Ozerova. Strangely enough, in this same letter Chekhov announces that he is at work on *The Seagull*, and one wonders whether the Ozerova episode might not have been at the back of his mind in describing Nina's failures as an actress. See *Works* 16, 271 and 503.
[2] *Works* 16, 413.
[3] *Works* 18, 266.
[4] This remark, like the reference to the smallpox epidemic in Tsitsihar, is reminiscent of the comic calendar of events, prophecies, etc., which Chekhov contributed to the magazine *Alarm-Clock* in 1882. Here one reads that 'there is an outbreak of diphtheria on the island of Borneo', that 'in Berdichev the refraction of light will take place', and that 'on this day in the

year 132 nothing very special happened in Portugal' (*Works* 1, 174, 178, 182).

[5] Valency, *op. cit.*, p. 212.

[6] Roskin, *op. cit.*, p. 375.

[7] M. N. Stroeva, '*The Three Sisters* in the Production of the Moscow Art Theater', in *Chekhov. A Collection of Critical Essays*, ed. Jackson, pp. 121–135. (My quotations are taken from the translation of Stroeva's article by Robert Louis Jackson.)

[8] *Works* 19, 24.

[9] Roskin, *op. cit.*, pp. 283–84. Before his untimely death A. I. Roskin (1898–1941) had written widely on Chekhov, and his study of *Three Sisters* is largely devoted to a fascinating comparison of the original Stanislavsky production with that of Nemirovich-Danchenko in 1940.

[10] *Ibid.*, p. 264.

[11] *Works* 18, 266.

[12] Letter to Maxim Gorky of October 16th, 1900 (*Works* 18, 406). Perm is situated to the west of the Ural Mountains, more than 700 miles from Moscow; in 1914 its population was 62,000. Chekhov's only story with a military setting is *The Kiss* (1887).

[13] This theme is anticipated in the story, *On Official Duty* (1889), where the hero visits a country estate and meets the four young daughters of the house: 'and he even felt sorry for these girls, living out their lives here in the backwoods, in the provinces, far from a cultural environment' (*Works* 9, 352).

[14] *Chekhov v vospom.*, p. 395.

[15] Roskin, *op. cit.*, p. 313.

[16] *Works* 19, 25.

[17] *Works* 11, 593. Cf. the remarks of Misail, the hero of the story *My Life* (1896), e.g.: 'Our town has existed for hundreds of years and during all that time it hasn't given the country a single useful person—not one!' (*Works* 9, 188).

[18] *Works* 9, 273.

[19] As, for example, by the Czech 'Theatre Behind The Gate' company, whose production of *Three Sisters* formed part of the 1969 World Theatre season at the Aldwych Theatre, London.

[20] Similar confrontations are to be found in Chekhov's short stories, e.g. *In Exile* and *Ward Six* (1892). In both instances Chekhov's sympathies seem to lie very much with the 'active' rather than the 'passive' protagonist.

[21] *Works* 19, 20.

[22] For a short story touching on this theme, see *Lights* (1888).

[23] *Works* 9, 248.

[24] See *Works* 11, 590.

CHAPTER FIVE

[1] Maurice Collis, *Somerville and Ross* (London, 1968), pp. 53–54.

[2] *Ibid.*, p. 53.

[3] Quoted by J. M. C. Davidson in his introduction to *The Cherry Orchard* (Letchworth, 1965), p. 10.

[4] *Works* 11, 605.

[5] See Yermilov's chapter on *The Cherry Orchard* (pp. 473–88), from which all the quotations in this paragraph are taken.

[6] Letter to Olga Knipper (*Works* 20, 159).

[7] Letter to Nemirovich-Danchenko (*Works* 20, 172).

[8] See *Works* 11, 605.

[9] See Nemirovich-Danchenko, *op. cit.*, p. 82.

[10] Letter to Stanislavsky of October 30th, 1903 (*Works* 20, 170).

[11] See *Works* 20, 258.

[12] *Works* 19, 54 and 76.

[13] *Works* 20, 131.

[14] *Chekhov v vospom.*, pp. 408–09.

[15] *Works* 20, 141.

[16] Magarshack, *op. cit.*, Preface, x.

[17] *Works* 20, 139.

[18] *Chekhov v vospom.*, pp. 410–11.

[19] *Works* 19, 401.

[20] *Works* 20, 170.

[21] Chekhov's only short story that anticipates the theme of *The Cherry*

Orchard at all is *Someone Else's Misfortune* (1886). This describes a young couple going to look over an estate which the owners are being forced to sell. When the sounds of sobbing are heard from an open window, the owner explains that it is his wife: 'you were saying a moment ago by the pond that you'd have to pull down something here and put up something there, and such words are like plunging a dagger into her heart' (*Works* 5, 357).

22 See his letters of October 30th, 1903, to Olga Knipper and to Stanislavsky (*Works* 20, 168–70). In letters to the actress, Vera Kommissarzhevskaya, Chekhov describes Ranyevskaya's role as the central one (*Works* 20, 29 and 205).

23 Yermilov, *op. cit.*, p. 485.

24 *Ibid.*, p. 483.

25 *Works* 20, 136.

26 *Works* 19, 10.

27 *Works* 20, 164.

28 *Works* 20, 129 and 149.

29 *Works* 20, 126–27. Cf. the description at the start of *Gooseberries* (1898): 'and if you stood on one of the little hills, then you could see the same huge expanse of open country, the telegraph poles, and the train which looked from a distance like a caterpillar crawling along; while in clear weather even the town would be visible'. (*Works* 9, 266.)

30 In *The Cherry Orchard* Chekhov's use of sound effects is more important than in any of the previous plays. 'Your shepherd played well. That was most essential,' he wrote to Stanislavsky of the pipe-playing shepherd at the end of Act I (*Works* 20, 177).

31 Magarshack, *op. cit.*, p. 286.

32 Francis Fergusson, 'The Cherry Orchard': A Theater-Poem of the Suffering of Change', in *Chekhov. A Collection of Critical Essays*, ed. Jackson, p. 154. Originally part of *The Idea of a Theater* (Princeton, N.J., 1949).

33 Valency, *op. cit.*, p. 286.

34 Cf. this passage about the unsympathetic father in *My Life* (1896):—'Look!', he was saying to my sister, pointing to the sky with the same umbrella that he had used to flog me with earlier. 'Look at the sky! Those stars, even the smallest ones, are all individual worlds. How insignificant man is before the universe!'

And his tone of voice suggested that he found it extraordinarily flattering and agreeable to be so insignificant. What an untalented man! (*Works* 9, 109.)

35 *Works* 20, 251.

36 The sound of a breaking string occurs on several occasions in the short stories. In *The Dream* (1886) the string of a guitar snaps unexpectedly in a dark and silent room (see *Works* 4, 475–76), while the following passage from *Happiness* (1887) clearly anticipates *The Cherry Orchard*:

—A sound echoed through the still air, spreading out rapidly across the steppe. In the far distance something had sighed menacingly and struck against stone, so that the sound reverberated through the steppe: *takh! takh! takh! takh!* When it had died down, the old man looked enquiringly at the unconcerned, motionless figure of Pantelei.

'Must have been a bucket falling in a mine-shaft', said the young man, after a moment's thought. (*Works* 6, 166.)

The hero of *A Rolling Stone* (1887) describes how he is flung to the bottom of the mine when the chain holding his bucket snaps (see *Works* 6, 210–11), and finally, in Chekhov's last story, *The Fiancée* (1903), a string breaks on a violin, but on this occasion it just gives rise to general amusement (*Works* 9, 436).

37 *Works* 9, 86–87.

38 See *Works* 11, 602–03.

39 Stanislavsky, *My Life in Art* (Harmondsworth, 1967), p. 387.

40 Cf. the description of the hero in *Good People* (1886):

—He was a writer in whose mouth

such expressions as 'There are so
few of us!' or 'What is life without
struggle? Forward!' sounded most
appropriate, even though he had
never struggled with anyone or
moved forward in his life. (*Works* 5,
234.)

41 Letter of September 21st, 1903, to
Olga Knipper (*Works* 20, 135).

42 'One shouldn't lose sight of the
fact', Chekhov wrote to Stanislavsky,
'that Lopakhin in loved by Varya, a
serious and religious girl; she wouldn't
have fallen for a money-grubbing
peasant.' (*Works* 20, 170.)

43 Recalled by I. Gurlyand. See *Iz
arkhiva A. P. Chekhova* (Moscow,
1960), p. 187.

44 Yermilov, *op. cit.*, p. 484.

45 Valency, *op. cit.*, p. 287.

46 *Works* 20, 251.

47 Princess Nina Andronikova Toumanova, *Anton Chekhov: The Voice
of Twilight Russia* (Columbia Paper-
back edition, New York, 1960), p.
214. First published in 1937.

48 *Works* 20, 164–65.

Index